# The Tip of the Tongue State

# ESSAYS IN COGNITIVE PSYCHOLOGY

North American Editors:
**Henry L. Roediger, III,** *Washington University in St. Louis*
**James R. Pomerantz,** *Rice University*

European Editors:
**Alan D. Baddeley,** *University of York*
**Vicki Bruce,** *University of Edinburgh*
**Jonathan Grainger,** *Université de Provence*

*Essays in Cognitive Psychology* is designed to meet the need for rapid publication of brief volumes in cognitive psychology. Primary topics will include perception, movement and action, attention, memory, mental representation, language, and problem solving. Furthermore, the series seeks to define cognitive psychology in its broadest sense, encompassing all topics either informed by, or informing, the study of mental processes. As such, it covers a wide range of subjects including computational approaches to cognition, cognitive neuroscience, social cognition, and cognitive development, as well as areas more traditionally defined as cognitive psychology. Each volume in the series will make a conceptual contribution to the topic by reviewing and synthesizing the existing research literature, advancing theory in the area, or some combination of these missions. The principal aim is that authors will provide overviews of their own highly successful research program in an area. It is also expected that volumes will, to some extent, include an assessment of current knowledge and identification of possible future trends in research. Each book will be a self-contained unit supplying the advanced reader with a well-structured review of the work described and evaluated.

FORTHCOMING

**Lampinen, Neuschatz & Cling:** *Psychology of Eyewitness Identification*
**Schmidt:** *Extraordinary Memories of Exceptional Events*
**Butler & Kang:** *The Mnemonic Benefits of Retrieval Practice*
**Weaver:** *Flashbulb Memory*

PUBLISHED

**Brown:** *The Tip of the Tongue State*
**Worthen & Hunt:** *Mnemonology: Mnemonics for the 21st Century*
**Surprenant & Neath:** *Principles of Memory*
**Kensinger:** *Emotional Memory Across the Lifespan*
**Millar:** *Space and Sense*
**Evans:** *Hypothetical Thinking*
**Gallo:** *Associative Illusions of Memory*
**Cowan:** *Working Memory Capacity*
**McNamara:** *Semantic Priming*
**Brown:** *The Déjà Vu Experience*
**Coventry & Garrod:** *Saying, Seeing and Acting*
**Robertson:** *Space, Objects, Minds, and Brains*
**Cornoldi & Vecchi:** *Visuo-spatial Working Memory and Individual Differences*
**Sternberg, et al.:** *The Creativity Conundrum*
**Poletiek:** *Hypothesis-testing Behaviour*
**Garnham:** *Mental Models and the Interpretations of Anaphora*

For updated information about published and forthcoming titles in the *Essays in Cognitive Psychology* series, please visit: **www.psypress.com/essays**

# The Tip of the Tongue State

ALAN S. BROWN

Psychology Press
Taylor & Francis Group

New York   London

Psychology Press
Taylor & Francis Group
711 Third Avenue
New York, NY 10017

Psychology Press
Taylor & Francis Group
27 Church Road
Hove, East Sussex BN3 2FA

© 2012 by Taylor & Francis Group, LLC
Psychology Press is an imprint of Taylor & Francis Group, an Informa business

Printed in the United States of America on acid-free paper
Version Date: 20110617

International Standard Book Number: 978-1-84169-444-3 (Hardback)

**Visit the Taylor & Francis Web site at**
**http://www.taylorandfrancis.com**

**and the Psychology Press Web site at**
**http://www.psypress.com**

# CONTENTS

# PREFACE

Memory problems are both fascinating and frightening. Fast and efficient retrieval of information is personally satisfying. When retrieval fails, it can be disturbing, confusing, and challenging, but it also provides research scientists with valuable clues into the complexities of routine cognitive experience. A personal fascination with the peripheral edges of memory function has led me to examine phenomena such as unconscious plagiarism (Brown & Murphy, 1989), transient amnesic states in normal adults (Brown, 1998), losing track of hidden valuables (Brown & Rahhal, 1994), déjà vu (Brown, 2003, 2004), and the tip of the tongue (TOT) experience (Brown, 1991). This book is a continuation of an earlier quest to better understand TOTs, one that began over two decades ago.

Some suggest that TOTs reflect an *aberrant* event, "...telling us about what happens on the rare occasions that lexicalization falters or fails, rather than about what happens when it succeeds" (Harley & Bown, 1998, p. 165). However, I believe that it embodies a normal function that is dramatically sidetracked, slowed, stalled, or incomplete. As such, TOTs provide a unique picture of an otherwise very rapid and automatic behavior, "...similar to how slow-motion photography clarifies the dimensions of a hummingbird's flight" (Brown, 1991, p. 204).

My prior review covered the first 25 years of published research on the TOT experience (Brown, 1991). Since then, the literature on this topic has quadrupled and continues to grow at an ever-increasing pace. The number of published articles with "tip of the tongue" or "TOT" in the title has essentially doubled decade by decade, expanding from 7 articles in the 1970s to over 70 in the 2000s.

A previous book on the TOT experience by Bennett Schwartz (2002b) provides an excellent summary of the state of the field at that point, and mine adds to his in several ways. First, over 85 new articles have appeared since Schwartz's book was published, and entire new areas of investigation have opened up, such as drugs that might be related to TOTs, the influence of gestures in eliciting and resolving TOTs, what areas of the brain light up during TOTs, and how the grammatical class of an interloper influences a TOT, just to name a few. A second difference is that Schwartz's primary focus is on the theoretical speculation related to TOT states, whereas my main emphasis is on empirical findings. Although theory and etiology are important, I believe that we can better understand this phenomenon by focusing primarily on the functionalistic aspects of the experience (cf. Watkins, 1990).

**Alan S. Brown**

# Historical Background

It is fitting to begin this book with the oft-cited description of the TOT experience written over a century ago by James (1893). He compellingly describes the manner in which we fail to grasp something just beyond our momentary linguistic reach, like having a stepstool too short to reach an item that we know to be up there, on the top shelf.

> Suppose we try to recall a forgotten name. The state of our consciousness is peculiar. There is a gap therein; but no mere gap. It is a gap that is intensively active. A sort of wraith of the name is in it, beckoning us in a given direction, making us at moments tingle with the sense of our closeness, and then letting us sink back without the longed-for term. If wrong names are proposed to us, this singularly definite gap acts immediately so as to negate them. They do not fit into its mould. And the gap of one word does not feel like the gap of another, all empty of content as both might seem necessarily to be when described as gaps. … The rhythm of a lost word may be there without a sound to clothe it; or the evanescent sense of something which is the initial vowel or consonant may mock us fitfully, without growing more distinct. (James, 1893, pp. 163–164)

Incidentally, this description appeared in a chapter on "the stream of consciousness," rather than one on memory. In contrast to this rather poetic view of TOTs, Angell (1908), who was a contemporary of James, presents a more jaded perspective on what TOTs mean:

> I know my friend's middle name perfectly well, and yet when asked for it a moment ago, I could not command it. Some momentary stoppage of the associated pathways in the cortex checked the attempt at recall. Many of the most serious disorders of insanity involve this

kind of disconnection and disintegration among ideas, of course much exaggerated. (Angell, 1908, p. 231)

Both quotes illustrate an early interpretation of TOTs as reflecting an aberration of normal mental function, a topic more fitting for clinical than experimental investigation. Given this early bias, it is not surprising that it took over a half a century before researchers applied scientific laboratory scrutiny to this phenomenon.

# ☐ Brown and McNeill's Original Research

A publication by Brown and McNeill (1966) dramatically changed the way psychologists approach TOTs. Up to this point, there were numerous informal and anecdotal reports based mainly on personal reflection. Brown and McNeill were the first to apply scientific methods, crafting an exemplary blueprint for the empirical evaluation of this subjective experience. Initially approaching the topic in an informal and introspective manner, Brown and McNeill tracked their personal TOT experiences for several months for clues on how to design a laboratory investigation. They next conducted a modest pilot study with 9 subjects to refine their methodology and materials, and then followed this by a large-scale study with 56 subjects. They were often apologetic about the difficulty of applying high standards of scientific rigor to the study of TOTs, yet they set a methodological example that few subsequent published reports have equaled. Their statistical approach was highly sophisticated, and they pointed out the potential limits of the statistical analysis and conclusions that were based upon the necessarily piecemeal data derived from a relatively infrequent experience.

Brown and McNeill (1966) peppered their report with colorful descriptions, noting that subjects were "seized" by a TOT "in mild torment, something like the brink of a sneeze," that the experimenter intruded on the subject's "agony" to ask pertinent questions about the missing word, that related words were often produced while the subject was "under the spell" of a TOT, and that subjects experienced "relief" when the sought-after word was discovered (pp. 326, 328). This engaging description conveys Brown and McNeill's (1966) belief that an emotional struggle was integral to the TOT phenomenon. Although some agree that an affective reaction is a central component of TOT experiences (Gruneberg, Smith, & Winfrow, 1973; Yarmey, 1973), this is more likely a by-product of frustrated retrieval efforts (cf. Brown, 1991).

Brown and McNeill's (1966) primary goal was to demonstrate how TOTs support the concept of "generic recall," where features of a word are accessible in the absence of the word itself. They posited two forms of generic recall: *partial*, consisting of linguistic pieces of the word (letter, prefix, suffix), and *abstract*, comprised of syllable number and syllable stress pattern. They sought to document the variety of word dimensions available during TOTs and piece together a more coherent general picture of language structure. The term generic indicated that any of these components "defines a class of words extending beyond the target" (p. 326) and that retrieval of any specific word in the lexicon involves winnowing through progressively smaller sets of words.

Their original investigation set a solid foundation upon which a considerable amount of subsequent research would be built. To keep the historical record straight, Freedman and Landauer (1966) published a TOT study the same year as Brown and McNeill (1966). However, it was very brief and provided little detail about TOTs. Freedman and Landauer (1966) intended to connect the feeling of knowing (FOK) and TOT experiences, and verify that recognition probability is directly related to one's subjective confidence in the accessibility of the missing target word. More specifically, words with the highest confidence rating signal TOTs and are more likely to lead to correct recognition. Whereas Freedman and Landauer (1966) demonstrate that the first letter of the target word facilitates subsequent retrieval, relative to the wrong letter or no letter at all, they provide no details on mean differences at each confidence level. Thus, their report does not allow us to determine whether the first letter was more effective at facilitating word retrieval during TOT (confidence 4) compared to non-TOT states (confidence 1–3).

# ☐ Post Brown and McNeill

After Brown and McNeill (1966) established the prototypical paradigm, research on TOTs has branched off in four different directions. For many years, most of the research was conducted by memory researchers. However, the TOT experience has attracted growing interest among linguists who use TOTs to test various theories of language production (e.g., Askari, 1999; Beattie & Coughlan, 1999; Caramazza & Miozzo, 1997; Faust, Dimitrovsky, & Shacht, 2003; Faust, Dimitrovsky, & Davidi, 1997; Faust & Sharfstein-Friedman, 2003; Gollan, Bonanni, & Montoya, 2005; Gollan & Acenas, 2004). A third direction involves a metamemory perspective, where TOTs are viewed as reflecting our personal awareness of cognitive processes rather than the actual contents or functions of memory (Schwartz, 2002b). The fourth direction is philosophical, framing TOTs as a window into the broader nature of consciousness. These philosophical articles claim that TOTs provide a wealth of information on the types of activities that are just out of reach of normal waking consciousness, at the fringes of mental activity (Baars, 1993; Brown, 2000a,b; Litman, Hutchins, & Russon, 2005; Lowenstein, 1994; Mangan, 2000). Although some empirical data are presented in these philosophical articles (e.g., Litman et al., 2005), the literature primarily focuses on peripheral dimensions of TOTs, such as epistemic curiosity states. These speculations do not fit the main purpose of the present book and, as such, are not covered.

Rather, my intent is to summarize the TOT experience, gathering the literature from three different perspectives: memory, linguistic, and metacognitive. The findings generated from these diverse approaches are sometimes difficult to fit together, given that each line of research examines different aspects of the TOT experience. More specifically, scientists who study language processes are generally separated, by both empirical methods and theoretical perspective, from scientists who study memory and metamemory. It is hoped that this book will help form a bridge to enhance more fluid communication and cross-fertilization across different approaches.

CHAPTER 2

# Defining a TOT

## ☐ Universality

The TOT experience is universal. Everyone understands the concept and acknowledges having the experience. Even the anatomical reference to "tongue" is consistent across cultures and languages, as Schwartz (1999) found in his informal survey. His sample of individuals is admittedly opportunistic, involving highly educated individuals who were available and willing to participate. All respondents were partially fluent in English, creating the possibility that knowledge of the English TOT expression biased evaluations of their other language(s). Despite these qualifiers, it is impressive that out of 51 languages sampled (at least two speakers sampled for each), 40 make reference to the tongue or some part of it: tip, point, head, end, top, or front. Aside from the consistent label, empirical research verifies the reliability of the experience across many languages and cultures, including German, French, Italian, Spanish, Farsi, Polish, Tagalog, Russian, Chinese, Japanese, and American Sign Language (see Chapter 10).

What about nonliterate cultures? Do they also understand the concept, in the absence of a verbal label? Brennen, Vikan, and Dybdahl (2007) investigated this question with people in Guatemala who used a primarily unwritten Mayan language. Although few had heard the Spanish expression for tip of the tongue, the majority understood the experience when described to them. Thus, Brennen et al. (2007) make the case that understanding the linguistic and phenomenal aspects of TOTs are separable, and widespread use of the tongue metaphor may not be the best proof for universality.

# ☐ Definitions

A central task in TOT research is defining the experience. Brown and McNeill (1966) suggest that "the class of cases defined by the conjunction of knowledge and a failure of recall is a large one. The TOT state … seems to be a small subclass in which recall is felt to be imminent" (p. 325). One can view the set of retrieval failures alluded to by Brown and McNeill (1966) as either a *continuum*, with one end marking a total absence of knowledge and the other the extreme feeling of accessibility characterizing a TOT, or a *dichotomy*, where TOTs represent a unique feeling of accessibility and certitude, and not simply a very intensely felt form of accessibility. This debate relates to the distinction between TOTs and FOKs (feelings of knowing), as well as the metamemory perspective on TOTs, both of which are covered more thoroughly later in this book.

The most important aspect of TOT research is the specific instructions given to subjects, detailing for them how to identify and monitor their subjective memory experience. Most investigations use Brown and McNeill's (1966, p. 327) definition or some modification of it:

> … that state of mind in which a person is unable to think of a word that he is certain he knows, the state of mind in which a word seems to be on the tip of one's tongue. … If you are unable to think of the word but feel sure that you know it and that it is on the verge of coming back to you then you are in a TOT state …

Many studies include the specific instructions to subjects in their Method section, and most stay relatively close to the wording used by Brown and McNeill (1966) (Brown & Nix, 1996; Ecke, 2004; Harley & Bown, 1998; Heine, Ober, & Shenaut, 1999; Jönsson, Tchekhova, Lönner, & Olsson, 2005; Koriat & Lieblich, 1974; Kozlowski, 1977; Schwartz, 1998, 2001b; Schwartz, Travis, Castro, & Smith, 2000; White & Abrams, 2002).

Some investigations do not include the phrase "tip of the tongue" in instructions to subjects. For example, Brédart and Valentine (1998, pp. 202–203) use the phrase "know the name while being momentarily unable to retrieve it." Some do not include any definition, and leave it up to the subject to determine what comprises a TOT (e.g., Brennen, Baguley, Bright, & Bruce, 1990). Others emphasize that it is insufficient to simply believe that one could later recognize the target word, but that the TOT must include a feeling that the word could be later recalled without assistance (Lesk & Womble, 2004). Some add a clarification that one should not report a TOT simply because the target word is from a subject area he or she knows well (Ravizza, 2003). A number of investigators include the term *verge* to emphasize the sense of imminence associated with TOTs (Rastle & Burke, 1996; Riefer, 2002; Schwartz & Smith, 1997).

Given that the assessment of TOTs requires an introspective evaluation on the part of the subject, the wording of instructions can easily influence TOT incidence. To illustrate this point, Harley and Bown (1998) suggest that a 40% drop in TOT incidence from their Experiments 1 to 2 may have resulted from a modest change in their instructions. Harley and Bown (1998) were suspicious that the TOT tally found in the first experiment may have been too high, and contaminated with high FOKs. For the second study, participants were told that they should not report targets that they thought they should know as TOTs, and their suspicions were confirmed by a drop in TOTs. Widner, Smith, and Graziano (1996) also found TOT incidence to be highly sensitive to instructions. Subjects who were told that the target words were *easy* ("95% of students had little difficulty answering them") reported nearly three times more TOTs than those who were told that target words were *difficult* ("95% of students had great difficulty answering them"). Both investigations (Harley & Bown, 1998; Widner et al., 1996) suggest that it is important to be sensitive to subjects' expectations, as this can have a substantial impact on what gets reported as a TOT.

## Recognition Criterion

On occasion, a TOT can involve a target word other than the one intended by the experimenter. The simplest way to verify this is by a yes/no recognition test, where the target is presented at the end of the trial and the subject indicates whether this is the one he had in mind (Brown & Nix, 1996; Gollan & Acenas, 2004). A better alternative is a multiple choice test, where the target is embedded in several distractors, some of which are related to the target word in meaning or structure. This is used less often because it is difficult to construct such a test (e.g., White & Abrams, 2002). It is also worth pointing out that some multiple-choice recognition tests may provide clues about the target word (tornado), especially when the foils include ones that are semantically related (hurricane), phonetically related (tomato), and unrelated (zebra) to the target (cf. Goodglass, Kaplan, Weintraub, & Ackerman, 1976).

An astute participant can triangulate on the target by evaluating which of the words is related to two of the others: one on first letter and one on meaning. As another example, Heine et al. (1999) used three foils that were related to the target (grout) in the following way: (a) a related word with the same first letter (glue), (b) a related word with a different first letter (plaster), and an unrelated word with the same first letter (glair). Again, a subject could pick the correct target word: select the one word among the three sharing the same first letter that matches the fourth word (different first letter) in meaning.

Other investigations have used less strict criteria to verify TOT states. For instance, following an incorrect response Lovelace (1987) had subjects rate their confidence in later identifying the correct word. A response of "I'm sure I would recognize the item" (p. 371) was sufficient evidence of a TOT. Vigliocco, Antonini, and Garrett (1997) used a similar modest criterion, defining TOTs as items for which recall fails but recognition succeeds (cf. Freedman & Landauer, 1966; Schwartz & Frazier, 2005). In both approaches, subjects are not asked whether they are experiencing a TOT but rather this is inferred from their pattern of responses. Such criteria seem too loose, and the best approach is to verify TOTs directly by the subject's personal assessment.

Brown and Burrows (2009) recently noted a potential problem with using recognition to verify TOT targets in those studies where subjects are asked to provide partial information about the target word (e.g., first letter; number of syllables) during a TOT and prior to recognition (e.g., Biedermann, Ruh, Nickels, & Coltheart, 2008; Caramazza & Miozzo, 1997; Miozzo & Caramazza, 1997; Shafto, Burke, Stamatakis, Tam, & Tyler, 2007). In Brown and Burrows, subjects identified which of three letters (C, S, or M) was the initial letter of the missing target word (sextant). The subsequent yes/no recognition decision for TOTs was significantly more accurate following a correct than an incorrect letter selection, and this same difference was also found for non-TOT trials where the target word was rated moderately familiar, somewhat familiar, and unfamiliar. Thus, it appears that subjects may use backwards reasoning to make their recognition evaluation: if I selected the correct first letter, then I must have had partial access to this word; if I selected the incorrect first letter, then I must have had some other word in mind.

# Alternative Approaches to Defining TOTs

## Merging TOTs and High FOKs

Some TOT studies combine high-confidence FOKs with TOTs. Harley and Bown (1998) were wary that subjects would take this approach unless given specific instructions on how to keep them separate (see earlier comment in this chapter), but other studies have intentionally combined these two categories in their analyses. For example, Gardiner, Craik, and Bleasdale (1973) used a four-point response scale (0 = no feeling of knowing; 1 = slight feeling of knowing; 2 = strong feeling of knowing; 3 = TOT state), and condensed these four rating categories into two for the analyses: non-TOT (ratings 0 + 1) and TOT (ratings 2 + 3). Gardiner et al. (1973) apparently assumed that TOTs are comparable with very strong FOKs, an issue examined in more detail later in this chapter.

## Extended Retrieval Criterion

Some have defined TOTs as synonymous with long or extended retrieval, assuming that if a word does not come to mind immediately then it must reflect a TOT. For example, Hamberger and Seidel (2003) define a TOT as a word retrieval that takes 2 seconds or longer, using Goodglass, Theurkauf, and Wingfield's (1984) assertion that normal retrieval consists of two stages: automatic (up to 1.5 s) and effortful (after 1.5 s). In short, all non-immediate retrievals that are eventually successful indicate a TOT. This is similar to how Kikyo, Ohki, and Sekihara (2001) defined TOTs in their fMRI study: any target word that takes more than 6 seconds to retrieve. Such time-based inferential criteria are less valid ways to identify TOTs, which should always be verified directly by the subject's own evaluation.

## Inferring Backwards from Partial Target Word Information

TOTs are often accompanied by various elements of the missing target word: first letter, number of syllables, syllabic stress (see Chapter 6). Inferring backwards from this, some assume that all occasions where such information is available reflect a TOT.

> … our review of the incorrect guesses … suggests that many of the subjects were in a "tip-of-the-tongue" state. In an experiment designed to induce "tip-of-the-tongue" phenomena, Brown and McNeill (1966) found that recall for the ending and beginning letters of a word was better than that for middle letters. Our data parallel those findings. (Meyer & Hilterbrand, 1984, pp. 49–50)

May and Clayton (1973) similarly assumed that when subjects remembered some aspect of the visual appearance of an object prior to name recall, they were experiencing a TOT. Again, subjects were given no instructions about TOTs, and were not asked to verify the experience. This selectivity by partial information has also been used to cut in the other direction. Vigliocco et al. (1997) define TOTs as only those occasions where some partial information about the target word could be retrieved (grammatical gender, number of syllables, letters, and related words). When subjects claimed to be experiencing a TOT but could not provide any correct partial information about the target word, these TOTs were excluded from the analysis as not genuine.

The problem with a partial information inclusionary criterion for defining TOTs is that some non-TOT experiences may be captured. It has been demonstrated that individuals can access structural (Koriat & Lieblich, 1974) and semantic (Durso & Shore, 1991; Shore & Durso, 1990) information about missing target words even during non-TOTs (see Chapter 5). Defining TOTs by partial recall is more common with studies on special groups (e.g., anomics) who seem to be especially prone to such word finding difficulties (Delazer, Semenza, Reiner, Hofer, & Benke, 2003; Georgieff, Dominey, Michel, Marie-Cardine, & Dalery, 1998; Ralph, Sage, & Roberts, 2000; Vigliocco, Vinson, Martin, & Garrett, 1999).

> It is tempting to assume that normal "tip-of-the-tongue" states are an analogous, albeit milder, form of the aphasic anomic deficit. As with the normal subject, the aphasic patient seems in some sense to "know" the word he is searching for and can often demonstrate this by pantomime or circumlocution.... (Marshall, 1979, p. 257)

Another version of backward inference of TOTs is through various verbal and nonverbal behaviors exhibited while attempting to think of a target word. Beattie and Coughlan (1999) inferred the presence of a TOT if one or more of the following behaviors were observed during the retrieval attempt: (1) verbal reactions ("Oh, God, I know it!"), (2) facial expressions (wincing), (3) body movements (holding head in hands), (4) head movements (head falling back), and (5) foot/leg movements (jiggling). When judges applied these five behavioral indicators to videotaped word retrieval efforts, Beattie and Coughlan (1999) found a high level of agreement among judges (88%) and proposed that TOTs can be identified via such observation.

This represents a creative and unobtrusive way to assess TOTs, but needs to be validated with the subjects' own assessment of prior use as sole criterion. Pine, Bird, and Kirk (2007) used a similar set of behavioral indicators to determine that children were experiencing a TOT, including both verbal remarks ("Oh! I forgot what they're called") and nonverbal behaviors such as wincing, rocking in their chairs and putting their heads in their hands (p. 749). Schwartz (2002b) labels such a backward-inferred TOT as a "third-person TOT" and also suggests that it would be valuable to confirm this operational definition through subject report.

## ☐ Positive and Negative TOTs

In laboratory research on TOTs, the target word sought by the subject sometimes differs from the one defined by the experimenter. This discrepancy may be due to a number of factors, including imprecise definitions, misperceived target word cue, or erroneous knowledge. On 35% of occasions where subjects claimed to have a TOT, Brown and McNeill (1966) discovered that the subject's target word differed from the one intended by the experimenter. They defined a TOT+ as one where the subject's and experimenter's target words matched, and a TOT– where these did not match. This designation has been routinely used in subsequent research, and is based on either retrieval (wrong word is produced) or recognition (correct word not identified) (cf. Koriat & Lieblich, 1974).

About half of all TOT investigations report both TOT+ and TOT– rates. The proportion of TOT– is usually lower than TOT+, although there are a few exceptions (Ferrand, 2001; Vigliocco et al., 1997, 1999). The mean TOT– rate in the set of outcomes in Table 2.1 is 7% whereas the mean TOT+ rate

**TABLE 2.1**  Comparison of % TOT– and TOT+

| Study | % TOT– / % TOT+ |
| --- | --- |
| Abrams & Rodriguez (2005) | 3/8 |
| Abrams et al. (2003)* | 6/13 |
| Bak (1987) | 5/7 |
| Biedermann et al. (2008)* | 6/7 |
| Brown & McNeill (1966) | 4/9 |
| Brown & Nix (1996) | 4/15 |
| Burke et al. (1991, Exp 2) | 2/9 |
| Caramazza & Miozzo (2005)* | 3/8 |
| Dahlgren (1998) | 1/4 |
| Ecke (2001) | 12/19 |
| Ecke (2004) | 12/13 |
| Ferrand (2001, Exp 1) | 14/10 |
| Gollan & Acenas (2004)* | 2/7 |
| Gollan & Brown (2006)* | 15/20 |
| Gollan et al. (2005, Exp 2) | 2/32 |
| Harley & Bown (1998)* | 3/14 |
| James & Burke (2000)* | 7/11 |
| Lesk & Womble (2004) | 5/11 |
| Maril et al. (2005) | 1/8 |
| Rastle & Burke (1996)* | 6/10 |
| Vigliocco et al. (1999, Exp 1) | 28/13 |
| Vigliocco et al. (1997) | 19/9 |
| White & Abrams (2002) | 6/15 |
| Yarmey (1973) | 10/14 |

* Data averaged across multiple experiments.

is 12%. Thus, over one third of reported TOTs are actually TOT–, a figure close to the 35% originally reported by Brown and McNeill (1966). Variation in the TOT– rate is likely to depend upon the difficulty of the cue material or instructions given to subjects (liberal or conservative criterion). As one would expect, TOT+s are associated with a higher confidence in subsequent target word recognition, compared to TOT–s (Caramazza & Miozzo, 1997).

One could make a case that a TOT– is a *legitimate* TOT, with respect to the subjective experience and retrieval dynamics. Using this logic, some studies combine TOT+ and TOT– to report general incidence (Caramazza & Miozzo, 1997; Lovelace, 1987). As Smith (1994) notes, a TOT– can be combined with a TOT+ if one is examining the subjective experience, but the two must be considered separately if one is evaluating such aspects as the availability of target word characteristics (e.g., first letter) or interlopers during TOTs. More often than not, TOT–s are excluded from the analyses, but the incidence should still be routinely reported (cf. Koriat & Lieblich, 1974).

# ☐ Levels of TOT

Some propose that TOTs can be classified in different levels. Schwartz (2002b) suggests that there is no reason to assume that a TOT is a monolithic experience, and some research has attempted to differentiate among levels of TOTs based on various quantitative and qualitative dimensions of the experience.

## Nearer and Farther TOTs

Brown and McNeill (1966) distinguished between *nearer* TOTs, where the target word comes to mind while filling out the questionnaire on the unretrieved target, and *farther* TOTs, where the target does not come to mind during this immediate time frame. First letter guesses were correct significantly more often with nearer (62%) than farther (42%) TOTs, suggesting that being closer to recovery is positively related to the availability of partial target word information. Koriat and Lieblich (1974) noted similar near versus far differences for availability of first letter (79% versus 35%, respectively), final letter (53% versus 47%, respectively), and syllable number (92% versus 65%, respectively). Yarmey (1973) also discovered significant differences for guesses about a famous person's profession (near = 96%; far = 92%), but not for place where this person was last encountered (near = 98%; far = 95%).

## Strong and Weak TOTs

Schwartz et al. (2000, Experiment 1) addressed the issue of TOT intensity, noting that "...some TOTs are so strong that they may bother us for days. Others pass without a second thought" (p. 19). They instructed subjects that "sometimes, the tip-of-the-tongue state may feel particularly strong; other times, the tip-of-the-tongue state may not feel as strong" (p. 20). Significantly more strong (22%) than weak (13%) TOTs were reported, and the resolution probability was higher for strong (13%) than weak (8%) TOTs. Replicating this outcome, Jönsson and Olsson (2003) found that odor-name TOT strength was directly related to resolution probability with 19% of "strong" and 37% of "very strong" TOTs resolved within 90 seconds. Jönsson et al. (2005) later replicated this resolution probability difference for both odors (strong = 3%; weak = 2%) and famous names (strong = 11%; weak = 6%). Similar to the lab research, Schwartz (2001a) found more naturally occurring TOTs were reported as strong (66%) than weak (34%) by diary subjects. But unlike the lab study, strength was unrelated to resolution probability: strong TOTs comprised approximately two-thirds of both resolved and unresolved TOTs.

Defining strength another way, Kozlowski (1977) had subjects indicate how confident they were that they were experiencing a TOT (0 = not at all confident; 4 = completely confident). TOT confidence was positively related to target word recognition, increasing from 46% for low (0) to 61% for moderate (1, 2) to 84% for high (3, 4) ratings. As a side comment on this particular study, a "0" TOT rating seems odd because the standard TOT definition involves a feeling of certitude about imminent retrieval: individuals are sure that they can retrieve the word, although not at the moment. A modified scale ranging from moderate to strong to extreme TOT might be more congruent with the manner in which TOTs are typically defined.

## Imminent and Nonimminent TOTs

The term "imminence" often appears in definitions and descriptions of TOTs, or a similar term like "verge" (Brown & McNeill, 1966; Rastle & Burke, 1996; Brown, 1991; Schwartz, 2001b; Schwartz & Smith, 1997). Some investigators see it as an essential feature of TOTs (Valentine, Brennan & Brédart, 1996), and especially useful in differentiating TOTs from FOKs (Smith, 1994). The concept of imminence also relates to James' (1893) characterization that TOTs make us "tingle with the sense of our closeness" (p. 251) (cf. Schwartz et al., 2000), and is related to the topic of far and near TOTs discussed earlier in this chapter. However, the near–far distinctions are *objective*, based on whether the target word does (near) or does not (far) come to mind (cf. Brown & McNeil, 1966), whereas imminent and nonimminent TOTs are *subjective* and defined by participants.

> Sometimes, you may feel as if you are about to recall the target, and will do so if given enough time – imminence. Other times, you may feel the TOT state, think that you know the answer, but may not feel the target is immediately imminent. (Schwartz et al., 2000, Experiment 3, p. 24)

If imminence *is* central to TOTs, then very few (or no) nonimminent TOTs should occur. Contrary to this expectation, Schwartz et al. (2000) found no difference between the incidence of imminent and nonimminent TOTs, suggesting that this attribute may not be essential to the experience. Despite this, imminence did predict both resolution and recognition: TOT resolution was higher after imminent (21%) than nonimminent (8%) TOTs, and target word recognition was higher for imminent (50%) than nonimminent (33%) TOTs.

Schwartz (2001a) also evaluated imminence in a diary study. Contrary to the laboratory investigation, there were many more imminent (65%) than nonimminent (35%) TOTs, but similar to the lab study, resolution success was positively associated with imminence: imminent TOTs comprised a larger proportion of resolved (68%) than unresolved (46%) TOTs. With respect to this latter finding, an alternative possibility is that the causal link goes in the opposite direction, with imminence evaluations based on assessments of target word resolvability. Schwartz (2001a, 2002b) further speculates that a feeling of imminence may reflect direct access to the target words, whereas a sense of nonimminence may signal an inferential TOT where one believes that a target word is accessible when actually it is not (see Chapter 9).

As a footnote on this topic, if imminence an integral aspect of TOTs (Schwartz et al., 2000), then a nonimminent TOT may actually be a high FOK item, instead. A second caution is that instructions such as these (Schwartz et al., 2000) may artificially create a set of items that do not normally exist. More specifically, subjects may recalibrate their assessments by assuming that nonimminent TOTs exist even if they have not experienced one.

## Brief and Protracted TOTs

To qualify as a TOT, does a retrieval effort have to extend for a *minimum* period of time? When one is briefly stymied in accessing a target word and this resolves within a few seconds, is this a true TOT? Or do TOTs require a more protracted period of time (e.g., more than 5 s) devoted to hunting for the missing target word? Gruneberg et al. (1973) note that "some blockages were only fleeting ..." (p. 190) and combine these brief TOTs with correct retrievals, thus defining TOTs as retrieval episodes lasting *at least* 2 seconds. Similarly, Meyer and Bock (1992) found that on a small percentage of trials, subjects provided the target word yet claimed to be in a TOT, but these were not counted as TOTs. Related to this, some investigations lump declared TOTs that are resolved relatively rapidly (within 15 s) into the correct recall category (Biedermann et al., 2008; Caramazza & Miozzo, 1997).

When analyzing subjects' verbal protocols during word retrieval attempts, Kohn, Wingfield, Menn, Goodglass, Berko Gleason, and Hyde (1987) did not even ask whether a subject was experiencing a TOT until after they spent at least 2 minutes searching for the target word. Relevant to this discussion, Goodglass et al. (1984) proposed that retrieval progresses through two stages: an initial automatic stage for 1.5 seconds, followed by an effortful stage. Are TOTs limited to the second, effortful, stage or can they happen during the first, automatic, stage, as well?

When subjects are told that some TOTs may be quickly resolved, Riefer, Kevari, and Kramer (1995) discovered that about two thirds (68%) of all TOT resolutions occur within 5 to 7 seconds following cue presentation. Thus, it seems possible that many TOTs resolve rapidly and are not labeled as such unless the subjects' attention is drawn to this fact. Schwartz (2001b, Experiment 4) examined this possibility by measuring "retrospective TOTs." Following each successful target word retrieval, subjects were asked whether they "... momentarily experienced a TOT just in advance of retrieving the word. The TOT may have only lasted an instant, but may have been felt prior to the retrieval of the answer" (p. 123).

These brief TOTs accounted for 9% retrievals (Schwartz, 2001b), whereas regular (protracted) TOTs occurred on 22% of trials. Thus, including brief TOTs would substantially increase the total number of TOTs. Average retrieval time for correct retrievals was substantially longer for those preceded by brief TOTs (16 s) compared to those that were not (10 s), but Schwartz (2001b) cautions that the assessment of a retrospective TOTs might be driven by fluency. More specifically, subjects may assume that slower correct retrievals are more likely to have been caused by a TOT, compared to faster retrievals.

We also examined this topic at Southern Methodist University (SMU), in an unpublished study. Using object picture cues, we told subjects that on those occasions where they hesitated for 2 seconds (or more) in producing the correct target word ("slow recall" trials), they would be asked whether they were initially *positive* of the correct word but it was slow to come to mind, or initially *unsure* of the correct word and had to search further. The former type of trial was defined as a brief TOT, although we did not use this term with the subjects. Nearly every subject (97%) experienced brief TOTs. Regular TOTs comprised 6% of all items, whereas brief TOTs accounted for 5% of all items (or 10% of correct retrievals). Slow correct retrievals not classified as brief TOTs (latter category, above) comprised 7% of all retrievals. In short, a substantial proportion of slow correct retrievals (about 40%) could be redefined as brief TOTs.

Both ours and Schwartz's (2001b) findings reveal a surprisingly high incidence of these brief TOTs. These are harder to identify, requiring more complex instructions and individual subject testing. Gathering peripheral information on brief TOTs (e.g., first letter, interlopers) would be impossible, but the incidence of such brief TOTs could be worthwhile to record when employing manipulations intended to influence TOT incidence, or when examining differences across subject groups or types of materials.

## Objective and Subjective TOTs

Another distinction made with TOTs involves the presence versus absence of peripheral target word information. If a subject reports some information about the missing target word, this is classified as an objective TOT because it indirectly confirms that the intended target is the correct word (as defined by the experimenter). Absent such information, the TOT is subjective because the only verification of the intended target is the subject's own assessment (Astell & Harley, 1996; Jones & Langford, 1987; Maylor, 1990a; Perfect & Hanley, 1992; Widner, Otani & Winkelman, 2005). Astell and Harley (1996) argue that the incidence of objective TOTs is generally lower than subjective TOTs because high FOK experiences are too frequently misinterpreted as TOTs. This objective/subjective distinction does imply that the lack of partial information lessens the importance, legitimacy, or accuracy of the subject's TOT assessment. However, one should keep in mind that the presence or absence of peripheral information during TOTs may be a function of the subject's threshold to volunteer such information when available, or explicit instructions to provide details of the target word that might come to mind.

## ☐ TOT versus FOK

An FOK judgment is a general assessment of one's sense of familiarity for inaccessible information (Hart, 1965, 1966). TOTs and FOKs are similar in that both relate to unavailable knowledge. However, these differ in several important dimensions. First, a TOT involves certitude that the information exists in one's knowledge base, whereas FOK assessments span the entire range of confidence levels. Put another way, an essential part of a TOT is a sense that the word eventually can be *recalled* given sufficient time, whereas FOK judgments involve the likelihood of subsequent correct *recognition*. A second distinction is that a TOT is generally viewed to be a "bottom-up" experience triggered by the retrieval effort, whereas a FOK evaluation is made in response to a request ("top-down") for such an assessment, usually on every trial. So an FOK is driven by the experimenter, whereas a TOT is triggered by a subject. A final distinction is that TOTs occur on a minority of items, whereas FOKs can apply to all items. Although these two evaluations bear a superficial resemblance, Schwartz (2002b) points out that the TOT and FOK literatures have evolved independently, with the study of TOTs driven mainly by memory and language researchers and the examination of FOKs guided by metamemory investigators (Schwartz, 2008).

## TOTs as Extreme FOKs

There is an extensive and lively discussion in the literature on the relationship between TOT and FOK (see Schwartz, 2006, 2008). At the heart of this debate is whether there is a quantitative or a qualitative difference between the two: is a TOT simply an extreme FOK (Bahrick, 2008), or are the two qualitatively distinct experiences (Schwartz, 2008)? From the quantitative perspective, some use a common response scale comprised of graded levels of increasing FOK, with a TOT as the extreme end point. One example is Gardiner, Craik and Bleasdale's (1973) four-point scale: 0 = no FOK, 1 = slight FOK, 2 = strong FOK, 3 = TOT. Similarly, Freedman and Landauer (1966) employed a four-point response scale that ranged from *don't know it* to *probably don't know it* to *probably know it* to *definitely know it* (TOT), and Ferrand (2001, Experiment 1) used a five-point rating scale for unavailable words, with *not at all* at one end to *it is on the tip of my tongue* at the other. Both Litman et al. (2005) and Lowenstein (1994) define TOTs as extreme FOKs, or a "TOT FOK state" (cf. Naito & Komatsu, 1989). Significant positive correlations between FOK and TOT ratings in several studies suggest that a similar mechanism underlies both responses (Schwartz et al., 2000; Yaniv & Meyer, 1987).

Some researchers request that both TOT and FOK ratings be made on the same item, but in a sequential manner. To illustrate this procedure, Yaniv and Meyer (1987) had subjects perform a two-stage rating on all unrecalled targets. Following an initial TOT assessment (yes/no), subjects were then asked to make a five-level FOK rating (low to high) on the missing target. The percentage of TOTs across the FOK rating categories (low to high) were 1%, 6%, 26%, 35%, and 33%. Note that many TOTs were associated with low to moderate FOK ratings, contrary to the standard conceptualization of TOTs as words that we are *sure* we know. A possible explanation for the low and moderate FOK/TOT ratings may be found in an unusual aspect of Yaniv and Meyer's (1987) procedure. Subjects knew that they would sometimes confront the missing target word moments later in a lexical decision task, and may have hedged their confidence ratings to avoid the awkwardness of having made an incorrect TOT evaluation. Yaniv and Meyer (1987) further found instances of high FOK ratings for non-TOT items, leading them to suggest that different processes may underlie FOKs and TOTs (cf. Brown, 1991).

Caramazza and Miozzo (1997) similarly segmented TOTs into various levels, asking subjects to rate "how confident they were 'to have the word at the tip of the tongue'" (p. 319). This might actually measure whether a subject believes that the TOT target word that they have in mind is correct (TOT+), with lower confidence ratings given for words that they believe may be TOT–s. Supporting such speculation, TOT+s were accompanied by significantly higher confidence ratings than TOT–s. Taking a more analytical approach, Metcalfe, Schwartz, and Joaquim (1993) found that both FOK and TOT responses increased directly with cue familiarity, which also supports the position that similar mechanisms underlie both types of responses.

## TOTs and FOKs as Separate

In contrast to the above speculation on the communality of TOTs and FOKs, there is evidence that TOT and FOK experiences are qualitatively separate cognitive functions. Widner et al. (1996) found that participants who were told that target words were easy to retrieve had more TOTs than those who were told that the words were hard, but this instructional manipulation had no effect on FOK ratings for nonretrieved words. Furthermore, when Widner et al. (2005) compared subjects with intact versus deficient prefrontal cortex (PFC) function, the relationship between FOK and recognition accuracy was poorer in the deficient than the intact PFC group (Experiment 1), with no difference between these two groups in the strength or accuracy of TOT reports. Widner et al. (2005) suggest that this outcome implicates a two-stage model of TOTs. The first involves an automatic and implicitly activated feeling of availability that does *not* involve the prefrontal cortex, which accounts for the lack of a TOT difference between intact and impaired PFC groups. However, the second stage is an effortful memory search guided by intentional cognitive processes associated with the prefrontal cortex, and this explains why the deficient PFC group is worse than the intact group on FOK evaluations.

Additional evidence on the independence of FOK and TOT is provided by Maril, Simons, Weaver, and Schacter (2005). Their participants classified each target word as: don't know (DK), know (K), can't get the word but know it (FOK), or can't get the word now but it is on the tip of the tongue (TOT). Compared to their prior investigation (Maril, Wagner, & Schacter, 2001) with similar procedure/materials but no FOK alternative (only DK, K, and TOT), they found the same percentage of TOTs. This led them to conclude that FOK ratings in Maril et al. (2005) were not simply extracted from the TOT response category because the percentage of TOTs would have been reduced from Maril et al. (2001) to Maril et al. (2005). Rather, FOKs appear to have come from the DK category, implying a clear distinction between FOKs and TOTs. Maril et al.'s (2005) response latencies also differentiated FOKs from TOTs: TOTs took significantly longer (2764 ms) than FOK (2569 ms), DK (1956 ms), or K (1942 ms) responses, again pointing to different mental processes underlying TOTs and FOKs.

Neuroimaging data from the above investigations also support a distinction between FOK and TOT. More specifically, right prefrontal activity is associated with TOTs (Maril, Simons, Mitchell, Schwartz, & Schacter, 2003) whereas left prefrontal activation characterizes FOKs (Maril et al., 2003). This comparison, however, is clouded by the fact that these two studies confounded FOK and TOT measurement with memory function: Maril et al. (2001) used a semantic memory task to evaluate TOTs, whereas Maril et al. (2003) used an episodic memory paradigm to examine FOKs. To disambiguate this comparison, Maril et al. (2005) compared FOK and TOT within a single study, using the same task. They found that TOTs but not FOKs were associated with activation in the anterior cingulate, right dorsolateral prefrontal cortex, and right inferior cortex. Interestingly, there was no brain region uniquely associated with FOK judgments that was not also active to some extent with TOTs.

Thus, Maril et al. (2005) suggest that TOTs and FOKs may reflect qualitatively different processes. However, because no brain regions showed greater activation with FOKs compared to TOTs, and that "FOK was observed to be associated with levels of activation that were either equal to or lower than the levels of activation associated with TOT" (p. 1137), they could not totally eliminate the possibility that a TOT was simply an extreme FOK (cf. Schwartz, 2006).

As no dissociation was observed in the present study, the results are inconclusive with regard to…a quantitative or a qualitative difference between them. However, with TOT but not FOK eliciting activations in frontal areas, it may be the case that TOT is a cognitive state that is not merely a strong instance of FOK, but rather that there may exist a qualitative difference between the two states." (Maril et al., 2005, p. 1137)

Schwartz (2008) presents additional evidence for a separation between TOT and FOK by showing a dissociation with a secondary task. When subjects perform a verbal working memory task (retaining digits) during their word retrieval task, the probability of TOTs declines (Experiments 1–3) whereas FOKs either increase slightly (Experiment 1) or are unaffected (Experiments 2 and 3). This outcome suggests that TOTs require working memory capacity, such that increasing the demand by having both a digit span task and TOT evaluations diminishes both. However, FOKs do not require this function, so the simultaneous requirement of FOK judgments and digit span does not diminish either.

In summary, it is most likely that TOT and FOK responses are highly related but distinctive cognitive functions. Variations in the degree to which these two responses are related may be dependent upon the instructions and materials used in a particular study. Because TOT and FOK ratings are dissociable does not necessarily mean that the two responses are uncorrelated. Most likely, some of the same underlying processes may be driving both assessments, even though clear differences exist between them (Schwartz, 2006).

# ☐ Illusory TOTs

Can a TOT happen in the absence of an actual target word? Schwartz (1998) floated this question as part of a test of the inferential position, that TOTs emanate from assessments of cue familiarity or own knowledge base rather than target word accessibility (see Chapter 9). If TOTs occur for nonexistent target words, then they must be based on inference rather than access.

The initial test of this idea required subjects to learn artificially created stimulus animals, or TOTimals (see Chapter 4). Six TOTimals were used, four of which had names (identified) and two of which had no names (unidentified) (Schwartz, 1998, Experiment 1). TOTs occurred for 23% of the TOTimals with names. But more important, TOTs were reported for 16% of unnamed TOTimals. Schwartz (1998) argued that TOTs are, at least on some occasions, inferential; otherwise, there should be no TOTs on unnamed TOTimals. Schwartz (1998, Experiment 2) extended this examination of illusory TOTs with the more standard stimulus material (definitions), mixing 20 definitions that had no correct answer (fictional) ("What is the name of the heroic innkeeper in the movie *Seems Like Old Times*

*Again?*"; "What is the capital city of Bormea?") with 80 regular (real) definitions. There were significantly fewer TOTs for items without answers (18%) than for those with answers (44%), but again Schwartz (1998) argues that the former percentage should be zero if TOTs reflect issues related to stored target word access.

In a followup, Schwartz et al. (2000) compared illusory and real TOTs on strength (Experiment 1), emotionality (Experiment 2), and imminence (Experiment 3). As before (Schwartz, 1998), subjects had more TOTs to real than illusory targets. In addition, real TOTs were rated strong more often than weak, whereas illusory TOTs reversed this being rated weak more often than strong. More real TOTs were rated to be emotional than nonemotional, whereas illusory TOTs were more often rated nonemotional than emotional. Finally, TOTs for real items were equally likely to be rated imminent as nonimminent, but TOTs for illusory items were seen as nonimminent more than imminent. In summary, illusory TOTs were relatively less frequent, strong, emotional and imminent, compared to real TOTs.

Although TOTs to nonexistent target words seems to support an inferential basis for TOTs, both Taylor and MacKay (2003) and Schwartz (2000) propose several alternative explanations for illusory TOTs. More specifically, an illusory TOT could result from a misunderstanding of the cue question, similar to what happens with the Moses illusion: "How many animals of each species did Moses take aboard the Ar[k]?" (Reder & Kusbit, 1991). Also, the question "What is the capital of Bormea" could be misperceived as "What is the capital of Burma" (Taylor & MacKay, 2003). Thus, illusory TOTs can be viewed as negative TOTs (TOT–s), where participants' intended target is actually a real word, but one mistakenly derived from the definition as presented. Schwartz et al. (2000) do not believe that this argument is credible because illusory TOTs differ from TOT–s in several dimensions described above (strong/weak; emotional/nonemotional; imminent/nonimminent). However, Taylor and MacKay (2003) suggest that postexperiment inquiry could address this issue. Subjects could clarify their TOT responses to unanswerable items, or take a multiple choice test that includes possible incorrectly encoded or misperceived targets as alternatives.

Schwartz et al. (2000) also note that demand characteristics may explain illusory TOTs: subjects assume that the experiment includes only real information, and acquiesce to the expectation to have TOTs on some items. But Schwartz et al. (2000) counter this argument by pointing out that illusory TOTs remain consistently strong, imminent, and emotional from the first presentation of the cue to the second, suggesting that demand characteristics do not play a role. Otherwise, these ratings should diminish with time. However, they do not clarify exactly why experimenter demand would result in these secondary dimensions associated with TOTs declining over time. Taylor and MacKay (2003) further propose that ultimately this argument is difficult to evaluate because real TOTs can be resolved whereas illusory ones cannot.

Perhaps the most important support for experimenter demand with illusory TOTs is the dramatic age difference. Schwartz (2002b) tried to test older adults using fictional questions, but they immediately detected that the questions had no answer and even informed the experimenter of this. Nearly 200 college students have been tested using illusory questions (Schwartz, 1998; Schwartz et al., 2000), but only 1 young adult reported noticing anything odd (Schwartz, 2002b). In contrast, most older subjects detected that the questions were impossible, and even inquired as to whether there were answer sheet errors or "no possible answer" could be an alternative (Schwartz, 2002b). Schwartz (2002b) attributes this discrepancy to higher vocabulary and general knowledge in older adults, but it could also be due to the lower level of acquiescence to experimental demands among older adults.

## ☐ Emotionality

Anecdotal descriptions of TOTs include emotional reactions such as *surprise* (Maril et al., 2005), *tingle* (James, 1893), *turmoil* (Faust et al., 1997), and *agitation* (Wellman, 1977). TOTs have been described as accompanied by *agony* during the experience and *relief* after resolution (Brown & McNeill, 1966), as well as evocative of smiles and gasps (Finley & Sharp, 1989). The experience has also been likened to "... a feral beast that struck without warning" (Jones, 1989, p. 215), and described as "all the wrong words and parts of words that I think of make me feel crazy" (Faust et al., 1997, p. 1034). Some view an emotional reaction as a defining property of TOTs (Gruneberg et al., 1973; Yarmey, 1973), although no research has directly confirmed this (cf. Brown, 1991).

In a diary study on TOTs, Burke, MacKay, Worthley, and Wade (1991, Experiment 1) had participants evaluate four physical/psychological dimensions as related to the experience of TOTs: worry, sick, fatigue, and excitement (1 = more than usual; 7 = less than usual). Ratings averaged in the mid-range on all dimensions (3.4 to 4.1) indicating no special emotional or physical intensity is associated with the typical TOT. Using a more general query, Schwartz (2001a) found that 61% of natural TOTs were emotional, with fewer resolved TOTs rated as emotional (58%) compared to unresolved TOTs (89%). Although Schwartz (2001a) suggests that greater emotionality with unresolved TOTs is puzzling, this makes sense if lack of resolution fuels negative emotions such as frustration (cf. Schwartz, 2010). This could be especially true in diary studies, where retrieval efforts may span longer time periods. Understandably, *relief* accompanied resolution for 80% of diary TOTs (Schwartz, 2001a).

Schwartz et al. (2000, Experiment 2) also explored emotional components of laboratory TOTs by instructing subjects that "sometimes you may feel frustrated or emotional that you cannot recall a word that you are sure you know" (p. 23). By their own admission, this assessment was moderately problematic in that a number of subjects were confused about this instruction and had to receive further clarification. Similar to the diary outcome, the majority of TOTs were emotional (55%) but unlike the diary finding, resolution was more likely for emotional (14%) than nonemotional (9%) TOTs (Schwartz, 2001b, Experiments 1 and 2). This was replicated in Experiment 3, with the majority of TOTs rated as emotional. Employing a more fine-grained assessment of emotionality in Experiment 4, 48% of TOTs were reported to be frustrating, 14% exciting, and 12% both frustrating and exciting. Thus, TOTs are more likely to be accompanied by negative than positive emotions.

Schwartz (2002a) complains that subjective phenomenology surrounding TOTs—strength, imminence, emotionality—is relatively ignored in published research. However, given the evanescent nature of TOT experiences, such evaluations are difficult. The vagueness and brevity of the cognitive state accompanying a TOT make precise metacognitive assessments problematic. Furthermore, emotionality (frustration, excitement) may relate more to situational and personality variables than to cognitive or memory function. More specifically, one would expect more emotionality with natural (diary) than artificially induced (lab) TOTs, and more arousal associated with a TOT to a friend's name in a social setting than to a state capital name in a laboratory study. Schwartz (2002b) does point out that the causal link between emotionality and TOTs is unclear: does emotion cause a TOT, does a TOT result in an emotional reaction, or does some glitch in the word retrieval process cause both? In fact, Schwartz (2010) recently published a manipulation to induce emotion through materials related to such topics as sex, violence, and profanity, and found that this increased TOT rate over neutral items. This topic of emotionality as a cause of TOTs is covered in greater detail in Chapter 4.

Widner et al. (1996) suggest that emotional arousal may explain why their high demand manipulation ("easy" targets) increased TOTs over the low demand condition ("hard" targets). High demand may have increased anxiety, which induced more TOTs. The instructional manipulation had no effect on FOK assessments (Experiment 2), supporting such speculation. One would expect stress to have a negative impact on retrieval, but not one's assessment of word retrievability. Widner et al. (1996) do not agree with this interpretation, and see the FOK data as evidence against a stress-TOT causal connection.

# ☐ Motivation

> A common experience associated with the TOT state is a driving force to bring it to an end by retrieving the sought-for target. … Regardless of the origin or validity of the feeling of knowing associated with a TOT state, this state seems to have motivational consequences. (Koriat, 2000, p. 152)

Although Koriat's observation corresponds to our ordinary experience concerning TOTs, there is little research on this topic because it is not readily apparent how to measure it.

Within an inferential interpretation of TOTs (see Chapter 9), Schwartz (2001b) suggests that TOTs have two associated processes: monitoring and control. Monitoring involves a general inference about one's knowledge, and a specific inference about the given cue. In contrast, the control function is the goal-directed behavior of retrieving the target word. Thus, the control function provides the motivation for an extended memory search during TOTs. Litman, Hutchins, and Russon (2005) confirmed this speculation by demonstrating that subjects are more likely to open a readily available envelope containing the target word during a TOT compared to a DK trial.

Schwartz (2001b, Experiment 1) suggests that longer retrieval latencies should also be considered to be a reflection of higher motivation. Given that retrieval times were longer during TOTs than non-TOTs in two studies (Experiments 1 and 2), he concludes that TOTs motivate us to conduct longer searches. He does, however, suggest a very plausible alternative causal direction: the TOT state may not extend retrieval time, but rather extended retrieval time increases the likelihood of one inferring that he or she is experiencing a TOT.

# ☐ Physical Evidence

Several studies have suggested that various types of observable behaviors may reflect that a TOT is occurring. Beattie and Coughlan (1999) propose that TOTs are often accompanied by verbal statements ("Oh, what are they called?!"), facial expressions (wincing), head movements (falling, dropping, turning), body movements (leaning head forward), and foot/leg movements (tapping, jiggling). In addition, Pine et al. (2007) used physical evidence (wincing, rocking in chair) to verify the presence of TOTs in children. Both studies report a high interrater reliability in these measures, but neither study confirmed that subjects were actually having a TOT by asking them. Thus, although intriguing, this behavioral evidence for TOTs needs more direct empirical verification.

Another form of physical evidence of TOTs, albeit indirect, comes from brain imaging research. A growing body of literature attempts to relate the activation of various brain structures to TOTs. Using neuropsychological assessment to identify subjects with intact versus deficient prefrontal cortex (PFC) function, Widner et al. (2005, Experiment 1) found no difference in TOT incidence between these groups, or in the strength and accuracy of TOT reports. Although this research suggests no involvement of the PFC with TOTs, brain imaging research suggests otherwise.

Using functional magnetic resonance imaging (fMRI), Maril et al. (2001) found that both the anterior cingulate cortex (ACC) and right middle frontal (or Broadmann's) area (PFC) are more activated during TOT states than during know or don't know trials. They speculate that the PFC and ACC are activated when a retrieval failure is accompanied by "a sense of impending success" (p. 656), and this circuit seems to be involved in managing and resolving the conflict between different streams of information processed during a TOT, such as related words and partial target word information. In short, ACC and PFC activation reflects the "cognitive struggle" during TOTs. Maril et al. (2005) further identified five areas that were selectively related to TOTs but not FOKs: ACC, right dorsolateral PFC (or DLPFC), right inferior PFC, left anterior PFC, and right anterior PFC.

Maril et al. (2005) note that both the ACC and PFC have been described as components of a cognitive control system, with the ACC involved in conflict monitoring and the PFC in managing partial information recovery during TOT. In addition, the anterior PFC has been associated with managing thought processes and handling multiple relationships, perhaps related to TOT activities of evaluating retrieval products and deciding whether to continue (or terminate) the search for the target word. Also, the right inferior PFC selectively handles "fine grained phonological processing of words, at the level of phonemes or single syllables" (p. 1136). Finally, the ACC, right DLPFC and frontopolar regions may be activated because TOTs have a great "richness of content of retrieved partial information" (p. 1137).

Shafto, Stamatakis, Tam, and Tyler (2010) subsequently confirmed the findings of Maril and colleagues, again using fMRI. Comparing TOT with K responses, the four greatest differences in activity level were found in (1) the left inferior frontal cortex, left anterior insula, left temporal pole; (2) right insula, right inferior frontal cortex; (3) right middle frontal cortex; and (4) right middle cingulate gyrus. Thus, the frontal lobes again appear to be highly involved in TOT activities. It should be noted that Kikyo et al. (2001) also used fMRI to investigate brain regions active during TOTs, but their findings may be difficult to interpret. They defined TOTs as any retrieval longer than 6 seconds, so their data probably combine TOTs with those non-TOTs that involve extended search.

Another brain recording procedure used to evaluate differential activation of various regions during TOTs is voxel-based morphometry (VBM), which compares gray matter concentrations across different brain regions (voxel by voxel). Shafto et al. (2007) evaluated a broad age range of subjects (19 to 88 years old; mean = 56) on celebrity name retrieval, using picture-plus-description cues. After identifying brain areas strongly related to TOTs, they partialled out areas associated with a general age-related cognitive decline. The primary area associated with TOTs was the left insula, and extending to the rolandic operculum, Heschl's gyrus, and superior temporal gyrus. Thus the left insula is strongly involved with TOTs, and seems related to phonological retrieval deficits that supposedly underlie TOTs (see Chapter 11). This outcome was also confirmed by Shafto et al. (2010).

Finally, scalp recording procedures have been used in evaluating the neurological correlates of TOTs. Díaz, Lindín, Galdo-Alvarez, Facal, and Juncos-Rabadán (2007) discovered that event-related potentials, or ERPs, revealed no difference between K and TOT trials in the early events in the brain response (P1, N1, P2, and N2). With respect to the early stages of the P3 (450 to 550 ms), there was again no K versus TOT difference. However, there was significantly lower amplitude on TOT compared to K trials for late P3 (550 to 750 ms) and the period following this (1350 to 1550 ms). Their interpretation is that the stimulus evaluation is not affected during TOTs, but the lack of sufficient activation of the lexical route is evidenced by lower amplitude in the later ERP stages (cf. Galdo-Alvarez, Lindín, & Díaz, 2009a, 2009b; Lindín, Díaz, Capilla, Ortiz, & Maestú, 2010). Díaz et al. (2007) further suggest that this outcome supports Burke et al.'s (1991) transmission deficit hypothesis about TOTs (see Chapter 9), where initial semantic activation of the word concept is successful but transmission of activation from the semantic to phonological nodes is insufficient for full word generation.

The research relating brain function and TOTs is at a very nascent stage of development, and promises to develop rapidly in the near future. However, the procedures and techniques may not be well suited to the subjective designation of a TOT state, and the fact that the temporal onset and resolution of TOTs are both rather poorly defined. Finally, the procedures and definitions of a TOT differ substantially across investigations, and are often at odds with standard laboratory studies on TOTs (see above), making it difficult to draw a reasonably definitive picture at this point of the connection between the TOT state and areas of selective brain activation.

# ☐ Variations on TOTs

Several different varieties of the TOT experience have been described in the literature. Two of these—tip of the eye (TOE; see Chapter 8) and tip of the nose (TON; see Chapter 3)—cannot technically be considered phenomena that are distinct from a TOT. The eye and nose simply denote the sensory mode (line drawings; odors) used to cue the target word, but word production still gets stymied at the end-stage output, or metaphorically at the tip of the tongue. Thus, both involve the same verbal production system as when other cues (definitions, faces, music) are used (cf. Valentine et al., 1996). However, there are several TOT variations that are distinctive and deserve separate mention.

## Tip of the Finger

One variation involves gestural rather than oral or written word production. Thompson, Emmorey, and Gollan (2005) examined the tip of the finger, or TOF, experience in deaf signers. Two different types of responses were examined: finger-spelled names cued by face pictures, and American Sign Language (ASL) signs cued by English words. There were twice as many TOFs associated with finger spelling than signing. Subjects recalled some phonological information for about half of proper names cued by pictures, and most of this involved the initial letter of the first, last, or both names. For TOFs associated with ASL, four out of five were accompanied by structural features of the hand sign (i.e., hand position). When reported, about half of these particular TOFs contained information about three of four parameters, including hand shape (44%), hand location (53%), hand orientation (40%), and hand movement (26%). All were well above chance levels, which Thompson et al. (2005) established to be at, or below, 10%. Thus, TOFs resemble TOTs in being more common for proper names (see Chapter 6), with various features of the word or sign often available (see Chapter 5). However, the sign TOFs were remarkable in that most were accompanied by information about multiple dimensions of the temporarily inaccessible hand sign. Given that resolutions were unrelated to the total number of sign features available during the TOF, Thompson et al. (2005) concluded that a TOF can occur when any one of several different word/sign parameters is insufficiently activated.

## Tip of the Pen

Written languages generally have a phonological basis, where sounds map onto letters. Chinese differs from most, using a logographic written language system where characters represent concepts rather than sounds. Sun, Vinson, and Vigliocco (1998) describe a tip of the pen (TOP) experience, where one momentarily loses the visual representation of the character associated with that semantic concept. The idiom in Chinese is Ti-Bi-Wang-Zi, which translates as "pick up a pen but forget how to write a character." During a TOP, subjects can successfully provide orthographic information about the inaccessible character (structural features such as the number of strokes and radicals) at a rate above a baseline established for non-TOTs. Two different language systems in Chinese provide separate pictorial and verbal routes to a semantic representation, and Sun et al. (1998) found it noteworthy that a TOP (character generation) can occur even when the target word is available, but a TOT never occurs when the character is available.

## ☐ Summary

TOTs are universal, and have been documented across a variety of languages and cultures. There is some discrepancy in how TOTs are defined in research studies, and given that the experience is primarily subjective and requires some introspection, the definitional precision that is conveyed to the subject is very important. Verifying that the subject's target word matches the one designated by the experimenter is essential, and normally accomplished through a recognition test. Unfortunately, this is still not standard practice (cf. Hanley & Chapman, 2008). Some have operationalized TOTs by extended retrieval time or availability of peripheral information, but these are indirect procedures and are in need of direct verification. The best verification is to have the subject provide his or her own personal assessment. A distinction is made between positive TOTs (TOT+), where the target word sought by both subject and experimenter match, and negative TOTs (TOT–), where the experimenter-intended target differs from the one sought by the subject. Although TOT–s are routinely excluded from analyses, this should not be automatic.

TOTs have been separated into different varieties, such as near versus far, strong versus weak, imminent versus nonimminent, brief versus protracted, and objective versus subjective. Research has addressed whether TOTs are simply strong FOKs (quantitative difference), or whether they are distinctly different experiences (qualitative difference), and this debate continues. TOTs can be elicited for nonexistent information (illusory

TOTs). This finding has implications for the etiology of the experience (see Chapter 9), but there is debate about the significance of illusory TOTs. An emotional component appears to be a part of TOTs, but it is still not clear whether this is part of the essential TOT experience or part of one's reaction to it. A search for objective physical verification of a TOT experience has involved bodily reactions and brain imaging (ERP, VBM, fMRI). Finally, there are intriguing variations on the TOT experience, involving words stuck at the tip of the finger (TOF) and the tip of the pen (TOP). Such conceptual extensions deserve additional exploration, as they could provide new inroads into understanding the mechanisms of TOTs.

CHAPTER 3

# Eliciting and Measuring TOTs

A variety of approaches has been used to evaluate the frequency and nature of TOT experiences. The simplest are retrospective, where one evaluates TOTs from prior experience. Another technique involves capturing TOTs as they happen in real time, through personal diary records kept over an extended time period (usually 1 month). Brown and McNeill (1966) originally tried out the diary procedure, but found that the rarity of TOTs would require an improved methodology for the research to move forward. Thus, they brought TOT research into the lab using a "prospecting" procedure: artificially eliciting TOTs using definitions. This laboratory approach dominates the published literature on TOTs, and employs a variety of different cues and procedures that are detailed below.

Harley and Bown (1998) point out that laboratory tasks may overestimate the incidence of TOTs and diary studies may underestimate it, or both. But more important than the incidence is whether TOTs elicited artificially in the laboratory resemble those that occur naturally in real life. Luckily, both types do appear comparable. As Brown and McNeill (1966) note, the nature of the TOT experience tends to be similar from word to word and from subject to subject, and such invariance means that response measurement does not have to be adjusted under varying conditions (cf. Burke et al., 1991).

## ☐ Retrospective Evaluation

### TOTs and Academic Tests

As any teacher can confirm, students commonly complain that TOTs occur regularly during standard academic tests, which involve a focused recall effort with multiple retrievals of often marginally learned material in a limited period of time. Thus, we might expect that any naturally occurring retrieval problem would occur with greater frequency. Another factor that may increase the incidence of TOTs is situational stress. Although only superficially addressed in the TOT literature (cf. Brown, 1991; Chapter 2), it seems reasonable that stressful factors may lead to more TOTs, given what we already know about the negative effects of stress on memory retrieval (Buchanan, Tranel, & Adolphs, 2006; Kuhlmann, Piel, & Wolf, 2005). Finally, an academic test situation probably makes a TOT more memorable because of immediate negative consequences associated with retrieval failure.

Over the last two decades, I surveyed 359 college students enrolled in upper-level psychology classes at Southern Methodist University. The incidence of TOT experiences during academic tests is nearly universal, at 99%. Most claim that this happens on every test, either one (34%) or more (20%) times. The rest of the students estimate that TOTs occur once (8%) or several times (37%) per semester. Recovery rates for missing target words associated with TOTs are shown in Figure 3.1. The majority are eventually recovered, with most students claiming between a 50% and 80% recovery rate. Asked about when the target word recovery typically occurs, 31% said during the test, 39% said immediately after the test (within 10 min), and 29% said 30 min or more after the test. Diary research has shown that 70% of TOTs are recovered within 10 minutes (Burke et al., 1991), which is identical to the present 70% estimate (31% plus 39%) over a comparable

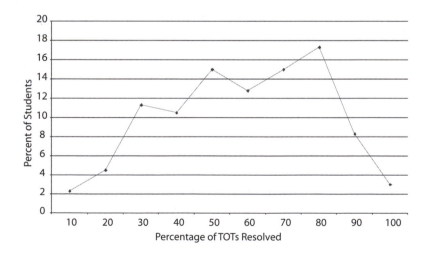

**FIGURE 3.1**   Academic test TOTS.

time frame. Perhaps the sudden reduction in test-induced stress as one leaves the room accounts for the greatest recovery, although this needs empirical verification.

# Naturally Occurring TOTs

Several retrospective queries regarding TOTs are embedded with a larger set of questions on other memory and cognitive issues. For example, The Error-Proneness Questionnaire contains 30 questions relating to memory problems, such as losing one's place in a sequence of behaviors, and picking up the wrong object. Among these are two items that resemble the standard definition of a TOT: "recall blank on known fact" and "blocked on name." With a college age sample, Reason (1984) found that recall blanks were experienced by 13% of persons on a daily basis, 26% weekly, and 32% monthly. Name blocks plagued 14% of respondents daily, 36% weekly, and 34% monthly. Also using a multiple-item (18) memory problem questionnaire, Thompson and Corcoran (1992) queried a large sample of adults across a broad age range and found that TOTs occurred daily for 14% of their sample, similar to that found by Reason (1984).

Using a memory problem questionnaire to survey older adults (64 to 75 years old), Sunderland, Watts, Baddeley, and Harris (1986) found that TOTs occurred once a week (modal response) and ranked at the top of 28 different memory failures. To obtain converging validation of this incidence, a relative of each study participant was also asked about how often he or she observed each memory problem in that family member. Relatives' evaluations were somewhat lower, with a modal frequency of TOTs occurring once a month. However, this may be due to the simple fact that they were not with the participant at all times, and the participant may not have commented on each incident to the relative. As with the self-report data, relatives also rated TOTs as the most frequent memory problem observed in their associated participant (actually, tied for first with "forgetting where you put something"). Comparing adults across the entire age span, and using only a question on TOTs, Burke et al. (1991, Study 1) discovered a TOT frequency estimate that fell in the average, or midrange (4.1), on the scale of 1 (never) to 7 (very frequently). Estimates of the number of TOTs per month averaged 3.2.

Although these retrospective reports vary considerably, TOTs seem to occur about once a week in everyday living (Burke et al., 1991; Sunderland et al., 1986), and one in seven persons experiences TOTs daily (Reason, 1984; Thompson & Corcoran, 1992). Furthermore, these retrospective estimates seem to change little with age (Burke et al., 1991; Reason, 1984; Thompson & Corcoran, 1992).

# ☐ Diary Studies

Most diary studies on TOTs extend across 4 weeks, during which time participants record all of their TOTs. Reason and Lucas (1984) suggest that diary investigations are like "wide-gauge trawl nets" which pick up the most salient of TOTs, and are limited by several problems:

> *Volunteer bias:* people who sign up may be more prone to TOTs.
> *Item selection:* noteworthy TOTs are selectively recorded, whereas others may be forgotten.
> *Information loss:* less information is recorded than actually occurs, because forgetting occurs between the TOT experience and when it is recorded.

The data from diary studies indicate that TOTs occur about once a week, and increase in frequency with age. Three of these investigations compare multiple-aged groups of subjects, but for the present chapter the data are collapsed across age groups, and details of these age differences are addressed later (Chapter 10). Burke et al. (1991) found the mean number of TOTs per month was 5.3 (range = 1 to 17), whereas Heine et al. (1999, Experiment 2) found a somewhat higher incidence of 7.0 per month in a slightly older sample. Finally, Cohen and Faulkner (1986) asked subjects to record only proper name TOTs and found a monthly average of 6.7, which is roughly comparable to the other two studies without such a restriction. In all studies, the youngest group had significantly fewer TOTs than the oldest group.

Studies evaluating only college-age participants have found slightly lower one-month averages of 3.4 (Gollan, Bonanni, & Montoya, 2005, Experiment 1), 4.7 (Schwartz, 2001a), 5.0 (Ecke, 1997), 5.2 (Ecke, 2004), and 5.4 (Gonzalez, 1996). Reason and Lucas (1984; Experiment 1) found a somewhat lower monthly average of 2.5 TOTs, but included only midage subjects (33 to 36 years) who were limited to a maximum of five TOTs total, all of which had to have been resolved.

The above data suggest that everyday TOTs probably occur at least once per week. This is probably an underestimate, given the nontrivial logistical limitations of having subjects remember to make note of an infrequently occurring behavior, and remember later to record it in their diaries. As Brown (1991) points out, one should expect an undercount because many of our ordinary TOTs may be resolved quickly, involve trivial information, or occur when preoccupied.

# ☐ Case Study

Linton (1996) conducted a unique 17-year investigation into the maintenance of knowledge (MOK), using herself as the sole participant. Her subject matter was Latin names for plants, and colored pictures were used
to cue these targets. Linton's goals in this research were to examine: (a)
the relationship between encoding difficulty and subsequent recall, (b)
changes in the knowledge base with repeated recall, and (c) TOT experiences. TOTs were defined in a broad and nonstandard manner, using
five different types: (1) a classic TOT (no further clarification given); (2)
the correct name retrieved, then rejected; (3) part of target word retrieved
with full recovery deemed likely; (4) no association with the target word
available; and (5) an incorrect name retrieved and acknowledged as such.

Over 8 years, 3,331 self-administered memory tests resulted in TOTs
36% of the time. Of 477 different botanical terms tested, 23% never elicited a TOT. The others were associated with TOTs from 1 to 11 times (see
Linton, 1996, p. 159 for a detailed distribution). Of the 14 terms that elicited
TOTs most often, 6 caused 8 TOTs, 6 caused 9 TOTs, 1 caused 10 TOTs, and
1 caused 11 TOTs. Within this subset of 14 mnemonically obstreperous
names, only 27% of the TOTs were resolved, a rate much lower than her
overall resolution rate of 47%. Linton (1996) speculated that perhaps the
lack of a resolution on one occasion increases the likelihood of a similar
outcome—an unresolved TOT—on the next encounter. Repeated TOTs
on the same items is an important empirical and theoretical issue, but
this has only been tackled in only one laboratory investigation. Warriner
and Humphreys (2008) confirmed Linton's speculation, showing that
a repeated TOT is three times more likely following a previously unresolved, compared to a resolved, TOT.

Linton (1996) made predictions about resolution likelihood while
experiencing a TOT, and was unimpressed with her accuracy. For TOTs
that were eventually resolved, her a priori estimate was 45%; for TOTs
that were not resolved, her prediction was 38%. To illustrate this point
more saliently, one botanical term elicited seven TOTs, none of which was
resolved, and the average resolution estimate was 43%. On another term
that also elicited seven TOTs, most of which were resolved (four times),
her average resolution estimate of 58% was not much different from the
consistently unresolved item.

Linton's procedure infuses some critical control features into a
naturalistic TOT investigation, and provides useful insights and careful observation. More specifically, she found a considerable variability
across items, a likelihood of repeated TOTs on the same items, and a
poor ability to predict resolution probability. Despite the limitations of a
very select set of materials (Latin botanical terms) and possible effects of

repeated testing (and repeated TOTs) with the same material, she should be applauded for this systematic and meticulous research design. Other such data collection efforts would be of great value with a broader range of materials.

# ☐ Laboratory Studies

## Comparability of Lab and Diary Studies

An important issue with laboratory research on TOTs is how well these resemble naturally occurring TOTs. With respect to qualitative resemblance, Ryan, Petty, and Wenzlaff (1982) found that over 90% of their participants claimed that their artificially induced lab TOTs resembled real ones. With respect to quantitative resemblance, two investigations have compared the same subjects in both laboratory and diary studies. Heine et al. (1999) found a modest but significant correlation (.21) between number of laboratory and diary TOTs. However, with age partialled out, this correlation became nonsignificant (.08). Burke et al. (1991) discovered a significant positive correlation between number of diary and lab studies TOTs, but only for young subjects (.58). Older adults, on the other hand, showed no relationship (–.23).

Thus, there is no meaningful or consistent statistical support for the comparability of incidence rate between natural and artificial TOTs. However, frequency is less of an issue because it may be dependent upon many factors, such as verbal ability, testing procedures, and specific knowledge set. Also, the relatively low incidence makes statistical comparison unstable. The more important question involves the quality of the experiences, and Ryan et al.'s (1982) inquiry suggests that they are comparable. However, additional research would be quite valuable, given the heavy reliance upon laboratory procedures in the TOT literature.

## General Laboratory Procedures

Much of the research conducted after Brown and McNeill (1966) has modeled their original design fairly closely. Definition cues predominate in lab investigations of TOTs, although a variety of nonlinguistic cues have also been used, including pictures, faces, odors, and sounds. Some studies also present target-related word(s) prior to (Chapter 4) or following (Chapter 8) the definition, with the aim of influencing either TOT rate or resolution probability through facilitating or inhibiting target word accessibility.

As noted earlier (Chapter 1), instructions can potentially affect the incidence of TOTs, as well as the presence of peripheral information about the target word (Chapter 5) and interlopers (Chapter 7) (cf. Harley & Bown, 1998). For this reason, it is important for published reports on TOTs to include the complete instructions given to subjects (Meyer & Bock, 1992). TOT lab studies have used both individual and group testing procedures. Brown and McNeil's (1966) original investigation was conducted on a large group of students. When students in the group experienced TOTs, they indicated such by raising their hands and the procedure was halted to allow them to fill out their response sheets concerning that particular TOT experience. Could such group procedures, where subjects witness others having TOTs, alter the threshold for the experience? One could argue that this could increase the incidence (suggestibility) or decrease it (not wanting to slow the procedure). This issue has not been raised, although a considerable amount of research has used group testing procedures because of their convenience and efficiency.

## Selecting Target Words (Piloting)

A TOT is a relatively rare event, and the majority of trials in lab studies are not of value because the correct target word is retrieved. Refining materials through pilot testing can improve efficiency and increase TOT yield (Brown & Nix, 1996; Dahlgren, 1998; Frick-Horbury & Guttentag, 1998; Pine et al., 2007). Brown and McNeill (1966) did this in their original investigation, using nine pilot subjects to refine their materials and procedure. Burke et al. (1991) also culled some target words reported by diary participants (Study 1) for their subsequent lab investigation (Study 2). As an extreme (and clever) example of maximizing efficiency, Rubin (1975) used only four target words, those that elicited the most TOTs in Brown and McNeill (1966): Ebenezer, philatelist, sampan, and ambergris.

To assist future TOTs research, the Appendix contains a list of target words with TOT incidence. These data come from studies using line drawing (Alario & Ferrand, 1999; Snodgrass & Vanderwart, 1980) and definition (Abrams, Trunk, & Merrill, 2007; Burke et al., 1991) cues. Table 3.1 is a more general reference for possible stimulus materials, listing studies that provide their target words or target word cues.

## TOT Incidence

Laboratory investigations reporting TOT rates appear in Table 3.2, organized by type of cue: definition, picture (line drawing), face, definition plus picture, TOTimal, paired associate, odor, and music. Different outcomes

---

**TABLE 3.1**  Studies Listing Targets or Target Word Cues

---

**Definitions Plus Targets**
Astell et al. (1996)
Beattie and Coughlin (1999)
Biedermann et al. (2008)
Burke et al. (1991)
Frick-Horbury and Guttentag (1998)
Harley and Bown (1998)
Jones (1989)
Kohn et al. (1987)
May and Clayton (1973)
Meyer and Bock (1992)
Perfect and Hanley (1992)
Viglioccco (1999)
Yaniv and Meyer (1987)

**Targets**
Gollan and Brown (2006)
Gollan and Silverberg (2001)
Pine, Bird, and Kirk (2007)

**Celebrity Descriptions Plus Targets**
Brennen et al. (1990)

**Celebrity Targets**
Jönsson et al. (2005)

**Famous Landmarks**
Brennen et al. (1990)

**Pictures Plus Targets (Number)**
Faust et al. (1997)
Georgieff et al. (1998)
Pine et al. (2007)
Pyers et al. (2010)

**Odors**
Jönsson et al. (2005)
Cleary et al. (2010)

**Illusory Definitions**
Schwartz (1998)

---

**TABLE 3.2** Laboratory Investigations Reporting TOT Rates

| | | SUB | TAR | COR | TOT |
|---|---|---|---|---|---|
| **DEFINITIONS** | | | | | |
| Abrams and Rodriguez (2005) | | 60 | (96) | 8 | 34.5 |
| Abrams et al. (2003) | Exp 1 | 50 | (78) | 10 | 34 |
| | Exp 2 | 60 | (90) | 16 | 27 |
| | Exp 3 | 87 | (80) | 13 | 30 |
| Askari (1999) | unrelated cue (Farsi) | 16 | (36) | 15 | 50 |
| Astell and Harley (1996) | | 12 O | (24) | 5.5 | 80 |
| | | 12 DAT | | 12.0 | 46 |
| Bacon et al. (2006) | | 15 | (100) | 11.9 | 78.7 |
| | | 15 LOR | | 12.9 | 69.6 |
| Bak (1987) | | 50 | (20) | 6.9 | 34.3 |
| Beattie and Coughlin (1999) | gesture | 30 | (25) | 14.8 | 66.8 |
| | no gesture | 30 | | 9.6 | 72.4 |
| Brennen et al. (1990) | Exp 1 | 15 | (50) | 21.0 | — |
| | Exp 2 | 30 | (50) | 17.0 | — |
| | Exp 3 | 30 | (40) | 14.5 | — |
| Brown and McNeill (1966) | | 56 | (49) | 8.5 | — |
| Brown and Nix (1996) | Pilot | 30 | (72) | 9.7 | 52.2 |
| | Main | 20 | (25) | 15.1 | 63.6 |
| | Main | 20 O | (25) | 14.2 | 74.0 |
| Burke and Laver (1990) | | 21 | (100) | 17.8 | — |
| | | 21 | | 23.2 | — |
| Burke et al. (1991) | Study 2 | 21 | (100) | 7.6 | 49.6 |
| | | 21 O | | 9.6 | 58.5 |
| Cleary (2006) | Exp 2 (primed) | 14 | (56) | 24 | 23 |
| | Exp 2 (unprimed) | 14 | (56) | 31 | 14 |
| | Exp 3 (primed) | 53 | (56) | 14 | 46 |
| | Exp 3 (unprimed) | 53 | (56) | 15 | 36 |
| Dahlgren (1998) | | 62 | (57) | 3.4 | 31.0 |
| | | 62 M | | 3.1 | 46.6 |
| | | 62 O | | 4.7 | 44.6 |
| Ecke (2001) | | 24 BL | (21) | 19.2 | 36.7 |
| Ecke (2004) | | 35 BL | | 7 | 55 |
| | | 34 BL | | 18 | 40 |
| Ferrand (2001) | Exp 1 | 60 | (40) | 10.3 | 63.5 |
| | Exp 2 | 90 | (40) | 12.4 | 74.9 |
| Finley and Sharp (1989) | | 16 O | (41) | 25.9 | — |
| Frick-Horbury and Guttentag (1998) | | 36 | (50) | 12.0 | — |
| Gardiner et al. (1973) | Pilot | 20 | (50) | 5.8 | — |

*(Continued)*

**TABLE 3.2** Laboratory Investigations Reporting TOT Rates (Continued)

| | | SUB | TAR | COR | TOT |
|---|---|---|---|---|---|
| Gollan and Silverberg (2001) | | 25 ML | (80) | 5.1 | 91.5 |
| Gollan et al. (2005 Exp 2) | English targets | 25 BL** | (80) | 10.8 | 80.8 |
| | Hebrew targets | 25 BL** | (80) | 15.4 | 75.0 |
| | Personal names | 28 ML | (46) | 31 | 50 |
| | Personal names | 28 BL | | 28 | 43 |
| | Famous names | 28 ML | (46) | 34 | 39 |
| | Famous names | 28 BL | | 38 | 36 |
| Harley and Bown (1998) | Exp 1, H frq, H ngh | 85 | (15) | 9.3 | 75.1 |
| | Exp 1, H frq, L ngh | 85 | (15) | 11.7 | 57.1 |
| | Exp 1, L frq, H ngh | 85 | (15) | 15.4 | 59.7 |
| | Exp 1, L frq, L ngh | 85 | (15) | 29.8 | 29.3 |
| | Exp 2, H frq, H ngh | 92 | (15) | 9.9 | 75.4 |
| | Exp 2, H frq, L ngh | 92 | (15) | 11.5 | 77.2 |
| | Exp 2, L frq, H ngh | 92 | (15) | 9.2 | 78.4 |
| | Exp 2, L frq, L ngh | 92 | (15) | 15.1 | 68.0 |
| Heine et al. (1999) | Study 1 | 30 | 112 | 18 | — |
| | | 30 O | | 23 | — |
| | | 30 OO | | 28 | — |
| James and Burke (2000) | Exp 1, unprimed | 36 | (57) | 11.7 | 36.3 |
| | Exp 1, unprimed | 36 O | | 13.8 | 42.6 |
| | Exp 2, unprimed | 36 | (57) | 7.9 | 36.0 |
| | Exp 3, unprimed | 36 O | | 11.4 | 40.4 |
| Koriat and Lieblich (1974) | | 56 | (62) | 11.2 | — |
| Kozlowski (1977) | Exp 1 | 19 | (75) | 21.7 | — |
| | Exp 2 | 26 | (50) | 12.6 | — |
| Lesk and Womble (2004) | Exp 1 | | | | |
| | placebo | 32 | (50) | 8.0 | 36.7 |
| | caffeine | 32 | (50) | 13.3 | 33.2 |
| Lovelace (1987) | | 21 | (45) | 21 | — |
| Maril et al. (2005) | | 15 | (336) | 8.2 | 38 |
| Meyer and Bock (1992) | Exp 1, unrelated | 411 | (12) | 13.3 | 18.6 |
| | Exp 2, unrelated | 348 | (12) | 13.5 | 16.0 |
| | Exp 3, unrelated | 261 | (10) | 15.0 | 22.1 |
| Murakami (1980) | | 300 | (20) | 3.7 | — |
| Perfect and Hanley (1992) | Exp 1 | 29 | (40) | 26.8 | 29.3 |
| | Exp 2a | 18 | (30) | 23.3 | 35.4 |
| | Exp 2b | 18 | (30) | 17.4 | 27.6 |
| Rastle and Burke (1996)* | Exp 1, unprimed | 30 | (45) | 8 | 32 |
| | Exp 1, unprimed | 30 O | (45) | 16 | 16 |
| | Exp 1, primed | 30 | (45) | 4 | 46 |

**TABLE 3.2**  Laboratory Investigations Reporting TOT Rates (Continued)

|  |  | SUB | TAR | COR | TOT |
|---|---|---|---|---|---|
|  | Exp 1, primed | 30 O | (45) | 10 | 54 |
|  | Exp 2, pleasant | 24 | (30) | 10 | 54 |
|  | Exp 2, pleasant | 24 O | (30) | 10 | 56 |
|  | Exp 2, syllable | 24 | (30) | 8 | 47 |
|  | Exp 2, syllable | 24 O | (30) | 11 | 49 |
|  | Exp 2, case | 24 | (30) | 12 | 44 |
|  | Exp 2, case | 24 O | (30) | 10 | 46 |
|  | Exp 2, baseline | 24 | (90) | 12 | 30 |
|  | Exp 2, baseline | 24 O | (90) | 20 | 34 |
|  | Exp 3, pleasant | 40 | (22) | 6 | 50 |
|  | Exp 3, syllable | 40 | (22) | 7 | 43 |
|  | Exp 3, unprimed | 40 | (44) | 10 | 32 |
| Rubin (1975) | Exp 1 | 259 | (4) | 9.7 | — |
| Schwartz (1998) | Exp 2 first attempt | 32 | (80) | 44 | 38 |
|  | Exp 2 second attempt | 32 | (80) | 34 | — |
| Schwartz et al. (2000) | Exp 1, answerable | 41 | (80) | 34.6 | 36 |
|  | Exp 2, answerable | 41 | (80) | 31.0 | 34 |
|  | Exp 3, answerable | 41 | (80) | 31.6 | 38 |
| Schwartz (2001) | Exp 1 | 80 | (80) | 28 | 38 |
|  | Exp 2 | 50 | (80) | 24 | 36 |
|  | Exp 3 | 45 | (40) | 44 | 28 |
|  | Exp 4 | 49 | (80) | 22 | 41 |
| Schwartz (2002b) |  | 84 | (80) | 32 | 35 |
| Schwartz (2010) |  | 30 | (99) | 26 | 34 |
| Vigliocco et al. (1999) | Exp 1 | 37 | (47) | 13 | 39 |
| Vigliocco et al. (1997) |  | 60 | (54) | 9 | 51 |
| Vitevitch and Sommers (2003) | Exp 1 | 24 | (120) | 2.1 | 35.9 |
|  |  | 24 O | (120) | 3.1 | 42.9 |
| White and Abrams (2002) |  | 37 | (90) | 16.6 | 28.2 |
|  |  | 22 O | (90) | 14.3 | 36.4 |
|  |  | 26 OO | (90) | 13.2 | 37.0 |
| Widner et al. (1996) | Pilot, high demand | — | (60) | 18.8 | — |
|  | Pilot, low demand | — | (60) | 6.3 | — |
|  | Exp 1, high demand | 20 | (60) | 10.8 | — |
|  | Exp 1, low demand | 20 | (60) | 3.7 | — |
| Widner et al. (2005) | Exp 2 | 30 W | (30) | 18.3 | — |
| Yaniv and Meyer (1987) | Exp 1 | 44 | (52) | 18.4 | — |
|  | Exp 2 | 46 | (52) | 15.9 | — |

*(Continued)*

**TABLE 3.2** Laboratory Investigations Reporting TOT Rates (Continued)

| | | SUB | TAR | COR | TOT |
|---|---|---|---|---|---|
| **PICTURES/LINE DRAWINGS** | | | | | |
| Alario and Ferrand (1999) | | 28 | (400) | 1.2 | — |
| Brown and Nix (1996) | Pilot | 30 | (72) | 8.4 | 56.2 |
| | Main | 20 | (25) | 12.9 | 69.2 |
| | Main | 20 O | (25) | 7.9 | 86.0 |
| Cleary and Reyes (2009) | Exp 1 | 70 | (120) | 33 | 9 |
| | Exp 2 | 76 | (120) | 42 | 11 |
| Cross and Burke (2004) | Primed | 24 | (32) | 8.6 | 72.1 |
| | Primed | 24 O | (32) | 26.2 | 57.8 |
| | Unprimed | 24 | (32) | 8.1 | 67.7 |
| | Unprimed | 24 O | (32) | 22.2 | 57.2 |
| Evrard (2002) | | 35 | (16) | 1.8 | — |
| | | 30 M | (16) | 1.1 | — |
| | | 33 O | (16) | 0.9 | — |
| Faust et al. (1997) | | 14 LD | (66) | 29.7 | 66.2 |
| | | 14 C | (66) | 10.8 | 85.7 |
| Faust et al. (2003) | | 15 LD | (90) | 33.7 | 77.9 |
| | | 15 C | (90) | 19.2 | 64.0 |
| Faust and Sharfstein-Friedman (2003) | | 23 LD | (70) | 13.4 | 86.1 |
| | | 23 C | (70) | 7.1 | 92.6 |
| Georgieff et al. (1998) | | 11 D | (53) | 1.0 | — |
| | | 11 W | (53) | 1.2 | — |
| Gollan et al. (2005) | Exp 2 | 28 ML | (50) | 23 | 66 |
| | | 28 BL | | 34 | 43 |
| Gollan and Acenas (2004) | Exp 1 | 30 ML | (217) | 4.0 | 93 |
| | Exp 1 | 30 BL | | 7.7 | 84 |
| | Exp 2 | 30 ML | (225) | 4.5 | 95 |
| | Exp 2 | 30 BL | | 12.2 | 84 |
| Gollan and Brown (2006) | Exp 1, easy targets | 22 | (30) | 13.5 | 81.1 |
| | Exp 1, easy targets | 22 O | (30) | 16.2 | 16.4 |
| | Exp 1, hard targets | 22 | (30) | 14.7 | 73.3 |
| | Exp 1, hard targets | 22 O | (30) | 22.3 | 46.8 |
| Hanly and Vandenberg (2010) | | 14 LD | (143) | — | 2.3 |
| | | 14 C | (143) | — | 1.4 |
| Mitchell (1989) | | 48 | (96) | 1.2 | 95.5 |
| | | 48 O | (96) | 1.4 | 96.0 |
| Snodgrass and Vanderwart (1980) | | 42 | 260 | 0.7 | — |

**TABLE 3.2** Laboratory Investigations Reporting TOT Rates (Continued)

|  |  | SUB | TAR | COR | TOT |
|---|---|---|---|---|---|
| **FACES** |  |  |  |  |  |
| Brédart and Valentine (1998) |  | 42 | (30) | 7.8 | 74.7 |
| Burke et al. (2004) |  | 50 | (86) | 12.0 | 42 |
|  |  | 40 O |  | 21.0 | 33 |
| Cleary and Speckler (2007) | Exp 2 | 25 | (120) | 14.0 | 32 |
| Delazer et al. (2003) |  | 19 A | (27) | 34.0 | 12.2 |
|  |  | 24 MI |  | 30.3 | 50.0 |
|  |  | 20 O |  | 34.0 | 44.4 |
| Evrard (2002) |  | 35 | (16) | 8.9 | — |
|  |  | 30 M |  | 13.3 | — |
|  |  | 33 O |  | 18.3 | — |
| Galdo-Alvarez et al. (2009b) |  | 13 Y | (200) | 42 | 21 |
|  |  | 10 O | (200) | 42 | 24 |
| James (2006) |  | 36 | (58) | 7 | 48 |
|  |  | 36 O |  | 11 | 50 |
| Jönsson et al. (2005, Exp 1) |  | 40 | (30) | 18 | 29 |
| Lindín and Díaz (2010) |  | 10 | (800) | 22 | 22 |
| Lindín et al. (2010) |  | 12 | (800) | 23 | 22 |
| Riefer (2002) |  | 15 W | (27) | 25 | 59 |
| Shafto et al. (2010) |  | 15 Y | (200) | 42 | 15 |
|  |  | 15 O | (200) | 38 | 15 |
| Yarmey (1973) |  | 53 | (40) | 13.7 | — |
| **DEFINITIONS + PICTURES** |  |  |  |  |  |
| Caramazza and Miozzo (2005) | Exp 1 | 53 | (152) | 5.7 | 79.9 |
|  | Exp 2 | 42 | (152) | 8.7 | 69.5 |
| Choi and Smith (2005) |  | 80 | (48) | 5.5 | — |
| Gollan and Brown (2006) | Exp 2, easy targets | 36 ML | (34) | 14 | 79 |
|  | Exp 2, easy targets | 36 BL | (34) | 28 | 64 |
|  | Exp 2, med targets | 36 ML | (34) | 26 | 54 |
|  | Exp 2, med targets | 36 BL | (34) | 33 | 33 |
|  | Exp 2, hard targets | 36 ML | (34) | 21 | 27 |
|  | Exp 2, hard targets | 36 BL | (34) | 16 | 9 |
| Miozzo and Caramazza (1997) | Exp 1 | 16 | (160) | 13.4 | 76.3 |
|  | Exp 2 | 32 | (152) | 13.1 | 76.1 |
| **TOTIMALS** |  |  |  |  |  |
| Schwartz and Smith (1997) | Exp 1 | 82 | (12) | 13.6 | 37 |
|  | Exp 2 | 96 | (12) | 14.8 | 35 |
|  | Exp 3 | 112 | (12) | 16.2 | 33 |

*(Continued)*

**TABLE 3.2** Laboratory Investigations Reporting TOT Rates (Continued)

| | | SUB | TAR | COR | TOT |
|---|---|---|---|---|---|
| Schwartz (1998) | Exp 1 | 101 | (6) | 11.5 | 50 |
| Smith et al. (1991) | Exp 1 | 41 | (12) | 25 | 33 |
| | Exp 2 | 61 | (12) | 34 | 27.8 |
| Smith et al. (2004) | Exp 1 | 41 | (6) | 42 | 23.7 |
| | Exp 2 | 44 | (6) | 29 | 41.7 |
| | Exp 3 | 115 | (6) | 35 | 37 |
| **PAIRED ASSOCIATES** | | | | | |
| Maril et al. (2001) | | 14 | (414) | 9.3 | 39.9 |
| Metcalfe et al. (1993) | Exp 3, A-B, A-B | 30 | (12) | 31[†] | 40 |
| | Exp 3, A-B, A-D | 30 | | 29 | 13 |
| | Exp 3, A-B, C-D | 30 | | 19 | 19 |
| | Exp 4, A-B, A-B | 24 | (12) | 43[‡] | 50 |
| | Exp 4, A-B, A-D | 24 | | 46 | 19 |
| | Exp 4, A-B, C-D | 24 | | 30 | 22 |
| Ryan et al. (1982) | 5 s study time | 99 | (14) | 8.0 | 61.0 |
| | 3 sec study time | | | 10.3 | 63.9 |
| | 1 sec study time | | | 15.5 | 72.0 |
| **ODORS** | | | | | |
| Cleary et al. (2010) | | 66 | (80) | 12 | 39 |
| Jönsson and Olsson (2003) | Exp 2 | 40 | (70) | 17.3 | 19.0 |
| Jönsson et al. (2005) | Exp 1 | 40 | (30) | 5 | 30 |
| Lawless and Engen (1977) | Exp 3 | 12 | (48) | 6.4 | — |
| **MUSICAL (TV SHOW THEME)** | | | | | |
| Riefer et al. (1995) | | 45 W | (50) | 20.8 | — |
| Riefer (2002) | | 15 W | (27) | 21 | 48 |

*Note:* Beattie & Coughlin, 1999, gave the first letter as clue after 30 s of no response. Although they argue that this increases TOT rate, there are no data given on the incidence of TOTs pre- and post-cue.

*Table Key:*  SUB = number of subjects; TAR = number of targets; COR = % correct responses; TOT = % TOTs.

*Subject Key:*  C = children; M = midage; O = older, OO = old–old; W = wide age range; BL = bilingual; ML = monolingual; A = Alzheimer's; MI = mild cognitive impairment; LOR = lorazepam; D = depressed.

\* Estimated from Fig. 2, p. 592 (Experiment 1), Fig. 4, p. 597 (Experiment 2), Fig. 5, p. 600 (Experiment 3).

\*\* These bilinguals were asked to retrieve two target words for each definition, in English and Hebrew. Thus, these rates may be higher because the incidence would be multiplied. Gollan & Silverberg (2001).

† Estimated from Fig. 3 (p. 858).

‡ Estimated from Fig. 4 (p. 859).

within an article are reported separately. Also provided are number (and type) of subjects tested, number of target words cued, mean overall percent correct, and mean percent TOTs. These data on TOT incidence suggest that about half (48%) of all outcomes have an incidence between 6 and 15% and 70% of outcomes yield an incidence of 20% or less. The mean incidence is 15% across all outcomes, in line with the prior estimate of 10 to 20% (Brown, 1991).

# Definitions

Most TOT studies use dictionary definition cues (see Table 3.2), usually consisting of a short sentence or phrase. The mean TOT rate across outcomes with definition cues is 15%. A potential problem with definitional cues is that, on occasion, words appearing in the definition could influence target word retrieval (cf. Brown & Nix, 1996). The mechanisms underlying TOTs probably derive from complex connections among the semantic and phonological aspects of words, and such relationships between words that appear in the definition and the target word could influence TOT rates in either a positive or negative direction (cf. Burke et al., 1991). In fact, the procedure for altering the elicitation (Chapter 4) and resolution (Chapter 8) of TOTs capitalizes on just this, prime words or cue words that are related to the target.

Brown and McNeill (1966) were cognizant of this potential problem and each word definition was "...edited so as to contain no words that closely resembled the one being defined" (p. 326). Brown and Nix (1996) illustrated this concern using a definition from Burke et al. (1991, p. 574): "What do you call a vessel, usually an ornamental vase on a pedestal, which is used to preserve the ashes of the dead?" This cue definition for the word "urn" includes the semantically related words *vase* and *vessel*, which could potentially affect target word access in either a positive or negative direction.

# Nondefinitional Visual Cues

The most commonly used nonverbal cue in TOT research is black and white line drawings, although color pictures have become more popular as technology has allowed easier access to these stimuli (Alario & Ferrand, 1999; Brown & Nix, 1996; Evrard, 2002; Faust & Sharfstein-Friedman, 2003; Faust, Dimitrovsky, & Shacht, 2003; Faust et al., 1997; Georgieff, Dominey, Michel, Marie-Cardine, & Dalery, 1998; Gollan et al., 2005, Experiment 2; Gollan & Acenas, 2004; Gollan & Brown, 2006; Mitchell, 1989; Snodgrass & Vanderwart, 1980).

Also popular are face picture cues of celebrities from TV, movies, sports, or politics (Beeson, Holland, & Murray, 1997; Brennen et al., 1990; Burke, Locantore, & Austin, 2004; Cleary & Speckler, 2007; Cross & Burke, 2004; Delazer, Semenza, Reiner, Hofer, & Benke, 2003; Evrard, 2002; James, 2006; Jönsson et al., 2005; Maylor, 1990b; Read & Bruce, 1982; Yarmey, 1973). Brédart and Valentine (1998) used face cues of characters from comics and cartoons, and Riefer (2002) used whole-cast group photos from TV shows to cue the show's title. The popularity of face stimuli is probably driven, in part, by the higher incidence rate of TOTs on proper names found in both real-world and laboratory studies (see Chapter 10). Finally, Cleary and Reyes (2009) employed pictures of famous structures (e.g., Eiffel Tower) as target word cues.

## Olfactory Cues

Given the difficulty in identifying odor names (see Table 3.2), these materials would seem to be ideal for eliciting TOTs. Lawless and Engen (1977) first examined TOTs to odors, and coined the acronym TON for tip of the nose. As noted earlier (see Chapter 2), this label implies a phenomenon separate from TOTs, whereas in fact the subjectively perceived problem is still connected with word output, regardless of the sensory input mode of the cue (eye, nose, ear, etc.) (cf. Valentine, Brennan, & Brédart, 1996).

Odor-cued TOTs appear to be distinct from other types of TOTs. With nonodor TOTs, subjects often have access to some aspects of the missing target word: first letter, number of syllables, and the like (see Chapter 5). However, with TOTs to odors, fragmentary aspects of the target word rarely come to mind. Jönsson and Olsson (2003) found that only 10% of odor-cue TOTs had any associated information reported, and these usually did not match the target word. Furthermore, Lawless and Engen (1977) noted that peripheral information available to the subject relates more to the conceptual properties of the odor, such as similar odors, category of the odor, origin of the object, and place associated with the smell. This difference suggests that the retrieval problem with odor-cued TOTs is earlier in the word selection process, relating more to semantic clarity than word label generation (see Chapter 9). More specifically, the primary problem may be identifying the object that is the source of the odor.

Supporting this interpretation, Jönsson et al. (2005) asked subjects whether they knew the odor identity but could not get the name (true TOT) or could not identify the odor source. They found that most formerly labeled TOTs with odors were actually failures to identify rather than failure to name. Jönsson and Olsson (2003, Experiment 2) further confirm that TOTs with odors appear to stem more from a feeling of imminent identification of the odor source rather than production of the odor name.

# Paired Associates

A methodological problem with most diary and laboratory TOT research is lack of control over the strength of cue-to-target word association (Smith, 1994). More precisely, we do not have a reliable measure of how well subjects actually know the target word being cued. One way to establish control over the target word strength is with artificial materials learned under controlled conditions. Ryan et al. (1982) had subjects learn 64 word pairs, and presented one of the words at test as a cue for the other. Similarly, Metcalfe et al. (1993) evaluated TOTs using paired associates in a traditional interference transfer paradigm, where two lists were learned in succession. As with Ryan et al. (1982), stimulus words were provided at test to cue the response words. Whereas these paired associate (PA) designs provide needed control; Valentine et al. (1996) point out a conceptual limitation with such materials. TOTs usually involve knowledge of semantics in the absence of phonology. Artificially acquired word pairs do not model this well because retrieval depends upon activating the associative connection between the two words instead of the phonological or lexical representation for a particular word. More specifically, the response word may be accessible in such PA designs, but the association with a stimulus word is weak (which response links to which stimulus?). In contrast, during TOTs the target word itself is inaccessible or difficult to activate.

# TOTimals

This problem of cue-to-target word strength has been addressed through use of a clever set of materials designed specifically for TOT research. These are artificially constructed animals, or TOTimals, devised to "induce high levels of TOT states through the use of stimuli whose acquisition and retention can be controlled and that refer unambiguously to recall targets designed by the experimenter" (Smith, Brown, & Balfour, 1991, p. 445). TOTimals were also constructed to boost TOT incidence for greater data collection efficiency, and to eliminate negative TOTs (TOT–) where the subject's intended target word differs from the one designated by the experimenter. Each of 12 TOTimals has a three-syllable name (with different initial letters), picture, size description, preferred food, and geographical habitat (country). An example from Schwartz and Smith (1997) is presented in Figure 3.2. TOTimals have been used to evaluate a broad range of empirical and theoretical issues regarding TOTs: can subjects have TOTs for unnamed targets (Schwartz, 1998), do TOTs vary with item strength (study trials) (Smith et al., 1991; Smith, Balfour, & Brown, 1994), and does TOT incidence vary with amount of cue information provided at test (e.g., country, size, picture; Schwartz & Smith, 1997)? TOTimals do

Yelkey

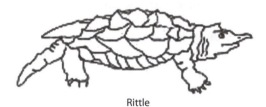

Rittle

**FIGURE 3.2** Examples of TOTimals.

yield higher TOT rates at around 25% (see Table 3.2), fulfilling one of the goals behind constructing such materials.

Despite the methodological advantages associated with TOTimals, there are some drawbacks. Given that the TOTimals combine physical features of real animals in different ways, prior knowledge may cause interference and influence TOT rates. For example, the Boshertin has a strong resemblance to a mongoose, whereas the Rittlefin looks something like a frog (see Smith, 1994, p. 33). Valentine et al. (1996) bring up another issue with the use of TOTimals: subjects unable to recall a TOTimal name may simply not have learned it earlier. Smith et al. (1991) argue that being able to correctly recognize the name demonstrates recall ability, but Valentine et al. (1996) disagree and suggest that some recognizable names could be too weak ever to be recalled. Valentine et al. (1996) suggest that this issue could be addressed by counting TOTs only for those TOTimals that had been previously recalled on at least one trial, which would demonstrate beyond a doubt that the particular name is potentially recallable.

Valentine et al. (1996) bring up one additional point pertinent to all artificial and recently learned materials (e.g., Ryan et al., 1982). If subjects have just learned information in the laboratory, they may experience a greater expectancy bias. More specifically, they may feel that recall should be imminent because they have learned the material only minutes before. Inserting an extended retention interval between learning and test could reduce this potential problem.

## Subject-Generated Cues

Rather than provide cues for specific target words, Gruneberg et al. (1973) had subjects prospect for TOTs on their own, instructing them to "... think of things that you know you know, but cannot give the actual word for" (p. 188). If subjects failed to generate TOTs on their own, Gruneberg et al. (1973) provided various memory categories to search through: personal acquaintances, capital cities, and sporting events. Subjects averaged 10 TOTs (range = 3 to 25) on their own, 38% of which were produced without category suggestions from the experimenter. Note that this outcome is not listed in Table 3.2 because there was no control over the target word cueing procedure, total number of success-ful retrievals.

## Cue Comparisons

Several studies have compared the relative efficacy of different types of cues in eliciting TOTs. Brown and Nix (1996) used both definition and picture cues for the same target words (different groups of subjects), and found no difference in TOT rate. This outcome seems at odds with the difference in average TOT rate for definition (15%) versus picture (11%) cue studies presented in Table 3.2. However, this disparity across studies using picture versus definition cues may result from differences between difficulty level of the typical items used in each study. Also, some stud-ies reporting TOTs for pictured objects were designed primarily to norm relatively high-frequency target words (Alario & Ferrand, 1999; Snodgrass & Vanderwart, 1980) and not to examine TOTs.

In other comparisons, Riefer (2002) looked at both visual (cast photo) and auditory (theme music) cues for TV show titles, and found no difference in TOT frequency, partial target word information, or interlopers. Furthermore, Ecke (2004) found that definition cues and translation-word equivalent cues yielded the same numbers of TOTs in bilinguals. Although limited, the above research suggests that the form of the target word cue does not appear to influence the likelihood of evoking a TOT.

## Response Mode

Many laboratory studies on TOTs require written responses from subjects. However, Kohn et al. (1987) point out a problem with this type of response: "The TOT phenomenon is a breakdown in spoken language, not written language. Therefore, to the extent that the stored orthographic representation for a word is different from its general phonological representation, spoken responses are more appropriate ... ." (p. 246)

Dahlgren (1998) used only oral, rather than written, responses in the belief that an oral response would facilitate TOT resolution. She reasoned that with oral responses, subjects could put more focus on the word search, whereas written responses would not aid this process. Dahlgren (1998) did not, incidentally, believe that response mode would affect TOT incidence, just resolution. Astell and Harley (1996) have argued that with written responses, subjects may include more high FOKs thereby inflating the TOT rate, and that oral responding provides more objective evidence on whether subjects are in a true TOT state.

It would seem reasonable (and easy) to address this issue by comparing TOT probability with oral versus written target word production. This particular comparison has not, to my knowledge, been conducted and would be of value both from an empirical and a theoretical position. The most influential theory of TOTs involves a breakdown in the connections between the semantic to phonological systems (Burke et al., 1991; see Chapter 9), and a comparison of written and oral response paradigms might be germane to this speculation.

## Onset Latency

How long does it take for one to consciously realize that a TOT is occurring? Heine et al. (1999) evaluated the time course of TOTs by marking three different points in the process:

1. Initiation of retrieval: cue presentation
2. Onset of a TOT: button press by the subject
3. Resolution: target word spoken

TOT onset (steps 1 to 2) took about 7 seconds, as estimated from their Figure 1 (p. 451). Given that the few seconds may be required to read the definition on the computer screen, this would probably make the actual onset of TOT following full cue processing to be closer to 5 seconds.

In a similar procedure, Maril et al. (2001) examined how long it took subjects to decide which state they were in, (button press) following presentation of the target word cue. Know (K) responses (1.8 s) were significantly faster than both don't know (DK) (2.2 s) and TOT (2.9 s). Similarly, Maril et al. (2005) found that identifying TOTs took significantly more time (2.8 s) than FOKs (2.6 s), DKs (2.0 s), and Ks (1.9 s) (cf. Goodglass et al., 1984).

TOTs take roughly 1 second longer than a K response in both investigations. The discrepancy between the TOT onset in Heine et al. (1999) and the Maril studies (5 versus 3 s, respectively) may reflect important procedural differences between their investigations: Maril's subjects made this decision while having their brain imaged in an MRI scanner, whereas Heine et al.'s (1999) subjects were not being scanned. In general, the above research consistently shows that TOTs take about a half a second longer than either DKs or Ks, with the latter showing little difference.

These efforts to measure TOT onset latencies are potentially useful in establishing temporal distinctions between TOTs and other retrieval outcomes, but this research is encumbered by the measurement issue of how to extract the time to read the definition from the total latency. A retrieval effort cannot be fully initiated until the cue is completely comprehended. How much time is needed for this initial processing? Díaz et al. (2007) eliminated this quandary by using pictorial rather than definition cues. TOT onset latencies were again significantly longer (1.5 s) than either K (1.1 s) or DK (1.0 s) latencies, with no difference between the latter. The magnitudes of these differences were similar in two subsequent investigations with face stimuli (Lindín & Díaz, 2010: TOT = 1.7, K = 1.5 s, DK = 1.2 s; Galdo-Alvarez et al., 2009b: TOT = 1.9 s, K = 1.4 s, DK = 1.4 s) (also see Galdo-Alvarez et al., 2009a).

# ☐ Methodological Issues

## Verifying TOTs

Given that a TOT report is based on subjective evaluation of a private mental experience, it is important to verify that the target word that the subject has in mind is the same as the one designated by the experimenter (TOT+). This is typically accomplished by a recognition test: *yes/no*, where the subject is presented the target word and asked whether this is the one she had in mind (Brown & McNeill, 1966; Brown & Nix, 1996), or *forced choice*, where the target word is accompanied by one to three distractor words (e.g., Abrams, White, & Eitel, 2003; Burke et al., 1991; Galdo-Alvarez et al., 2009b; Heine et al., 1999; White & Abrams, 2002). Some also provide *don't know* as an alternative on the forced choice recognition test (Burke et al., 1991). This topic was covered earlier in Chapter 2, but bears repeating because the exclusion of TOT– items from the overall TOT total is inconsistently applied across studies. This lack of a standardized way of dealing with these items makes across-experiment comparisons difficult and potentially decreases the accuracy of within-experiment comparisons of priming/cueing efficacy.

The choice of foil words in forced choice recognition tests may bias a recognition evaluation. Some investigations use a set of three distractor words where one shares a semantic relationship with the target, another has an orthographic relationship with the target, and one has no relationship (cf. Abrams, Trunk, & Merrill, 2007). With this particular assortment, an attentive subject could identify the target word through elimination. To repeat an illustration used earlier, Heine et al.'s (1999) recognition test for the target word "grout" had (a) a related word with a different first letter ("plaster"), (b) a related word with the same first letter ("glue"), and (c) an unrelated word with the same first letter ("glair"). Given this same pattern across test items, one could identify the two synonyms from among the three choices sharing a common first letter. As another example, White and Abrams' (2002) target word "abdicate" was accompanied by a semantically related word ("relinquish"), a phonologically related word ("abrogate"), and an unrelated word ("presume"). Again, an astute subject could select the target word by first identifying the two synonyms and then picking the one that matched the first letter of one of the other two alternatives. Many other investigations have a similar potential issue with multiple choice recognition tests (e.g., Hanly & Vandenberg, 2010), and these two studies are simply selected to illustrate the point. One could also argue that most subjects are not sufficiently motivated to outsmart the experimenter, and these forced choice tests are sufficient to assess word knowledge.

## Measuring TOT Incidence: Absolute Versus Relative?

For most TOT research, the proportion of target words that elicit TOTs is of little interest. This proportion is determined by many factors, including difficulty level of the target words and idiosyncrasies of subjects' knowledge base. TOT incidence does, however, become an issue when comparing different groups on TOT incidence within the same investigation: older versus younger, monolingual versus bilingual, LD versus language-proficient children. Between-group differences in language proficiency can influence TOT opportunities.

There are two ways to view a TOT. From one perspective, a TOT is a *partial retrieval failure* and more similar to DK than K responses. Within this framework, TOT incidence should be expressed relative to all trials where the target word retrieval was not completely successful (DK + TOT). Brown (1991) suggested this adjustment, and a number of studies have used this transformation in analyzing and reporting TOT probabilities (Askari, 1999; Brown & Nix, 1996; Burke et al., 1991; James & Burke, 2000;

Rastle & Burke, 1996; White & Abrams, 2002). Logically, a TOT can only occur on those trials where the correct word did not come to mind, and correct trials are removed from the calculations because these trials allow no opportunity to experience a TOT.

A second way to view TOTs is that they represent a *partial retrieval success* (Gollan & Brown, 2006). Retrieval successes come in two varieties: *complete success*, where the target word is retrieved, and *partial success*, reflected in TOTs. As Maril et al. (2005) suggest, "...the TOT represents an interme- diate level of recall success in which the sought-after information is not recalled, but at the same time, it is distinctly different from a retrieval fail- ure" (p. 1130). To make a simple analogy, under the first position the retrieval glass is half empty, and under the second position it is half full.

This problem mainly applies to between-group comparisons and is applied in Chapter 10 to help understand group TOT differences. As a brief illustration, let us use an age-group comparison. In most research in this area, older adults are more language-competent than younger adults, by standardized comparisons. Assume that Susan, an older adult, was presented with 10 target word cues. She generated 8 targets correctly (K), missed 2 (DK), and had 2 TOTs. Amanda, a young adult, was tested with exactly the same cues and got 5 K, 6 DK, and 1 TOT. By raw percentages, Susan had more TOTs. If one computes TOTs as failed retrievals (TOT/ (TOT + DK)), Susan again had more TOTs (50%, or 2/4) than Amanda (14%, or 1/7). However, if TOTs are viewed as partial retrieval successes (TOT/(K + TOT)), then the difference disappears: both Susan (2/10) and Amanda (1/5) had 20% TOTs.

If TOTs are considered in the context of correct retrievals, age differences usually decrease or disappear (Gollan & Brown, 2006). However, if consid- ered in the context of DKs, the age difference often becomes larger than the raw (unadjusted) percentages. The problem is that the standard procedure in laboratory studies represents a zero-sum game among three categories. All items have to fall into K, DK, and TOT. Increasing one category has to decrease the number of items in one (or both) of the other categories.

This issue also applies to comparisons across different materials within a single study. Riefer (2002) found no difference between the *raw* percent of TOTs with visual (21%; cast photo) versus auditory (25%; theme song) cues for TV show titles. When Riefer (2002) adjusted these percentages consid- ering TOTs as unsuccessful retrievals (DKs) (Brown, 1991), a substantial TOT difference emerged between visual (60%) versus auditory (41%) mate- rials because DKs were lower for visual than auditory cues. However, if these percentages are recomputed considering TOTs as partially correct retrievals (Gollan & Brown, 2006), the difference disappears with 30% TOTs for both types of cues.

As a general rule, when one compares groups or conditions where there are substantial differences in both correct responses and TOTs, it is important to adjust the TOT rate. But before doing so, one should appreciate that each is based on a different perspective, regarding TOTs as either partial retrieval failures or partial retrieval successes.

# ☐ Fragmentary Data Problem

The "fragmentary data problem" in TOT research was eloquently elucidated by Brown and McNeill (1966). TOT incidence varies widely both across words and participants, and it unlikely that two participants will have TOTs on the same subset of target words. In many studies, there are words that never elicit TOTs and subjects who never experience TOTs. For example, Brown and McNeill (1966) found that 16% of subjects had no TOTs. Other studies have found the percentage of non-TOT subjects in the range of 12% (Smith, Brown, & Balfour, 1991) to 46% (Thompson et al., 2005) (cf. Brennen et al., 2007; Widner et al., 1996). Thus, such investigations have a hidden subject-selection bias, where a substantial proportion of participants who experience no TOTs are excluded from the analyses.

It is more common for all subjects to experience some TOTs (Brennen et al., 1990; Caramazza & Miozzo, 1997, Experiment 2; Finley & Sharp, 1989; Gruneberg et al., 1973; Jönsson & Olsson, 2003; Miozzo & Caramazza, 1997; Vitevitch & Sommers, 2003), but the number can vary widely from person to person. Yarmey (1973) presented a detailed accounting of this type of spread: 5 subjects had 0–5 TOTs, 17 had 6–10 TOTs, 28 had 11–20 TOTs, and 3 had 21+ TOTs. A troubling aspect of this large variability is that a relatively small number of subjects can contribute a disproportionate amount of data to the TOT analyses.

Fragmentary data are also a problem in subanalyses examining the presence of peripheral information (i.e., related words, first letter, number of syllables). Brown and McNeill (1966) report that the initial letter of the target word was guessed correctly on 57% of TOTs, but subjects contribute differently to this percentage depending upon how many TOTs they experience. It is possible that individuals who experience more TOTs are also more adept at accessing first letter information, as well. If so, the incidence of first-letter availability would drop if every subject contributed only one data point (average for their TOTs).

Brown and McNeill (1966) suggest that standard statistical tests are severely limited with high levels of fluctuation (item to item; subject to subject), and their solution was to analyze the data in multiple ways, both by participants and by items. A good illustration of this cautious approach is their evaluation of syllable knowledge about the missing target word. Brown and McNeill (1966) analyzed this five ways, and proposed that confidence in a finding derives from consistency across different analyses. It is worth noting that their multiple-analysis approach is very time consuming, and rarely used in subsequent research. Gardiner et al. (1973) also tackled the missing data problem by creating "macro-Ss," pooling data from three successively tested participants to form one subject unit. This approach also failed to catch on.

Another problem in analyzing the data from TOT designs is the variation in TOT rates from word to word. For example, there was a range of 0 to 13 TOTs elicited by the 50 targets used in Burke et al. (1991, Study 2), and 0 to 28 TOTs evoked by the 50 targets used by Yarmey (1973). As another illustration, Lawless and Engen (1977) found that 21 (of 48) odors elicited no TOTs, 18 evoked 1 TOT, 8 caused 2 TOTs, and 1 precipitated 3 TOTs. This item-to-item variation in TOT rate presents a problem similar to across-subject variation: a handful of target words is overrepresented in the TOT analyses, with most TOTs harvested from 10% to 20% of all targets.

Given this, an important goal in TOT research should be to identify what dimensions differentiate target words that elicit high versus low TOT rates. This issue remains relatively neglected, aside from a few studies examining TOT differences across levels of target word frequency (Astell & Harley, 1996; Gollan & Brown, 2006; Harley & Bown, 1998; Vitevitch & Sommers, 2003) and neighborhood density (Harley & Bown, 1998; Vitevitch & Sommers, 2003; see Chapter 6).

Providing information on TOT rate per target word in published reports (cf. Alario & Ferrand, 1999; Bak, 1987; Burke et al., 1991; Snodgrass & Vanderwart, 1980) (see Appendix), would improve the efficiency of data gathering by documenting targets with the highest TOT probability, as well as facilitating research into target word features that are more likely to elicit TOTs. Abrams, Trunk, and Margolin (2007) have taken an important step to move the field along in this direction. They have summarized TOT incidence for 163 different target words, compiled from five studies appearing in four articles (Abrams et al., 2003; Abrams & Rodriguez, 2005; Robinson, Abrams, & Bahrick, 2004; White & Abrams, 2002). In addition to TOT+, TOT–, correct, DK, and incorrect "know" responses, they also list incorrect answers given by subjects. Most words (135) have data on both younger and older subjects (the remaining 28 have data for young subjects only). The word-by-word TOT percentages for both Abrams, Trunk, and Margolin (2007) and Burke et al. (1991) are presented in the Appendix.

# ☐ Summary

TOTs have been studied using a variety of different procedures. Most use laboratory evocation; however, some have employed diary procedures (usually across one month) or retrospective evaluations. The naturalistic incidence is about once a week, and lab studies yield TOTs on approximately 15% of items. This lab incidence varies considerably across different cue materials, which include definitions (most typical), line drawings/pictures, odors, paired associates, and artificially constructed materials (TOTimals). Several methodological issues are associated with TOT research, the most important of which is verifying that the subject's target word is the same as the one intended by the experimenter, and this is generally accomplished through recognition tests. A statistical problem in TOT research results from "fragmentary" data, or the high variability in TOT incidence rate across both subjects and items. A systematic exploration of which target word features are more likely to elicit TOTs would be extremely helpful. Although most researchers assume that TOTs are more likely with low-frequency words, this has not been convincingly demonstrated. A readily available source for gathering more information about TOTs is academic tests, although no research exists on this topic. One could not only have students identify TOTs as they occur, but also connect them to the strength of the item (how well was it studied?) and to resolution (time course, probability).

# ☐ Appendix: TOT Frequencies for Specific Target Words

The following are TOT frequencies for various target words cued by line drawings. Snodgrass and Vanderwart (1980; SV) tested 219 English-speaking subjects, and Alario and Ferrand (1999; AF) tested 28 French-speaking subjects. AF selected their line drawings from SV and Cycowicz, Friedman, Rothstein, and Snodgrass (1997).

|           | SV | AF |
|-----------|----|----|
| Accordion | 3  |    |
| Acorn     |    | 1  |
| Alligator | 1  |    |
| Anteater  |    | 3  |
| Anvil     |    | 3  |
| Arch      |    | 1  |
| Armadillo |    | 3  |
| Artichoke | 3  | 1  |
| Asparagus |    | 1  |
| Avocado   |    | 1  |

|  | SV | AF |
|---|---|---|
| Axe |  | 1 |
| Baby Carriage | 1 |  |
| Basin |  | 2 |
| Beetle | 1 |  |
| Bird House |  | 2 |
| Blimp |  | 5 |
| Bowl | 1 |  |
| Camel | 2 |  |
| Cannon | 1 |  |
| Celery | 1 | 3 |
| Cherry | 1 |  |
| Chisel | 2 | 7 |
| Clothespin | 2 |  |
| Colander |  | 1 |
| Cutting Board |  | 3 |
| Cymbals |  | 1 |
| Doorknob | 1 |  |
| Drum | 1 |  |
| Easel |  | 1 |
| Eel |  | 1 |
| Fan |  | 1 |
| Fire Hydrant |  | 4 |
| Fishhook |  | 1 |
| Football Helmet | 1 |  |
| French Horn | 2 | 2 |
| Funnel |  | 1 |
| Globe |  | 2 |
| Goat | 1 |  |
| Grapes | 1 |  |
| Hoe |  | 2 |
| Harmonica |  | 1 |
| Harp | 3 |  |
| Ironing Board | 2 |  |
| Kettle |  | 1 |
| Lantern | 1 |  |
| Leopard | 2 |  |
| Llama |  | 3 |
| Lock |  | 1 |
| Maracas |  | 6 |
| Microscope |  | 2 |
| Moose |  | 3 |

(*Continued*)

|               | SV | AF |
|---------------|----|----|
| Mushroom      | 1  |    |
| Nut           | 2  | 2  |
| Onion         | 1  | 1  |
| Orange        | 1  |    |
| Ostrich       | 2  |    |
| Peach         | 1  |    |
| Peacock       | 4  |    |
| Pepper        | 1  | 2  |
| Pliers        | 1  |    |
| Plug          | 2  | 1  |
| Pumpkin       | 1  |    |
| Raccoon       | 3  | 3  |
| Ray           |    | 1  |
| Record Player | 1  |    |
| Rhinoceros    | 2  |    |
| Rolling Pin   | 1  | 3  |
| Saxophone     |    | 1  |
| Scale         |    | 1  |
| Screw         | 1  |    |
| Screwdriver   | 1  |    |
| Seal          | 1  | 3  |
| Sheep         | 1  |    |
| Spatula       |    | 1  |
| Spinning Wheel| 3  | 4  |
| Squirrel      | 2  |    |
| Strawberry    | 1  |    |
| Stethoscope   |    | 4  |
| Suitcase      | 1  |    |
| Tambourine    |    | 2  |
| Telescope     |    | 7  |
| Tennis Racket | 1  |    |
| Thimble       | 3  |    |
| Tiger         | 1  |    |
| Totem Pole    |    | 1  |
| Toucan        |    | 1  |
| Turkey        |    | 2  |
| Vulture       |    | 1  |
| Vest          |    | 2  |
| Wagon         | 1  | 3  |
| Walrus        |    | 1  |
| Watering Can  | 4  | 1  |
| Watermelon    |    | 1  |

|  | SV | AF |
|---|---|---|
| Weather Vane |  | 5 |
| Whale |  | 1 |
| Wheel | 1 |  |
| Worm |  | 1 |
| Wrench |  | 1 |

The following are TOT percentages experienced by young (Y) and older (O) adults for targets cued by *definitions*. Burke et al. (1991, Study 2) tested 21 subjects in each age group. Abrams, Trunk, and Margolin (2007) combined data across five different studies, three of which used only young adults from Abrams et al. (2003) and Abrams and Rodrigues (2004), and two of which used both young and older adults from White and Abrams (2002) and Robinson, Abrams, and Bahrick (2004). The total sample of subjects for Abrams, Trunk, and Margolin (2007) was 327 young and 132 older adults, but this varied from word to word depending upon the number of studies in which the word(s) appeared.

|  | Burke et al. (Y, O) | Abrams, Trunk, & Margolin (Y, O) |
|---|---|---|
| Abacus | (14, 14) | (28, 26) |
| Abdicate | (24, 14) | (13, 15) |
| A Capella | (5, 19) | (15, 11) |
| Actuary |  | (7, 36) |
| Affirmation | (0, 14) | (4, 18) |
| Agnostic |  | (10, 14) |
| Albatross |  | (9, 16) |
| Alchemy |  | (11, 24) |
| Amber |  | (5, – ) |
| Ambergris | (5, 19) | (12, 31) |
| Ambrosia |  | (13, 21) |
| Amnesty |  | (7, –) |
| Amorous |  | (5, 0) |
| Anachronistic |  | (7, –) |
| Anagram |  | (14, 24) |
| Anarchist |  | (17, 24) |
| Anecdote |  | (10, 21) |
| Aorta |  | (14, 5) |
| Astrology |  | (7, –) |
| Atone |  | (8, 31) |
| Bandanna |  | (4, 4) |
|  |  | (*Continued*) |

| | Burke et al. (Y, O) | Abrams, Trunk, & Margolin (Y, O) |
|---|---|---|
| Barnacle | | (8, 12) |
| Barter | (10, 5) | (10, 7) |
| Beaver | | (0, –) |
| Biography | | (2, –) |
| Bola | (14, 5) | |
| Boomerang | | (15, 27) |
| Cadaver | | (22, –) |
| Caduceus | | (8, 19) |
| Calibration | | (13, 15) |
| Calisthenics | | (10, 17) |
| Calligraphy | | (12, 21) |
| Canonize | | (7, –) |
| Capillary | | (18, 14) |
| Carcinogen | | (16, 15) |
| Cartographers | (5, 19) | |
| Castanets | | (11, 10) |
| Catharsis | (5, 10) | (4, –) |
| Chameleon | | (12, 15) |
| Cherub | | (6, –) |
| Contingency | | (7, 5) |
| Corona | | (7, 11) |
| Coroner | | (7, –) |
| Cosmonaut | | (4, 9) |
| Covenant | (14, 5) | (10, 22) |
| Decanter | | (9, 20) |
| Desecrate | | (23, 34) |
| Determinist | | (12, 16) |
| Detonate | (10, 14) | (11, 15) |
| Dorsal | | (10, 5) |
| Dowry | | (25, 24) |
| Drill (team) | (0, 10) | |
| Egocentric | | (12, 13) |
| Ellipsis | (5, 5) | (10, 15) |
| Embryo | | (18, 19) |
| Emerald | | (2, –) |
| Encrypt | | (7, –) |
| Endorse | | (19, 12) |
| Ephemeral | (5, 14) | (6, 3) |
| Epidermis | | (8, 5) |
| Epilogue | | (33, 27) |
| Equestrian | | (4, 8) |

| | Burke et al. (Y, O) | Abrams, Trunk, & Margolin (Y, O) |
|---|---|---|
| Esoteric | | (13, 5) |
| Estrogen | | (14, –) |
| Euphemism | | (10, 22) |
| Evangelist | | (6, 3) |
| Filament | | (8, 11) |
| Foal | | (31, 5) |
| Fovea | | (46, 27) |
| Fratricide | | (27, 24) |
| Gazebo | | (10, –) |
| Gerrymander | (19, 14) | (19, 20) |
| Haiku | (10, 5) | (12, 23) |
| Hegemony | (24, 5) | |
| Helix | (5, 5) | |
| Hemophilia | | (36, 47) |
| Hemorrhage | (19, 5) | (35, 19) |
| Heretic | | (16, 11) |
| Hieroglyphics | | (12, 16) |
| Hydrogen | | (3, 4) |
| Hypochondriac | | (30, 28) |
| Imminent | | (5, –) |
| Incisors | | (10, 4) |
| Incubate | | (17, 16) |
| Insomnia | (14, 14) | (24, 21) |
| Intransitive | (14, 14) | (6, 7) |
| Javelin | | (19, 9) |
| Jettison | (0, 29) | (21, 51) |
| Kaleidoscope | | (21, 49) |
| Kibitz | (14, 5) | |
| Lampoon | | (23, 42) |
| Liaison | | (5, 11) |
| Libretto | | (8, 19) |
| Ligament | | (9, 8) |
| Locust | (14, 5) | |
| Lynch | | (10, 37) |
| Malevolence | | (9, 15) |
| Manna | | (7, 5) |
| Marinade | (14, 14) | (16, –) |
| Marsupials | (14, 10) | (21, 32) |
| Mausoleum | (29, 10) | (11, 8) |
| Mercenary | | (12, 25) |
| | | (Continued) |

| | Burke et al. (Y, O) | Abrams, Trunk, & Margolin (Y, O) |
|---|---|---|
| Meteorology | | (3, –) |
| Meticulous | | (13, 15) |
| Metronome | | (20, 20) |
| Migraine | (10, 5) | |
| Mince | (5, 10) | (25, 19) |
| Minstrel | | (7, –) |
| Misdemeanor | | (10, 30) |
| Misogynist | | (11, 12) |
| Molasses | | (7, 8) |
| Molt | (10, 14) | (33, 37) |
| Moraine | (14, 10) | |
| Mutiny | | (17, 16) |
| Narcissism | | (10, 27) |
| Negotiable | | (18, 12) |
| Nepotism | | (23, 37) |
| Numismatist | | (0, –) |
| Omniscient | | (14, 11) |
| Omnivore | | (15, 32) |
| Onomatopoeia | | (22, 24) |
| Origami | (29, 10) | (20, 19) |
| Ornithology | | (17, –) |
| Orthodontist | | (6, 10) |
| Oscillation | | (6, 9) |
| Palindrome | (33, 19) | (29, 41) |
| Pantomime | | (31, 29) |
| Papyrus | (14, 0) | (13, 7) |
| Paradox | | (19, 34) |
| Parasite | | (16, 21) |
| Parody | | (27, 38) |
| Parsimony | | (14, 33) |
| Pasteurize | | (17, 11) |
| Pawn | (24, 24) | (48, 48) |
| Pendulum | | (8, 10) |
| Perjury | | (23, 21) |
| Perpendicular | | (5, –) |
| Petrify | | (17, 34) |
| Philatelist | (10, 14) | (9, 30) |
| Photosynthesis | (14, 19) | |
| Placebo | | (16, 29) |
| Plagiarize | | (17, 20) |
| Planetarium | | (33, 53) |
| Polo | (0, 5) | |
| Potpourri | (14, 24) | (8, 40) |

| | Burke et al. (Y, O) | Abrams, Trunk, & Margolin (Y, O) |
|---|---|---|
| Pride | | (27, 18) |
| Procrastinate | | (8, 15) |
| Proselytize | | (10, –) |
| Reef | (5, 0) | |
| Reincarnate | | (12, 7) |
| Reiterate | | (21, 24) |
| Rhetorical | (10, 0) | (14, 9) |
| Rosary | | (7, –) |
| Samurai | | (6, 8) |
| Seismology | | (27, 32) |
| Serenade | | (4, 15) |
| Serrated | | (10, 11) |
| Sextant | (38, 14) | |
| Silhouettes | | (17, 15) |
| Silo | | (9, –) |
| Simile | | (10, 24) |
| Sloop | | (6, 18) |
| Soliloquy | | (24, 25) |
| Spatula | | (6, –) |
| Spelunker | | (16, 36) |
| Stamina | | (8, 9) |
| Strop | (5, 0) | |
| Subscription | | (5, –) |
| Synagogue | | (5, –) |
| Teak | (19, 0) | |
| Thatch | (0, 5) | |
| Tic | (5, 10) | |
| Toga | | (9, 5) |
| Torpedo | | (6, 17) |
| Tranquilize | | (19, 29) |
| Translucent | | (12, 12) |
| Trot | (0, 14) | |
| Troy | (0, 14) | |
| Tryst | (14, 14) | |
| Tsunami | (0, 14) | (10, 15) |
| Umbrage | (10, 14) | |
| Urn | (19, 10) | |
| Utopia | | (16, 26) |
| Vaudeville | (10, 0) | |
| Velcro | (10, 33) | |
| Venison | | (8, 9) |
| Vigilante | (10, 14) | |

CHAPTER

4

# Manipulating TOT Probability

Can we alter the likelihood of experiencing a TOT? Practically speaking, most of us would like to reduce the incidence but information about both increasing and decreasing TOTs can provide valuable information about the causes (and cures?) for this word retrieval problem. The likelihood of experiencing a TOT appears to be related to certain individual and group differences, and these nonmanipulated subject differences are summarized in Chapter 10. The present chapter presents evidence for changing TOT likelihood (and resolution) through manipulated variables.

## ☐ Instructions

TOTs are universal, and subjects readily comprehend the concept when described. Most studies published on TOTs use verbally adept, high-achieving participants (college students) who are immersed in a culture of constant information retrieval. Thus, there is considerable endogenous drive to succeed in any laboratory task involving word retrieval. And when faced with a temporary retrieval problem, student subjects are adept at identifying the TOT experience.

Instructions to subjects, however, can have an impact on TOT incidence. To illustrate, in Widner et al. (1996), some subjects were told that the target words were *easy* and that nearly all students (95%) have little difficulty retrieving these words. This was referred to as the high-demand (HD) condition, with implied pressure to retrieve most or all of the target words. In contrast, subjects in their low-demand (LD) group were told that the target words were *hard* and that nearly all students (95%) had great difficulty retrieving them. This set a low bar for word retrieval success, taking the pressure off. The instructional manipulation resulted in a TOT rate three times higher in the HD (11%) than the LD (4%) group. The groups did not differ on the incidence of accurate peripheral target word information (e.g., first letter; related words), but HD subjects felt compelled to offer more guesses. Apparently, Widner et al.'s (1996) instructional manipulation did not alter correct information accessibility, only the threshold for reporting TOTs and partial information guesses.

An alternative possibility for the TOT difference is that the HD manipulation increased stress in HD subjects (Widner et al. (1996), which in turn increased TOT rate (see Chapter 11). Regardless of the mechanism underlying this shift, it appears to be remarkably easy to alter TOT reports via instructional expectations. In light of this outcome, it is important to note that some TOT investigations include instructions to participants that the questions are difficult and that they should not feel bad if they can't answer all of them (Burke et al., 1991; Dahlgren, 1998). This supposedly helps subjects avoid feeling bad about not retrieving all of the targets, but do such instructions create a situation similar to the LD group of Widner et al. (1996)? Could we increase TOT yield by excluding such well-intended clarification to the subjects?

# ☐ Cueing

The most common procedure to influence TOT probability involves presenting information related to the target word along with the definition. One approach is to present information prior to the target cue, and this design is referred to as *priming*. As James and Burke (2000) note, "The empirical effect of priming is a change in the availability of target information that is caused by prior processing of identical or related information" (p. 1378). The other approach is to present material soon after the target definition, which is referred to as *cueing*. Note further that there are two different varieties of cueing: where cueing occurs after every definition (Askari, 1999), and where the cueing is presented only after TOT or DK responses (Abrams et al., 2003; James & Burke, 2000, Experiment 2). All priming designs are intended to manipulate TOT probability, and are covered in the present chapter. Cueing designs can be used to either influence TOT *probability* or TOT *resolution,* and only the former design is covered here (the research on cueing and TOT resolution is covered in Chapter 8).

To clarify a semantic issue related to this topic, some investigations where information is presented after the definition refer to their procedure as priming (Abrams et al., 2003; Askari, 1999; White & Abrams, 2002). However, for present purposes these designs are classified here as cueing because the target retrieval is most likely already under way after the definition is presented. As Maylor (1990a) cogently points out, "Subjects may have been able to retrieve the target word *before* the presentation of the potential blocking word" in her cueing experiment. Simply put, in this chapter primes precede and cues follow the initiation of a target word search procedure.

In the first study employing postdefinition cueing, Jones and Langford (1987) provided one of four types of cue words immediately after each definition: (a) semantically related to the target (S), (b) phonetically related to the target (P), (c) semantically and phonetically related to the target (SP), or (d) unrelated to the target (U). Phonologically related cue words matched the target on first letter, first phoneme, and number of syllables. Both high-frequency (HF) and low-frequency (LF) versions of each cue type were generated. To illustrate, for the target *banshee,* the S cues were *ghost* (HF) and *incubus* (LF); for the target *braise,* the P cues were *bride* (HF) and *baulk* (LF); for the target *anachronism,* the SP cues were *anniversary* (HF) and *abnormality* (LF).

Jones and Langford (1987) report a significant effect of phonological cueing, but no effect of semantic cueing. More TOTs followed phonologically related (P and SP) compared to phonologically unrelated (S and U) cues, whereas the presence (S and SP) or absence (P and U) of a semantic relationship did not influence TOT rate. Incidentally, normative frequency of the cue (HF, LF) had no effect on TOTs. Both Jones (1989) and Maylor (1990a) followed up this investigation with similar materials and procedure and confirmed Jones and Langford's (1987) finding of more TOTs associated with phonetically related than phonetically unrelated cues, and no effect of a semantic relationship. It should be noted that none of these investigations (Jones, 1989; Jones & Langford, 1987; Maylor, 1990a) reported TOTs separately for each cue condition, but rather collapsed by pairs of conditions (see above).

Although this was ground-breaking research on cueing, a methodological complication limited its generalizability. None of the three studies (Jones, 1989; Jones & Langford, 1987; Maylor, 1990a) counterbalanced cue words across target words. Rather, each target word had only one of the four types of cue words associated with it. Two subsequent investigations (Meyer & Bock, 1992; Perfect & Hanley, 1992) addressed this counterbalancing concern. Both used the definitions and target words from Jones (1989), but constructed a set of four different cue words for each target word. Meyer and Bock (1992, Experiment 1) found no difference in TOTs following phonological (13%), semantic (14%), and unrelated (13%) cues. SP cues were not used because these were too difficult to construct. Meyer and Bock (1992) performed a second analysis, combining TOTs and correct retrievals. They correctly assumed that both should be influenced in a similar manner by cue type, so this combination should provide a more sensitive index of the positive or negative influence of cues. Again, there was no significant difference across phonological (33%), semantic (33%), and unrelated (32%) cues.

In Experiment 2, Meyer and Bock (1992) provided cue words only on trials where initial retrieval failed. Under these conditions, TOTs occurred significantly more often after semantically related (15%) than either phonologically related (14%) or unrelated (14%) cue words, although this difference was quite modest. There was again no evidence of an increase in TOTs with phonetic cues, contrary to Jones (1989), Jones and Langford (1987), and Maylor (1990a). Coming full circle, Meyer and Bock (1992, Experiment 3) duplicated the Jones and Langford (1987) study using the same definitions and cue words. This replicated the earlier findings of more TOTs with phonologically related (17%) (P + SP) than with nonphonologically related (13%) (S + U) cues, and no TOT difference between semantically related (15%) (S + SP) and semantically unrelated (15%) (P + U) cues. Examining each condition separately, the semantic plus phonological cue (SP) yielded the most TOTs (19%), the unrelated (U) and phonological (P) conditions yielded somewhat fewer TOTs (15% each), and semantic (S) cues produced the fewest TOTs (11%).

Perfect and Hanley (1992) also conducted a follow-up study on Jones' (1989) findings. In Experiment 1, one group of subjects was given the four different types of cues, duplicating Jones (1989), and a comparison group was given *no* cue words. Their cueing outcome replicated Jones (1989) and Jones and Langford (1987): phonologically related cues resulted in more TOTs than nonphonologically related cues, with no TOT difference between semantically and nonsemantically related cues. However, the no-cue group showed the same pattern for TOTs, suggesting inherent differences across the four sets of definitions/targets in evoking TOTs, unrelated to the nature of the cue–target relationship. Whereas Meyer and Bock (1992) addressed the materials' inequity by testing another set of definitions and cue words, Perfect and Hanley (1992, Experiment 2) handled this in a different way. Using the subsets of definitions used by Jones (1989), they created cue-sets matched on difficulty level based on correct response and TOT rates from their own Experiment 1. Similar to Meyer and Bock (1992), they eliminated the PS cue condition because it was too difficult to match up with the other three conditions. After this adjustment for inherent difficulty level of the target word sets, Perfect and Hanley (1992) found no difference as a function of type of cue word.

Meyer and Bock (1992) raise an important issue with respect to interpreting outcomes from cueing investigations. They point out that three retrieval states exist, representing an ordinal progression from lower to higher states of target word activation: (1) inaccessible (DK) to (2) partially accessible (TOT) to (3) fully accessible (know, or K). Given that a fixed set of materials is used in all laboratory investigations, this represents a zero-sum game. When the number of items in one category is increased or decreased, it must result in a change in the number of items in one or both of the other categories. Thus, an increase in TOTs could result from items shifting upwards in activation from the DK category, or items shifting downwards in activation from the K category.

To be more specific, from the activation perspective a related cue could increase TOTs by boosting activation of some words forward from DK to TOT. However, an increase in TOTs could also be accounted for from the suppression perspective. If a related cue impairs access, then this could increase TOTs by pushing some words *backward* from K to TOT. This issue can be easily resolved, however, by examining correct retrievals. With activation, correct retrievals should increase as items are pushed from TOT to K. However, suppression would predict the opposite, with correct retrievals decreasing because cue impairment pulls items from K to TOT.

One additional postdefinitional cueing study is worth noting. Beattie and Coughlan (1999) attempted to increase TOTs by providing just the initial letter of the target word following the definition. However, they used the unusual procedure of waiting 30 seconds after the target definition to give subjects the first-letter cue. They did not address the efficacy of this procedure, but a cue provided so long after the target word definition would be unlikely to elicit additional TOTs, but could play a role in resolving them.

In summary, investigations on cueing have not provided clear evidence of the positive or negative influence on TOTs of either semantic or phonetic information about the target word. Meyer and Bock (1992, p. 724) suggest further caution about such procedures:

> Although the results of previous experiments that used the cuing... paradigm have been brought to bear on arguments about lexical selection, the paradigm has features that may prevent it from capturing such processes. Even when cues directly follow definitions, they may appear well after lexical selection has occurred and with correspondingly little opportunity to influence it, having their effects instead on more strategic retrieval efforts.

# ☐ Priming

A number of investigations have attempted to manipulate TOT probability by presenting words prior to the target definition that either (a) have some semantic or phonetic relationship to the target word, (b) constitute the target word itself, or (c) share some features with the target word. Prime words are presented either transparently, immediately prior to the target cue, or in an obscured manner, embedded in a list of words processed in a seemingly unrelated task.

## Words Related to Target

Jones (1989) extended the cue word procedure, borrowed from Jones and Langford (1987; see preceding section), by using these same words as primes *preceding* the target word definition. Although the TOT percentage was lower with primes (8% TOTs) than with cues (12%), the difference across word type was similar: phonetically related primes (P and SP) resulted in more TOTs (11%) than phonetically unrelated primes (S and U; 5%), with no difference between semantically related (SP and S; 8%) and semantically unrelated (P and U; 8%) primes. However, the design problems discussed in the prior section make interpreting these differences problematic.

Using a different approach to priming, Burke et al. (2004) compared the impact of processing a noun prime word that was either phonetically related (*pit*) or unrelated (*cane*) to the name of a subsequent celebrity (*Brad Pitt*). Their four-stage trial sequence involved the following steps: prime word definition cue, filler name picture cue, unrelated word target definition cue, and target name picture cue. The prime word was always evoked by the first definition in step 1 ("the hard stone as of the plum or cherry, which contains the seed is called the p _____") and the target celebrity name was always cued by the second picture in step 4. In this sequence, the second (proper name) and third (word) stages were fillers meant to moderately obscure the prime (stage 1)–target (stage 4) relationship.

Phonetically related primes significantly reduced TOTs relative to unrelated primes, and this occurred to a similar extent for both young (10% versus 12%) and older (16% versus 21%) adults. One problem encountered with this procedure is that many younger (68%) and older (30%) adults noticed the prime–target correspondence and used this to assist retrieval. When Burke et al. (2004) reanalyzed the data using only unaware subjects, the TOT reduction from unprimed to primed remained for the older adults (23% and 18%, respectively), but disappeared for younger adults (12% and 11%, respectively). Thus, the phonological prime facilitation is limited to older adults, and Burke et al. (2004) speculate that this is due to an age-progressive deficit in phonological activation which the phonologically related prime corrects (see Chapter 10).

This same four-stage trial procedure (definition, picture, definition, picture) was used again in Cross and Burke (2004) to evaluate the influence of *semantically* related primes on TOT probability, with the prime name again elicited by the first definition (step 1) and the proper name target elicited by the second picture (step 4). In the semantically related condition, the primed name ("Eliza Doolittle" to definition "the flower girl from the musical *My Fair Lady* whom Prof. Higgins transforms into a fashionable lady presentable to society, Eli ____ Do ____") was a character that the subsequent target actor (Audrey Hepburn) had played. In the unrelated condition, the primed character name (Scarlett O'Hara) had not been played by the target actor. Cross and Burke (2004) found no difference in TOTs for targets previously primed with a related versus an unrelated name. A semantic priming design was also employed by Schwartz and Smith (1997), with similar null effects. Prior to the TOT trials, they presented the names of 24 countries, which subjects rated on pleasantness. Within this list were country names linked to half of the 12 TOTimals to be tested in a later task. However, in two different tries (Experiments 2 and 3), they found no difference in TOT rate between primed and unprimed TOTimals.

In brief, there is evidence that phonologically related primes can reduce TOTs (Burke et al., 2004), but primarily for older adults. However, semantically related primes appear to have no influence on TOTs (Cross & Burke, 2004), although additional work on this topic is needed.

# Target Word

TOT priming studies have also used the actual target words, embedded in a list processed in a supposedly "unrelated" task preceding the TOT session. Rastle and Burke (1996, Experiment 1) had subjects read a list of 45 words, and then answer 90 general knowledge questions. The answers to half of the questions had appeared in the prior word list. Target word priming significantly decreased TOTs for both older and younger adults and for both proper and common noun targets. In Experiment 2, subjects engaged in one of three different processing tasks instead of simply reading the words in the prime list: pleasantness rating, syllable count, or case (number of capital letters). For younger adults, no prime condition reduced TOTs relative to the unprimed condition; with older adults, TOTs were significantly reduced in all primed, relative to the unprimed, conditions. Concerned that the null effect for young subjects may have resulted from their awareness that targets had appeared in the prime list, Rastle and Burke (1996, Experiment 3) reduced the percentage of target words in the prior list from 100% (as used in Experiment 2) to 50%. With pleasantness and syllable processing, priming now occurred for young subjects, as reflected in a significant reduction of TOTs relative to nonprimed targets.

Additional evidence supporting the efficacy of target word priming to reduce TOTs comes from research on recognition without identification (RWI) by Cleary and associates (Cleary, 2006; Cleary, Konkel, Nomi, & McCabe, 2010; Cleary & Reyes, 2009; Cleary & Speckler, 2007). The RWI research involves a two-stage design where one list is presented for processing, followed by target word cues. The first list usually consists of a list of words (mercury), some of which are the targets for cues in the second list (what is the only metal that is a liquid at room temperature?).

Participants are also asked whether each target word cued in the second list had appeared in the first, and make this discrimination above chance both for targets that are successfully recalled (not surprising) and for those that cannot be generated (surprising). This latter effect is labeled the RWI phenomenon.

On some of these studies, participants are also asked about TOTs for unrecalled target words. Whereas Rastle and Burke (1996) tried to obscure the relationship between the target word list and subsequent test series, Cleary directly informed subjects prior to the study list that it would contain some answers to the trivia questions presented on the second task. Thus, the subjects are encouraged to remember list 1 words.

Germane to the present discussion, the TOT rate was consistently lower for primed than for unprimed targets, with general knowledge questions (Cleary, 2006, Experiments 2 and 3), famous faces (Cleary & Speckler, 2007, Experiment 2), famous scenes (Cleary & Reyes, 2009, Experiments 1 and 2), and odors (Cleary et al., 2010). Although the raw probability of a TOT was roughly equivalent for primed and nonprimed targets across five outcomes noted above, TOTs were substantially lower for primed targets when using Gollan and Brown's (2006) adjustment that considers TOTs relative to all successful semantic (stage 1) retrievals (see earlier discussion). Cleary and Reyes (2009) discovered this in their own outcome, as well as in a reanalysis of both Cleary (2006) and Cleary and Speckler (2007). Although not appearing in the published report, a similar reanalysis of Cleary et al. (2010) yielded 20% higher TOTs for nonprimed versus primed items. The reliability of this finding is consistent with the transmission deficit interpretation (Burke et al., 1991; see Chapter 9), where a TOT results from insufficient activation being passed from the semantic to phonological word representations. The lack of recent activation of the target word is one of the key factors leading to insufficient transmission of activation, and priming procedures reduce this problem.

## Target Word Features

The possibility exists in nearly all cueing and priming designs that subjects detect the relationship between the cue/prime word and target word, and use this to guide their memory search (cf. Burke et al., 2004; Rastle & Burke, 1996). A paradigm intended to obscure the relationship between tasks uses a set of several words that share some phonological feature(s) with the target word. The assumption is that experiencing these words simultaneously activates structural elements of the target that are shared with these prime word(s). James and Burke (2000) preceded each target word cue with a 10-word set. Half were related sets, where 5 of the 10 words shared a single phonological component with the target word: the first, middle, or final sound. The other half were unrelated sets, where none of the 10 words shared any phonological components with the target. For example, the related prime set for the target word "abdicate" included the words (related portion in italics): in*di*gent, *ab*stract, trunc*ate*, loc*ate*, and tra*di*tion. In Experiment 1, TOTs were significantly reduced following phonetically related (11%) compared to unrelated (13%) prime sets, suggesting that phonological feature activation aggregates to a degree sufficient to facilitate word retrieval and reduce TOTs.

Lesk and Womble (2004, Experiment 1) also used James and Burke's (2000) procedure, and made subjects rate each word in the prime set on pronunciation difficulty. Furthermore, prior to the procedure, half of the subjects were given caffeine and the other half a placebo. The caffeine group replicated James and Burke (2000) with significantly fewer TOTs following related (7%) than unrelated (13%) primes, but the opposite occurred for the placebo group, with more TOTs after related (11%) than unrelated (8%) primes. In Experiment 2, Lesk and Womble (2004) manipulated the degree of phonological relationship with two different types of related prime sets. In the *low* condition, 2 or 3 words (out of 10) were phonologically related to the target, whereas in the *high* condition 7 or 8 words were related. For the caffeine group, there were more TOTs in the low (8%) than the high (5%) prime conditions, but the placebo group showed the opposite with more TOTs after the high (13%) than the low (9%) prime sets.

Given that the findings flipped direction between the two experiments, the outcome does not lend itself easily to a straightforward interpretation. Lesk and Womble (2004) use a biological mechanism, proposing that caffeine consumption increases activation of *unrelated* primes, and that this abundance of active phonological components competes with target word via retrieval interference. Having more unrelated words increases the amount of irrelevant phonological activation, leading to even greater interference with the target word activation. This makes sense for the outcome of Experiment 2, and could possibly account for the findings of James and Burke (2000). However, this interpretation does not account for why their placebo group shows the opposite effect. Thus, they propose two different mechanisms: positive priming from increased phonologically related primes, as well as interference from unrelated primes.

Lesk and Womble (2004) further suggest that an unwitting combination of caffeine users and nonusers may have influenced James and Burke's (2000) outcome. Averaging across both groups in their own Experiment 1, Lesk and Womble (2004) found modest positive priming similar to James and Burke (2000). However, Lesk and Womble's (2004) proposed resolution for the discrepant findings between studies does not seem especially parsimonious, especially given the relatively small differences. Further research on this topic would be valuable, especially to evaluate their unusual proposal that caffeine consumption can have a negative influence on priming activation. Perhaps such omnibus activation via caffeine facilitates less constrained verbal output (i.e., conversation) but inhibits a focused word search (typical of TOT studies).

One general methodological caution should be raised with all priming (and cueing) outcomes using phonological elements of the target word. Presenting such information can potentially bias the subjects' personal assessment of whether they are in a TOT state. If they possess information that they believe to be structurally or phonetically related to the missing target word, they may convince themselves that they are experiencing TOTs when they are not (Brown, 1991; Burke et al., 1991). Furthermore, their use of such information may either facilitate or hamper retrieval efforts, depending on whether the information is relevant (related trials) or irrelevant (unrelated trials). This ambiguity can be avoided by using trials with no prime (or cue) words as the control comparison. A post-experiment questionnaire should be used in all prime/cueing studies to assess whether subjects detected the relationship between the prime (cue) and the target word, and, if so, whether they utilized this knowledge in their target word search (cf. Abrams, Trunk, & Merrill, 2007).

# ☐ Study Time

The influence of target word familiarity on TOT probability has been discussed often (see Chapter 6) but remains unclear because manipulating target words' exposure history is difficult. Objective word frequency norms are a starting point, but there remains considerable variability across individuals in word exposure history. Target word familiarity has been manipulated through a number of study trials (artificial materials). Smith et al. (1991, Experiment 2) found slightly (but not significantly) more subsequent TOTs with less familiar (35%; two trials) compared to more familiar (33%; four trials) TOTimals. This was replicated in Smith, Balfour, and Brown (1994, Experiment 3), with more TOTs in the lower-exposed (one study trial) (37%) than the higher-exposed (three study trials) (32%) condition, but this difference was again nonsignificant.

Employing a different approach to item strength, Smith et al. (1994) varied *amount* of study time rather than number of study trials with TOTimals. They proposed a distribution shift hypothesis, similar to Meyer and Bock (1992; cf. Cleary, 2006), whereby strengthening items will shift some from DK to TOT, and others from TOT to K. If practice selectively enhances lexical nodes, TOTs should increase: some DKs shift to TOTs, but no TOTs would shift K. In contrast, if practice selectively enhances phonological nodes, TOTs should decrease: some TOTs shift to K, but no DKs change to TOT. Smith et al. (1994, Experiment 1) found no difference in TOT rate between the 5- versus 15-second study, thus supporting neither hypothesis. Ryan et al. (1982) similarly found that study times of 1, 3, or 5 seconds per word pair had no impact on TOT incidence. In Experiment 2, Smith et al. (1994) modified the degree of study practice: some subjects wrote down the name during study, and others did not (the usual procedure). Writing significantly reduced TOTs (16%) relative to not (41%), a difference replicated in Experiment 3 (27% for write; 42% for no write), leading Smith et al. (1994) to conclude that writing strengthens phonological connections thus reducing TOTs.

In general, there is little evidence that an experimental manipulation of target word familiarity with study time or study trials influences TOTs. One problem with these designs may be that the variation in our range of familiarity with (exposure to) target words, even for relatively rare words (philatelist; sphygmomanometer), far exceeds anything that can be reasonably modeled in brief laboratory procedures. In addition, in these investigations it is important to establish that a particular target has been encoded sufficiently well to be retrieved on demand, before evaluating TOTs (Valentine et al., 1996).

# ☐ Amount of Cue Information

Can we influence TOT probability by the amount of cue information provided about the target word? Most research employs one (unitary) clue, such as the definition. Would additional details about the target—definition, picture, and context—influence TOTs? One could predict either direction: more information could nudge one from no knowledge (DK) to partial knowledge (TOT), thus increasing a sense that one is having a TOT. On the other hand, more target word information could help resolve TOTs, pushing one from partial (TOT) to full knowledge (K), thus reducing TOTs.

Schwartz and Smith (1997) manipulated the amount of cue information with TOTimals, by using a *minimum* condition where subjects learned two aspects of each TOTimal (name, country), a *medium* condition where they were shown three aspects (name, country, picture) and a *maximum* condition where five characteristics were presented (name, country, picture, diet, size). More TOTs occurred in both the medium (15%) and maximum (15%), compared to the minimum (10%) condition (Experiment 1), and Schwartz and Smith (1997) suspected that this difference could be attributed simply to the presence of the picture cue. Their hunch was confirmed in both Experiment 2, yielding more TOTs in medium than minimal cue condition (no maximum condition), and in Experiment 3, which replicated Experiment 1 with more TOTs in both the medium and maximum than in the minimum cue condition. Confirming the potency of picture information, Schwartz and Smith (1997) discovered more picture-related information comes to mind during TOTs (50%) than non-TOTs (27%), but there is no difference in recall of diet or size information. Based upon these findings, Schwartz and Smith (1997) suggest that TOTs are more likely when a mental picture of the intended target comes to mind during the word search.

Reinterpreting this outcome, Taylor and MacKay (2003) suggest that manipulating cue information does not increase actual TOTs, but rather the subjects' belief that they are experiencing TOTs. With more cues available, subjects are more likely to switch from declaring DK to TOT because they feel that they should be more likely to know the TOTimal. If this speculation is correct, correct recognition should *decrease* across increasing cues, but Schwartz and Smith (1997) do not provide data to address this. Taylor and MacKay (2002) further support their interpretation by pointing out that TOTimals' first letter availability during TOTs did not vary with amount of cue information.

# □ Drugs

As described earlier in this chapter, Lesk and Womble (2004) found that caffeine influenced TOT rate, but in a complex manner. Although there was no overall group difference in number of TOTs, they found a crossover interaction of drug with the type of prime word list (unrelated versus phonologically related). For unrelated primes, the caffeine group had fewer TOTs than the placebo group. However, with phonologically related primes, the caffeine group had more TOTs than the placebo group. Lesk and Womble (2004) related this outcome to the higher activation levels of unrelated word phonology under the influence of caffeine, which then competes with target word phonological activation (see earlier discussion).

A growing body of research suggests that benzodiazepines, a class of sedative drugs used to address anxiety, diminish episodic memory. In fact, the medical use of this medication is designed, in part, for this purpose. Benzodiazepine medication is often administered prior to surgical procedures to sedate the patient and to decrease later recall of presurgical procedures. The evidence is less clear, however, concerning the drug's effects on semantic memory retrieval. Bacon, Schwartz, Paire-Ficout, and Izaute (2007) found that lorazepam, a specific type of benzodiazepine, had no differential impact on TOT rate compared with a placebo control. Also, the predictability of TOTs for later recognition accuracy was equivalent for both groups, whereas one would expect a lower rate under lorazepam if this diminishes retrieval function. Thus, there seems to be no impact of this particular type of sedative on those retrieval functions associated with TOTs.

# ☐ Stress and Emotional Arousal

In a prior review of the TOT experience (Brown, 1991), I suggested that stress may be a potentially important contributing factor to TOTs and devoted an entire section to this possibility. In retrospect, I may have been misled by my classroom observations that students frequently experience TOTs (or at least claim to) under stressful exam conditions. I was also influenced by my colleague David Mitchell, who told me that one subject he had tested for a published report had an inordinate number of TOTs. After testing the subject, David discovered that he was in a highly stressed condition, having just come from a funeral for a family member (Mitchell, 1989).

I had also taken note of the relatively high incidence of TOTs during personal introductions, which is a particularly stressful occasion. In a broad sample of college students, 39% had had the experience of forgetting the name of a close friend or relative while introducing him or her to someone else (Brown, 1989). One woman even forgot her own father's name during an attempt to introduce him. Finally, Cohen and Faulkner (1986) noted that a number of their participants claimed that TOT incidence for proper names was noticeably higher when they were "tired, stressed or unwell." (p. 189)

Subsequent research, however, has paid scant attention to the connection between stress, or other emotional factors, and TOTs. Burke et al. (1991, Study 1) asked diary study participants how four physical and mental dimensions pertain to their typical TOT experience (1 = less than usual; 7 = more than usual). The mean ratings of 3.75 for worry, 3.83 for excitement, 4.04 for fatigue, and 3.21 for sickness were all at or below the midpoint of the scale, thus giving no indication of physical or psychological arousal/distress associated with TOTs.

Schwartz (2002b) does speculate that stress may have played a role in Widner et al.'s (1996) outcome. Subjects who were led to believe that targets were difficult (high demand, or HD) had fewer TOTs than those told that targets were easy (low demand, or LD; see Chapter 4). One interpretation is that LD subjects assume that they should know more targets, and thus shift a percentage of DK trials to TOTs to accommodate this demand. An alternative interpretation suggested by Widner et al. (1996) is that LD subjects experienced greater stress than HD subjects because they were having difficulty coming up with supposedly easy target words. Taking this one step further, the manipulation may have resulted in an *actual* increase in TOTs through stress rather than higher acquiescence to demand characteristics. Schwartz (2002b) claims that stress can create an "illusion of knowing," which is then experienced as a TOT.

One commonly experienced real-life link between stress and TOTs involves "confrontation naming" related to surprise encounters and spontaneous introductions. Schwartz (2002b) confesses that he commonly experiences a TOT when he bumps into a student from a prior semester. Perhaps the stress of a sudden encounter coupled with the rapidly dissipating name memory from last semester leads to such a TOT. A more complex documenting of real-life TOT experiences might enhance our understanding of the relationship between moderate stress and TOTs.

Whereas the above discussion relates to situation-induced stress, Schwartz (2010) recently published an evaluation of target word emotionality on TOT incidence, with a direct manipulation of emotion value of materials allowing causal inferences. Embedded in a larger set of general information questions was a small proportion (20%) involving emotionally sensitive topics (sex, disease, bodily functions, violence, and profanity). There were significantly more TOTs with emotionally charged (euthanasia, enema) than neutral targets, implying that arousal may increase TOTs. Furthermore, there were more TOTs to questions immediately after emotion-inducing question trials than following neutral question trials, suggesting a carryover impact of the emotional state. Schwartz (2010) interpreted this as supporting the inferential view of TOTs, in that one is likely to misinterpret an emotional reaction as reflecting a failed or difficult retrieval effort. It is also possible that a state of heightened physiological arousal may directly interfere with word retrieval processes, increasing TOTs.

As a final comment, the relationship between stress and TOTs (Schwartz, 2002b) could be addressed in diary studies by including evaluations of both chronic stressors (disease processes, divorce) and acute stressors (recent funeral) concurrent with the TOT experience (cf. Leeds, 1944). As a final comment, Schwartz (2002b) speculates that the increase in TOTs with age may, in part, be due to the elevated stress felt by older adults as they experience their word retrieval processes working less efficiently than before.

## ☐ Summary

A number of factors may have an influence on the likelihood of a TOT. One of the most important is the instructions given to the subject. An expectancy bias can possibly change the incidence in either direction, depending on how easy or difficult the target word retrieval is portrayed. Also, providing information related to the target word either before (prime) or after (cue) the definition can alter TOT frequency. In most cases, related information involves words with a phonetic/orthographic or semantic relationship to the target. Some priming studies have used the target word itself or partial features of the target word embedded in other words. The cueing studies have, in general, been unsuccessful in altering the TOT incidence with either semantically or phonologically related material. There is some evidence, however, that priming a phonological connection to the target word can reduce TOT incidence, but this evidence is not consistent across outcomes. Priming with the target itself does not appear to have a clear and consistent effect on TOTs. One consistent issue across all priming and cueing studies is identifying the degree to which subjects identify the relationship between the prime/cue and target word, and how they then use this information to alter their retrieval strategy. Target word study time has also been manipulated, with little clear impact of this strength manipulation on TOT rate. Several drugs (caffeine, lorazepam) have been evaluated but shown to be ineffective in altering the incidence of TOTs. Finally, stress may play a role in the etiology of TOTs, but a strong conclusion about such a link awaits additional laboratory research.

# 5

# Partial Target Word Information

Perhaps the most striking aspect of the TOT experience is that while hanging in linguistic limbo, unable to pull up the missing word, bits and pieces of it often come to mind. This dimension of TOTs was the primary motivation for the original scientific laboratory investigation by Brown and McNeill (1966). In their view, the availability of such information supported their concept of generic recall: a word search originates within a larger generic cluster of related words before narrowing down to the specific target. The fragments of the target word available during a TOT supposedly reflect aspects of this larger family of words, within which the target is embedded.

The partial target word information available during a TOT can consist of structural aspects (letter, phoneme), the sound or rhythm (number of syllables, syllabic stress), or some connotative meaning (gender, numerosity). TOTs are sometimes accompanied by other words related to the intended target, and this topic is covered in more detail in Chapter 7. Maril et al. (2005) provide some intriguing findings from brain imaging, suggesting that partial word feature activation occurs in a brain region separate from that involved with whole-word activation. More specifically, the right inferior frontal cortex is one of several areas that selectively lights up during TOTs, and this portion of the brain appears to handle the "fine grained phonological processing of words, at the level of phonemes or single syllables" (p. 1136).

Some view the availability of partial target word information as a defining feature of TOTs. For example, Nelson (2000) suggests that "...the TOT is the label we apply when a person reports partial aspects of the target. If there is any excess meaning of TOT beyond that, I do not know what it is" (p. 220). Although others agree with defining TOTs based on such indirect linguistic residue (Hamberger & Seidel, 2003; Kikyo et al., 2001;

Kohn et al., 1987; Vigliocco et al., 1997), most allow that partial information is not always available and that the subjects' personal assessments are adequate to define a TOT experience (cf. Schwartz, 2006).

# ☐ Cautions in Evaluating Partial Information

Before discussing the significance of partial target word information during TOTs, several cautions are in order. A variety of factors influences the availability of such information, and the manner in which this information is typically reported may possibly be misleading, and produce a misimpression about how often this occurs.

## Instructional Inconsistency

There is considerable variation across studies regarding how partial target word information is requested. It is important to separate how often such information comes to mind spontaneously versus in response to an experimenter's requests (Brown, 1991). The ideal situation is to require all participants to provide guesses during TOTs for every category of information (cf. Burke et al., 1991), but this is rarely done. Brown and McNeill (1966) made reporting some information mandatory for each TOT, but reporting other types of information was optional: "...the guess as to the number of syllables and the initial letter are required. The remaining entries should be filled out if possible" (p. 327). Their "remaining entries" included words of similar sound and similar meaning. Using a more systematic probe, Burke et al. (1991, Study 2) guided subjects sequentially through a set of information requests following each TOT: first letter or group of letters, last letter or group of letters, number of syllables, similar sounding word, and word that repeatedly comes to mind.

Many studies record only spontaneous reports by subjects who were given no specific instructions or guidance about providing such information (Askari, 1999; Brennen et al., 1990). Others provide a general framework without a structured report format. Gollan and Acenas (2004) suggest to their subjects that "...sometimes during a TOT experience, a person can report certain physical characteristics of the word (e.g., starts with a *b*)" (p. 250) and Heine et al. (1999) inform subjects that "...during a TOT state, partial information would be available about the target word, such as its number of syllables, its first letter, ideas associated with the word, an image of the word, or a similar word" (p. 448).

Lovelace (1987) constructed a comprehensive inquiry into types of target word information available during TOTs, but left his instructions intentionally vague:

> Often when a person cannot bring a certain word to mind, he can nevertheless produce things *about* the word itself. Perhaps you can tell me certain things about this word that you are looking for, or perhaps you can tell me something that the missing word reminds you of. ... Do not be inhibited because you feel that some point may be insignificant or silly. I would like to know whatever you can tell me about the missing word and any feelings you may have about the word. (p. 371)

The wide variability in procedures used to gather related information across investigations—ranging from indirect hints to direct probe—makes it difficult to get a precise picture of exactly what comes to mind, and how often it does. We have a good idea of the range of possible types of information, and a rough idea of which information is more likely to occur, but more structured research efforts are badly needed to gain more clarity on this important matter.

## Low Incidence of Information

To establish an accurate measure of the incidence of *correct* partial information during TOTs, it is important (a) to have subjects make an attempt for each category on all trials, and (b) to report the percentages of correct, incorrect, and no guesses. This is rarely done in the published literature. When the percentage of correct responses (e.g., first letters) is reported, this is often calculated with respect to all guesses, rather than all TOTs. If a subject had four correct, four incorrect, and four no guess TOT trials, accuracy may be reported relative to guesses (50%) or all TOTs (33%) and often it is impossible to determine which baseline is used.

To illustrate this ambiguity, Brown and McNeill (1966) report that first letter guesses were correct 57% of the time, but do not indicate how often guesses were made. Ecke (2001) provides a table with *percentages of fragmentary information reported* but fails to clarify whether these percentages were (a) TOT states where anything was reported, (b) TOT states with correct information reported, or (c) correct information expressed as a percentage of total information. Lovelace (1987) asked subjects how often they thought information was available during their TOTs, and found that *any* partial information is available on, at best, 10 to 20% of TOTs. This is much lower than reported in most research studies, which suggests that the literature may give a biased impression about the likelihood of such information.

For studies that do report the percentage based on all TOTs, the incidence of partial information is generally low (cf. Yarmey, 1973). Harley and Bown (1998) report that first letter guesses were made on 5% of TOTs, but this unusually low rate may be due to their vague instructions: "If you are in a TOT state and can remember something about the word, please write this down..." (p. 172). Jönsson and Olsson (2003) also found extremely low response rates for any partial information guesses with odor TOTs (7% syllable guesses, 2% syllabic stress guesses, and 5% letter guesses), but odor targets are notoriously problematic even to name.

Brown and Nix (1996) report a higher percentage of TOTs with partial information guesses (26% first letter; 30% syllable number), which may be higher due to the systematic and repeated probe for such information throughout the procedure. Partial information guesses were given for 30% of TOTs in Yarmey (1973), 41% of TOTs in Brennen et al. (2007, Experiment 3) and 50% of TOTs in Read and Bruce (1982). Contextual information about the person (roles played, national origin, etc.) was available on 42% of TOTs, and visual/auditory (looks, sound of voice) on 17% of TOTs (Read & Bruce, 1982). Rubin (1975) reports a substantially higher percentage of TOTs accompanied by letter guesses (72%), but this was on a small sample of high TOT-rate targets from Brown and McNeill (1966).

Widner et al. (1996) report that first letter guesses were made on 2% of TOTs, and that last letter and number of syllables were never guessed. They speculate that the request to provide partial information may actually decrease TOT reports, pointing to a pilot study yielding twice as many TOTs when partial information reports were not requested. Subjects may perceive a request for partial target word information as a validity check: if you are really having a TOT, demonstrate this by providing some partial information about the word. Thus, it is possible that such pointed instructions may make subjects more conservative in reporting TOTs, as well as fragmentary information.

These relatively low partial information report percentages suggest caution in interpreting their significance. Even if such information is frequently correct, the total number of guesses may be relatively low (cf. Whitten & Leonard, 1981). It is worth noting that partial information is reported for a greater percentage of diary TOTs: 91%, Ecke (2004); 56%, Cohen and Faulkner (1986). Confirming this difference, Burke et al. (1991) found that 2.07 pieces of target word information accompanied diary TOTs (Study 1), but only 0.73 pieces were reported with laboratory TOTs (Study 2), using the same subjects in both studies. This could suggest that more information accompanies natural TOTs, or that diary TOTs with partial information are more likely to be reported. The presence of peripheral information about the target word may make real-world TOTs more memorable, and therefore more likely to be recorded.

## Establishing Chance Probability

Another issue related to the availability of partial target word information is establishing a chance probability of correct guessing for first letter and number of syllables (cf. Brown, 1991). More specifically, if subjects provide correct first letter guesses on 21% of TOTs, is this greater than one would expect through educated guesses? One way to establish a chance baseline is to force a guess on every trial, and compare TOT with DK trials (Koriat & Lieblich, 1974). The problem with this procedure is that subjects exhibit some knowledge of the structural features of words even when they claim not to know the word (Brown & Burrows, 2009; Koriat & Lieblich, 1974). Koriat and Lieblich (1974) present a comprehensive discussion of the difficulties in establishing chance probabilities using guessing procedures. A better way to address chance levels is to force a recognition decision on a trial-by-trial basis (Brown & Burrows, 2009; Gollan & Acenas, 2004; Miozzo & Caramazza, 1997), but this has been rarely used mainly because it makes the experimental procedure considerably more tedious and time consuming.

## Spotty Publication Reports

A final problem involves the inconsistency and lack of detail concerning partial information reports in published articles. Often, this information is simply not reported because the incidence is too low (Vitevitch & Sommers, 2003; cf. Schwartz & Smith, 1997). Often, the method section indicates that peripheral information was requested during TOTs, but these data do not appear in the results. This latter situation leaves us wondering whether the study found that too few TOTs elicited such information, or excluded the information for reporting efficiency. For example, Ferrand (2001) requested gender, syllables, letters, and other words but reported no summary statistics on any of these data.

## ☐ Types of Information

The kind of information requested during TOTs is consistent across most investigations, and based largely upon the categories set up in Brown and McNeill (1966): first letter, similar words, and number of syllables. Lovelace (1987) took exception with this narrow set of dimensions and encouraged investigators to cast a wider net by not telling subjects what type(s) of information to expect.

Using an open-ended procedure to find out what subjects experience during a TOT state, Lovelace (1987) suggested that many categories of target word information can come to mind during TOTs: first letter (12%), syllable number (17%), word length (14%), context (32%), ending letter (2%), beginning sound (2%), ending sound (2%), frequency of occurrence (11%), language/country of origin (14%), and descriptive attribute (20%). These incidence rates are generally low, suggesting that peripheral information is relatively infrequent. However, Lovelace defined TOTs rather broadly—failed retrieval accompanied by high recognition confidence—so his results may apply more generally to unrecalled items than being specific to just TOTs.

# ☐ Letters and Phonemes

## Initial

The most common partial information available during TOTs (Gollan et al., 2005), is target word letter(s) with the most salient being the first letter. Across investigations, these first-letter guesses are accurate approximately half of the time (cf. Brown, 1991). Diary studies generally do not provide information about the incidence of specific types of target word information. Rather, diary reports provide more general information, such as the incidence of any type of partial information (Burke et al., 1991; Schwartz, 2001a) or the percent of TOTs where a specific type of information is reported without noting accuracy (Gollan et al., 2005). An exception is research by Ecke (1997, 2001, 2004), who reports that the initial letter/ sound is correct for 34% (Ecke, 2004) to 42% (Ecke, 1997) of TOTs.

With respect to laboratory research, Brown and McNeill (1966) report that the correct first letter accompanied 51% of TOTs in their pilot study, and 57% in their main study. As shown below, there is a wide variation across laboratory studies in first letter (or phoneme) accuracy, but the overall average is around 50%, supporting Brown's (1991) earlier summary.

---

2% (Widner et al., 1996)

7% (Smith & Schwartz, 1997)

29% (Schwartz, 2008)

40% (Brown & Nix, 1996)

47% (Biedermann et al., 2008)

54% (Caramazza & Miozzo,1997)

54% (Harley & Bown, 1998)

56% (Dahlgren, 1998)
58% (Brennen et al., 2007)
64% (Yarmey, 1973)
71% (Koriat & Lieblich, 1974)
71% (Biedermann et al., 2008)

---

Several investigations using prime/cueing procedures also report first letter guesses (Jones, 1989; Meyer & Bock, 1992), but these data are not included above because it is unclear how seeing the related (or unrelated) word may bias the frequency or accuracy of target word first-letter guesses.

Brown and McNeill (1966) also used an indirect approach to evaluate first-letter accuracy. They culled through the interlopers (related words) reported by subjects while experiencing TOTs and discovered that the target word shared a common first letter with 49% of similar sounding (SS) interlopers and 8% of similar meaning (SM) interlopers. Brown and McNeill (1966) suggest that although it is difficult to establish a chance baseline, the SS percentage was *certainly* above chance and that the SM was *probably* above chance. Similarly, Browman (1978, cited in Vihman, 1980) found that for 51% of natural TOTs, interlopers shared the same first phoneme with the target.

Still another approach is to compare first-letter guesses during TOT and DK trials. Across eight different comparisons, the difference between TOT (41%) and DK (15%) is consistent and usually dramatic (Biedermann et al., 2008, Experiment 1; Caramazza & Miozzo, 1997, Experiments 1 and 2; Koriat & Lieblich, 1974; Schwartz, 2008, Experiment 3; Smith et al., 1991, Experiments 1 and 2). Recognition tests have also been used to evaluate knowledge of a target word's initial *phoneme*, rather than letter. With a two-choice recognition test on only TOT items, Miozzo and Caramazza (1997) found 75% accuracy in Experiment 1. They replicated this accuracy in Experiment 2 (72%), and additionally demonstrated that this was significantly above DK trials (58%). Similarly, Gollan and Acenas (2004) also found greater accuracy on TOT than DK trials (respectively) in both Experiments 1 (85% versus 60%) and 2 (73% versus 52%).

Using a three-alternative forced-choice recognition test for first letter, Brown and Burrows (2009) found knowledge of the first letter of the target word during TOTs to be 67%, and significantly above chance (33%). Interestingly, knowledge of the first letter was also significantly above chance when the target word was unfamiliar (43%), vaguely familiar—(47%), moderately familiar—(57%), although TOT performance was significantly higher than each of these three DK states.

In summary, evidence of knowledge of target word first letter/phoneme during TOTs is strong and consistent in a number of different studies.

Furthermore, in nearly all cases where such a comparison is made, it is well above DK trials. What is curious, however, is the evidence that subjects may have insight into the target word's first letter during DK trials, as assessed by guessing (Smith et al., 1991) and recognition (Brown & Burrows, 2009; Gollan & Acenas, 2004; Miozzo & Caramazza, 1997). Apparently, a TOT is not a privileged state with respect to partial word access, although it is clearly quite strong and more likely to intrude into conscious awareness during a word search.

## Final

The final letter/sound of the missing target word also appears to be accessible during TOTs. There are fewer published reports on final compared to first letter knowledge (cf. Brown, 1991). Furthermore, the frequency of reports and accuracy level tends to be lower for final than for first letters, as illustrated by Brown and Nix (1996) who found final letter (or sound) guessed on 16% of TOTs (young adults) (versus 38% for first letter) of which 35% were correct (versus 40% for first letter). A higher success rate was discovered by Koriat and Lieblich (1974; 69%) who forced final-letter guesses on all trials, and this was significantly above that found for DK trials (17%). With a two-choice recognition test, performance was significantly above chance for both final phoneme in Caramazza and Miozzo (1997, Experiment 1; TOT = 67%; DK = 49%), and final vowel in Miozzo and Caramazza (1997; TOT = 61%; chance = 50%).

Using an indirect measure of last letter correspondence, Brown and McNeill (1966) note that 45% of SS interlopers matched the associated target words on last letter (estimated from their Figure 1, p. 330), a rate substantially above the 28% correspondence level for SM interlopers. Browman (1978, cited in Vihman, 1980) also found that 35% of related words generated during real-life TOTs matched the target on at least one letter at the end.

## Comparisons Across Multiple Letter Positions

The above outcomes clearly point to better initial letter compared to final letter (phoneme) knowledge during TOTs. Three investigations have compared knowledge of multiple letter positions by examining the correspondence between SS interlopers and targets for the first three and last three letters (Brown & McNeill, 1966; Rubin, 1975, Experiment 2; Koriat & Lieblich, 1975). These data for SS interlopers are presented in Figure 5.1, and include two control comparisons with SM interlopers (Brown & McNeill, 1966; Koriat & Lieblich, 1975). Note that these comparisons are necessarily

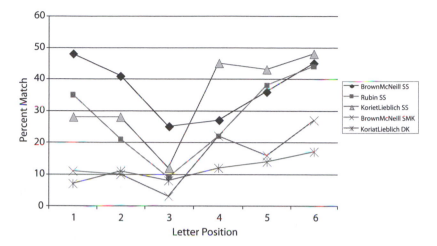

**FIGURE 5.1**    Letter position matches comparing target with SS, SM, and DK words.

limited to instances where both targets and interlopers are at least six letters long.

In Brown and McNeill (1966), the match between TOT target and SS interlopers was higher than for SM interlopers on all six positions, and significantly so for all but the third letter from the end (see Figure 5.1). Koriat and Lieblich (1975) focused their entire article on the match between SS interlopers and TOT targets, using the data from Koriat and Lieblich (1974). SS words generated during TOTs matched all six positions significantly more often than did SS words generated during DK states (see Figure 5.1).

Finally, Rubin (1975) assessed multiple-letter position matches in two different ways. In Experiment 2, he used the same procedure described above, comparing SS interlopers against TOT targets (see Rubin SS; Figure 5.1). This yielded a pattern very similar to the other two studies (Brown & McNeill, 1966; Koriat & Lieblich, 1974). In Experiment 1, he evaluated all letter guesses rather than just those from SS words, instructing subjects that when experiencing a TOT to "write down any letters that you know. Please feel free to guess. Please put in one dash for each letter you think is in the word, but that you do not know" (p. 393). He scored successive letters as correct only if the subject got all of the other letter(s) correct that appeared between it and the appropriate end of the word. In other words, unless the first letter was correct neither the second nor third letter guess was scored, and if the second letter was incorrect then the third letter was not evaluated. Put another way, at the start of the word all letters preceding that letter had to be correct for it to count as correct; for the end of the word, all letters following that particular letter had to be correct. The start and end letters were most likely to be correct, and accuracy trailed off in both directions toward the middle of the word, again revealing a U-shaped function of percentage of correct letter matches. In summary, all three investigations show a similar function, with letter information about the target word better at the beginning and end of the words. Furthermore, this information is significantly more accurate with SS interlopers, compared to either SM interlopers or word guesses made on DK trials.

Ecke (2001) also found higher correct guessing rates for letters/sounds at the first (59%) than either the middle (34%) or last (44%) portions of the missing target word, and this predominance of the initial knowledge was even more pronounced in his diary investigations (Ecke, 1997, 2004): first = 38%, middle = 15%, last = 16%. As a final note, several studies report that the accuracy of nonspecified letter information is moderately high (40%, Jönsson & Olsson, 2003; 44%, Vigliocco et al., 1999, Experiment 1), although chance levels are higher because the subject did not need to specify the position that the letter held in the target word.

## Phonology Versus Orthography?

It is difficult to separate the effects of phonology from orthography in the above comparisons. More specifically, the first-letter guess could derive from partial access to either the sound or form of the unavailable target word. There has been no direct evaluation of orthography apart from phonology, or vice versa, perhaps because these would be difficult to tease apart. Schwartz (2002b) briefly discusses this "neglected" but important dimension of partial access. In sorting through a large corpus of interlopers produced during naturally occurring TOTs, Schachter (1988) provides anecdotal examples of where orthography can be separated from phonology deductively. For example, the interloper Charles for *Chris* and Peg for *Phyllis* have a common orthography without shared phonology. It is hoped that this important question of the role which word sound versus structure plays in TOT elicitation (and resolution) will be more extensively addressed in future research.

## ☐ Syllables

Some evidence points to the availability of the syllabic structure of the elusive target word during a TOT experience. Empirical evidence supporting this type of "generic" recall is less definitive than that for letter availability, primarily because syllabic length shows limited variability across target words. The majority of target words used in TOT research are two or three syllables long (Brown & Burrows, 2009; Brown & McNeill, 1966; Caramazza & Miozzo, 1997; Koriat & Lieblich, 1974; Gollan & Silverberg, 2001). In addition to a high probability of a correct guess by chance, a strategically guided guessing based upon general knowledge of linguistic structure may also assist correct syllable number identification during TOTs. For instance, a medical term is likely to contain more syllables than a word for a fruit.

# Number

Brown and McNeill (1966) had participants guess the number of syllables in the missing target during TOTs, allowing choices of 1 through 5. In their main study, 60% of the guesses were correct (47% in their pilot study). Although there is a wide range of accuracy for guessing syllable number in subsequent outcomes, the listing below (by increasing percentages) shows that syllable number guesses are generally accurate more than half of the time.

27% (Brown & Nix, 1996)
34% (Jönsson & Olsson, 2003)
37% (Caramazza & Miozzo, 1997)
45% (Gollan & Silverberg, 2001)
50% (Ecke, 2001)
54% (Dahlgren, 1998)
55% (Vigliocco et al., 1999, Exp1)
67% (Rubin, 1975)
70% (Harley & Bown, 1998)
76% (Yarmey, 1973)
81% (Koriat & Lieblich, 1974)

Brown and McNeill (1966) analyzed syllable number information using five different approaches, a statistical attack more thorough than in any subsequent TOT study. First, they combined all syllable number guesses across participants and targets, and found a perfect (rank-order) correlation between actual and modal number of judged syllables. They also reported percentage of correct guesses separately for subgroups of target words of each syllable length. A similar summary was provided by Koriat and Lieblich (1974), and the combination of both of these data sets is presented in Figure 5.2 for target words that are one, two, three, and four syllables long (five-syllable targets and five-syllable guesses were both very rare). For target words one, two,

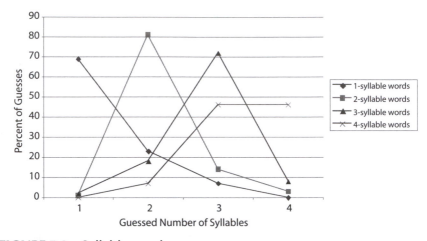

**FIGURE 5.2**    Syllable number guesses.

or three syllables long, the predominant guess (70 to 80%) is the correct one. For four-syllable words, syllable guess accuracy is not as high, perhaps due to the rarity of such words. As a control comparison, Koriat and Lieblich (1974) had subjects guess the number of syllables during DKs, and found a substantially lower accuracy of 38% compared to 81% when in a TOT.

Brown and McNeill (1966) also analyzed the syllable data separately by words and by participants. For target words, the mean syllabic number guess for each target word was averaged across all participants with a TOT on that particular word. For subjects, this analysis was reversed, with each subject counting once, and averaging guesses across each word length. Each of these analyses revealed the same systematic and linear relationship between actual and judged syllabic length. Then, a select analysis including only subjects with TOTs on both two- and three-syllable words (N = 21) revealed that the average guess for two-syllable words was significantly lower than than for three-syllable words. Finally, 48% of SS interlopers had the same number of syllables as the target, compared to 20% of SM interlopers. Correspondence between interlopers and targets in syllable number was also reported by Yarmey (1973; 80%), Browman (1978, cited in Zwicky, 1982; 56%), and Burke et al. (1991; 43%).

Data on syllable guess accuracy are also available from two diary investigations. In Gollan et al. (2005, Experiment 1), syllable number was correctly guessed on 29% of TOTs, whereas Ecke (2004) found a 61% success rate. Finally, studies using prime and cue procedures have reported relatively low syllabic guess accuracies during TOTs (34%, Jones, 1989;

24%, Meyer & Bock, 1992) but as noted earlier, presenting ancillary words during the TOT experience may bias these reports.

In summary, subjects seem to have a reasonable sense of syllabic number during TOTs. However, this is much less impressive than first-letter knowledge, especially given the limited syllabic range for most target words. Furthermore, chance levels of accurate guessing are relatively high, occluding the clear interpretation of such findings.

## Syllabic Stress

Knowledge of the syllabic stress (accent) of the missing target word occasionally has been evaluated during TOTs. Although Brown and McNeill (1966) did not ask subjects to provide such information, they inferred it from SS interlopers. This analysis was limited because (a) only multisyllable target words could be considered, and (b) only SS interlopers having the same number of syllables as the target word could be included. The 20% of SS interlopers that fit these two criteria showed a greater than chance probability of matching the target word in syllabic stress. Brown and McNeill (1966) were appropriately guarded in their conclusion, suggesting that "… we are left suspecting that *S* in a TOT state has knowledge of the stress pattern of the target, but we are not sure of it" (p. 330). Ecke (2001) also found that subjects correctly guessed the syllabic stress pattern 50% of the time, but provided no chance baseline comparison. Furthermore, Jönsson and Olsson (2003) found that syllabic stress was correct 60% of the time, but guesses were made on only 2% of TOTs. Thus, there is very modest evidence that the syllabic stress pattern is accessible during TOTs, and more research is needed before any firm conclusions can be drawn about this rhythmic component of implicit target word access.

## Word Number

For most TOT studies, nearly all targets are single words. However, a clever parallel to syllable number variation can be obtained using targets that all contain multiple words, such as proper names. Hanley and Chapman's (2008) innovative procedure included celebrity names containing three (Jamie Lee Curtis) or two (Demi Moore) words. For each TOT and DK trial, subjects guessed the number of words contained in the celebrity name. Subjects were informed that there were an equal number of two- and three-word famous names. The correct guess probability was significantly above chance during TOTs (56%) but not DKs (49%), suggesting that subjects had some knowledge of this structural dimension of the proper-name target. However, this evidence is not strong, as it is only slightly above chance (50%) during TOTs.

# ☐ Syntax

The availability of TOT target word syntax has been investigated in the form of gender and numerosity. The inquiries into both of these dimensions are primarily driven by linguistically oriented research on TOTs. As Schwartz (2001b) points out, one-stage versus two-stage theories of language production make different predictions about the availability of target-word syntax. One-stage theories assume that syntax and phonology are both accessed *after* the word's semantic representation. In contrast, two-stage theories posit that the semantic and syntactic information are compiled *prior to* accessing phonology (Caramazza & Miozzo, 1997; Levelt, 1989; Schwartz, 2001b). Thus, TOTs provide a good crucible to compare these two orientations because during TOTs there is often partial but not full access to the target word features. The two-stage models assume that syntax is highly accessible (as is semantics) during TOTs, but that phonology is only partially accessible. A one-stage model, in contrast, assumes that access to both syntax and phonology of the target word are problematic, and that they should be independent of each other (Caramazza & Miozzo, 1997).

## Gender

Research on target word gender access during TOTs has involved five different languages: Spanish, German, French, Italian, and Hebrew (cf. Schriefers & Jescheniak, 1999). Italian investigators did the initial examinations of this topic. Italian has only masculine and feminine (no neuter) forms, and although word endings tend to be correlated with gender, there are numerous exceptions. Because Vigliocco et al. (1997) use a loose definition of TOT (any nonretrieved word where subjects can supply some partial information), their results may be broadly relevant to gender access in the absence of phonological accessibility, rather than narrowly pertaining to TOT states (see earlier caution in Chapter 2). Vigliocco et al. (1997) found that subjects were significantly more accurate at word gender during TOT+ (84%) than TOT– (53%) states, and that this rate was essentially the same for TOT+s without phonological information available (80%) and for irregular target words with gender unrelated to word ending (80%).

Two additional Italian-language studies involve more traditionally defined TOTs. Miozzo and Caramazza (1997) found clear evidence supporting the availability of gender in the absence of phonology. In two experiments, subjects correctly guessed gender during TOTs (75%) at a rate significantly above DKs (47%). In addition, in Experiment 2 correct identification for both gender and phonology (first letter) were nearly identical, an outcome that challenges two-stage theory because syntactic information should be substantially more available if both semantic and syntactic elements of the word are integrated and fully accessible prior to phonology. In a follow-up, Caramazza and Miozzo (1997) found additional support for one-stage theory. Retrieval of gender during TOTs (71%) was significantly above DKs (51%), and the correlation between accessing gender and accessing phonology was essentially zero, clearly establishing the independence between these dimensions and supporting the single-stage theory.

Above-chance access to gender information during TOTs has also been demonstrated in three additional languages. For French, Ferrand (2001) found highly accurate assessment of gender during TOTs (80%) that was significantly above both TOT– (53%; Exp 1) and DK (48%; Exp 2) trials. In Spanish, Ecke (2004) noted that 73% of gender guesses (among Spanish bilinguals) were accurate in diary TOTs. And finally, Biedermann et al. (2008, Experiment 2) discovered that gender information was available to German language speakers on 73% of TOTs compared to 40% of DKs. Their outcome also supports the independence of syntax (gender) and phonology (first phoneme) because phonological information was available even when syntax was not. They also replicated this demonstration of independence using mass/count, rather than gender, as a measure of syntax (Biedermann et al., 2008, Experiment 1) (see additional discussion later in this chapter)

Access to gender information about the target word during TOTs may not be universal across all languages, however. Gollan and Silverberg (2001) found no evidence in Hebrew. Gender identification was at 55% in a two-choice identification test, which is essentially at chance. Thus, although there appears to be consistent and strong support for gender access across a number of different languages, there is an exception (Hebrew). This discrepancy should motivate a more thorough exploration of this topic across a broader range of languages.

## Numerosity (Count/Mass)

The other syntactic dimension evaluated during TOTs is numerosity, a concept referring to mass versus count. Applicable only to nouns, numerosity pertains to whether the word refers to a count (discrete) entity (e.g., "professor") that can be pluralized, or a mass entity (e.g., "rain") that cannot be pluralized. In English, this distinction can be identified by applying the adjective "fewer" or "less" to the word. "Fewer" applies to count (e.g., "there were fewer professors at the picnic this year"), whereas "less" pertains to mass (e.g., "there was less rain at the lake this summer").

This is a subtle aspect of syntax, and unlike gender has no obvious connection to either phonology or orthography (see above discussion of Italian). Vigliocco et al. (1999) assessed subjects' knowledge of this dimension by having them choose which of two statements was more appropriate to the missing target. The first shell is appropriate to mass words, and the second to count words:

| there is _____ | *versus* | there is a(n) _____ |
|---|---|---|
| there won't be much _____ | *versus* | there won't be many _____ |

Repeating a previous caution, Vigliocco et al. (1999) did not define their TOTs with reference to subjects' evaluations but rather by target word residuals reported during noncorrect trials.

In Experiment 1, for count words subjects were correct significantly more often during TOT+ (78%) than TOT− (59%) trials, but only marginally significantly correct more often for mass words during TOT+ (85%) than TOT− (82%) trials. Although numerosity assessments were above chance for both TOT+ and TOT− items, TOT+ were significantly higher than TOT− trials. Schwartz (2002b) later replicated this outcome using a more traditional definition of TOTs, with numerosity correct for 74% of TOTs compared to 65% of DKs. Similar to Vigliocco et al. (1999), both values were above chance and TOTs were significantly higher than DKs. Also replicating Vigliocco et al. (1999), Biedermann et al. (2008, Experiment 1) found mass/count accuracy to be significantly higher during TOTs (84%) than DKs (63%). They also showed that access to phonology (first phoneme) and syntax (mass/count) were independent (see above), again arguing against a two-stage, or serial, access of syntax-then-phonology during word retrieval.

# ☐ Imagery (Visual/Auditory)

Brown and McNeill's (1966) investigation had a strong verbal orientation, inquiring only about linguistic aspects of the TOT target word on the questionnaire probe (first letter, syllable number, related words, etc.). Subsequent research has generally followed in a similar linguistic framework, but Yarmey (1973) raised an objection:

> For several years, I have noticed that when I try to recall the names of people, introspective experiences such as images and affect and verbal descriptions are easily aroused. This suggests that TOT experiences may involve both verbal and nonverbal imagery processes. … (p. 287)

Several outcomes support Yarmey's suggestion that nonverbal elements may play an important role in TOTs (cf. Whitten & Leonard, 1981). Schwartz and Smith (1997, Experiment 3) compared the type of information about TOTimals that occurred during TOTs versus DKs (respectively): diet (23% versus 22%) and size (22% versus 17%) information revealed no difference, but picture-related information (50% versus 27%) did, leading Schwartz and Smith (1997) to suggest that image processes may be an important (and undervalued) aspect of TOTs.

Furthering this point, May and Clayton (1973) report that on 35% of those trials where the target name was not produced, the *appearance* of the target word's referent object was available. Although they did not use standard TOT procedures, they likened their subjects' reports to TOTs. Finally, Brennen et al. (1990, Experiment 2) found that 26% of TOTs for famous celebrity names were accompanied by an image of the celebrity's face, 22% by their physical appearance, and 1% by their voice. Although the experimental support for the involvement of imagery in the TOT experience is primarily ad hoc and anecdotal, it is sufficiently interesting to warrant further experimental exploration. Especially intriguing is Erdelyi and Kleinbard's (1978) discussion of tip-of-the-eye, as it relates to this point.

# ☐ Target Word Associations

Information loosely connected to the missing target word occasionally becomes available during TOTs, and tends to occur when target words are cued by nonverbal or nondefinitional cues. For example, when identifying TV shows by theme song, Riefer et al. (1995) found that 32% of TOTs were accompanied by recall of a character from the show, 19% by the lead actor's name, and 79% by plot outline. Subjects were also significantly more accurate during TOTs than DKs in guessing genre (85%; comedy, drama, action, western) and era (82%; decade 1950s through 1990s). Odor TOTs are also accompanied by associated information, such as similar odors (8%), odor category (17%), odor source (13%), and odor place (20%; Jönsson & Olsson, 2003). These findings on target word associations, although sparse and piecemeal, support Lovelace's (1987) encouragement to expand our conception of what aspects of the missing target are accessible during TOTs.

# ☐ Summary

Many TOTs are accompanied by peripheral information related to the missing target word. There are, however, serious issues with evaluating such information because the rate at which it is volunteered is often low, and selective on the part of the subject. In addition, it is difficult to establish chance levels for guessing target word features. Instructions may bias which type, and how much, information is reported by subjects, and TOT studies as a whole are inconsistent on if, and how, such information is reported. The first letter appears to be available on about half of TOTs, as estimated by voluntary reports, forced guesses, and the correspondence between target words and interlopers. Information about final letters (phonemes), syllable number, and syllabic stress also appear to be accessible above chance, although the evidence is not as strong or compelling as for first letter availability. Syntactical information has been repeatedly shown to be available during TOTs, in the form of both word gender and numerosity. It is worth emphasizing that partial information availability is a remarkable component of the TOT experience. The ability to know something about an inaccessible word suggests that word retrieval is not a digital, or all-or-none, process. Rather, it appears to be constructive, with various bits and pieces available in steps or stages.

# 6
CHAPTER

# Dimensions of TOT Target Words

Are certain types of target words more likely to elicit TOTs than others? Given the huge variability in TOT-eliciting capacity across the different target words used in laboratory investigations, this would seem to be a natural direction for this research (see Chapter 3). The one target-word dimension that consistently stands out as a potent elicitor of TOTs is proper names, leading to more TOTs than other types of target (Burke et al., 1991). A variety of other target-word dimensions have been examined with respect to the propensity to elicit a TOT, and these are detailed below.

## ☐ Frequency

An assumption found in much of the literature is that TOTs are more likely with lower- than with higher-frequency words. This assumption makes intuitive sense, because less frequently used words are more difficult to retrieve and TOTs should parallel retrieval difficulty. However, recent research challenges this assumption, especially for older adults (Gollan & Brown, 2006).

In their original investigation, Brown and McNeill (1966) attempted to construct a set of target words at the "margin of word knowledge" (p. 337) and "…in the passive or recognition vocabularies of our Ss but not in their active recall vocabularies" (p. 326). They assumed that TOTs are more likely for words used less frequently, and many subsequent studies have followed this by selecting low-frequency words for study materials (Askari, 1999; Biedermann et al., 2008; Burke et al., 1991; Burke & Laver, 1990; Ellis, 1985; Faust et al., 2003; James & Burke, 2000; Koriat & Lieblich, 1977; Lesk & Womble, 2004; Naito & Komatsu, 1989; Pine et al., 2007; Rastle & Burke, 1996; Tweney, Tkacz, & Zaruba, 1975).

Four diary study outcomes, however, challenge this assumption. Cohen and Faulkner (1986) found that most diary participants rated the proper names eliciting TOTs as *usually recalled easily* (62%) and *well-known* (71%). They add that this finding may seem counterintuitive and "... that retrieval failure results from a temporal fluctuation in the retrieval process, rather than defective encoding or storage" (p. 189). Similarly, Reason and Lucas's (1984, Experiment 1) diarists rated most of their TOT target words as very (39%) or moderately (35%) familiar, as opposed to slightly (27%) familiar.

Two additional studies had participants use a more detailed Likert scale rating procedure to evaluate the target word that elicited each personal TOT. Using a familiarity scale of 1 (very unfamiliar) to 7 (very familiar), Burke et al. (1991) found an average rating of 5.6, clearly above the scale mean of 4 and toward the familiar end. With a smaller familiarity range of 1 (not very well) to 5 (sure, I know it), Ecke (2004) similarly found mean TOT target word familiarity to be 4.3, again well above the scale mean of 3 and toward the high end.

Brown and McNeill (1966) selected their target words with an objective frequency of occurrence in the written language of between 1 and 4 per million (M) words (Thorndike & Lorge, 1952). Some have used rarer words (<3/M: Beattie & Coughlan, 1999; ≤1/M: May & Clayton, 1973; 0.25–1/M: Jones, 1989; ≤8/M: Abrams, Trunk, & Margolin, 2007). However, others have been successful in eliciting TOTs with words as high as 10/M (Abrams et al., 2003; Abrams & Rodriguez, 2005; Bak, 1987; White & Abrams, 2002), and Bak (1987) suggests "the fact that relatively high-frequency words ... elicit the TOT phenomenon suggests that the important variable is less a word's frequency than its place in semantic space ..." (p. 26). This topic remains open, and is worth further evaluation. The complexity of this issue may be daunting, however, given the number of word dimensions that tend to co-vary with objective frequency.

## Background Frequency in Diary Studies

When Burke et al. (1991) evaluated resolved TOT target words from diary study subjects, nearly half (47%) were so infrequent that they did not even appear in standard word frequency norms (Francis & Kučera, 1982). Those TOT target words that could be found were substantially lower than the overall normative frequency (84/M), for both abstract word (7/M) and object name (3/M) targets. Ecke (2004) found similar low frequencies for English (7/M) and Spanish (12/M) language diarists.

Ecke (2004) also found an interesting frequency difference between primary and secondary language TOTs. More specifically, TOT target word frequency was substantially lower in the dominant than the nondominant language (respectively) for both American bilinguals (7/M versus 20/M) and Mexican bilinguals (12/M versus 48/M). Thus, the frequency threshold of TOT words may shift with experience: with greater familiarity (dominant language), the TOT threshold shifts down toward lower-frequency words. A more controlled test of this idea could involve a comparison of TOT incidence for students at differing competence levels in learning a second language. This could be accomplished by either *longitudinal* comparisons as one student progresses through multiple semesters, or *cross-sectional* comparisons of current students at different points in a progressive language sequence (number of prior semesters).

It is worth pointing out that for both Burke et al. (1991) and Ecke (2004), the mean subjective familiarity rating for TOT target words among diarists was high (see earlier section), even though the objective frequency was relatively low. This suggests a disconnect between objective and subjective familiarity of target words. Individuals may believe that TOT targets are more familiar (or frequent) than they actually are.

## Background Frequency in Laboratory Studies

Several experimental studies on TOTs have compared target words of varying frequency levels. Comparing high-frequency (HF; >25/M) with low-frequency (LF; <10/M) target words in older adults, Astell and Harley (1996) discovered that HF targets elicited no TOTs at all, whereas LF targets elicited 3.5 TOTs per word. Vitevitch and Sommers (2003) also found more TOTs with LF (4%) than HF (2%) words, although the absolute difference is modest and all target words were monosyllabic. Harley and Bown (1998) also found significantly more TOTs with LF versus HF targets (respectively) in both Experiments 1 (14% versus 11%) and 2 (12% versus 11%), although again the difference is small. Finally, with young children ages 8 to 10, Hanly and Vandenberg (2010) discovered that nearly all of the TOTs (95%) were elicited by LF (<10/M) compared to HF (>20/M) words.

Several other methodologies have been used to examine the relationship between target frequency and TOTs. Gollan and Silverberg (2001) found a small but significant overall negative correlation between word frequency and TOTs. However, when separated out by language competence, this correlation remained significant for bilinguals but vanished for monolinguals. González (1996) also found a moderate negative correlation between target-word frequency and number of TOTs.

In a cross-experiment comparison, Harley and Bown (1998) point out that the TOT rate in Yarmey (1987) was greater than that found by Brown and McNeill (1966) even though Yarmey used higher-frequency targets (on the average). Harley and Bown (1998) argue that this superficially contradicts speculation that TOTs are especially likely with lower-frequency words. However, one must be very cautious in such inferences between studies because TOT rates are sensitive to a number of different aspects of procedure and participant group.

Gollan and Brown (2006) suggest that frequency level can have a big impact on the TOT rate. Individuals can experience TOTs on words at any frequency level, but there appear to be both a high and low TOT threshold. TOTs are unlikely to occur above the high threshold, because these words are simply too easy. TOTs are also unlikely to occur for words below the low threshold because subjects do not know these (cf. Gollan & Silverberg, 2001). In the middle range, the incidence of TOTs is usually higher for relatively rarer words, probably because the baseline activation level of these is lower. Gollan and Brown (2006) divided target words into relatively easy and difficult subsets, and the outcomes for these separate sets of words support the idea that TOTs are directly connected to word frequency. However, even this straightforward relationship is modified by aging. Among older adults, more frequent words are more susceptible to TOTs (see Chapter 10). Meyer and Bock (1992) voice a similar opinion, speculating that TOTs might reflect either superior or inferior access to target words, depending on the difficulty of the words. Among difficult (low-frequency) words, TOTs may reflect improved access, whereas among easier (higher-frequency) words, TOTs may reflect deficient access (cf. Meyer & Bock, 1992). These specific levels, of course, vary depending upon the linguistic competence of the particular participant.

Another approach to establishing target word familiarity, aside from objective frequency, is to define a target word's familiarity based upon the probability of correct target word retrieval among participants in the study. This should yield a negative correlation between correct retrieval and TOT probability if the frequency assumption is correct. Brown and Nix (1996) failed to find support for this. Correlations between retrieval success and TOT rate were actually positive, not negative, in both the pilot (.31) and main (.18) studies, although only the pilot correlation was significant. A caution associated with this finding is that the outcome is based upon a relatively restricted range of item difficulty.

Finally, Bonin, Perret, Méot, Ferrand, and Mermillod (2008) approached this issue of target-word familiarity through subjective evaluations by study participants. One group of subjects rated French celebrity faces on how often they had heard/read/produced the individual's name: never, once a year, once a month, once a week, every 2 days, every day, or more than once per day. Using TOT data derived from a second group, Bonin et al. (2008) discovered a significant negative correlation (−.32) across items between subjective frequency rating and TOT rate, suggesting that less frequently encountered names result in more TOTs. In contrast to this, Hanley and Chapman (2008) compared the TOT rate on celebrity names that had been rated high or low in familiarity by a separate group of subjects. They found no significant difference in TOTs between high (16%) and low (19%) familiar names, although the trend is in the same direction as for Bonin et al. (2008).

In general, the relationship between target word frequency and TOT probability will be difficult to definitively establish, mainly due to the complexities of personal usage experiences among individuals and between groups tested in any particular study (cf. Gollan & Brown, 2006). This point bothered Smith et al. (1994), who emphasize that "the relationship between TOTs and prior experiences with retrieval targets has not been clearly established by empirical studies" (p. 32). This imprecision motivated them to experimentally manipulate background exposure frequency via study time of the target words, using their artificially constructed and controlled TOTimals stimulus materials. However, their manipulation was unsuccessful, as increasing study time for target words did not influence TOT rate (see Chapter 4). As suggested before, perhaps their strength manipulation was not sufficient to model the large differences in exposure frequency with real usage experiences.

It is probably safe to conclude that word difficulty is related to TOT experience, but difficulty may be determined by multiple factors related to personal usage, recency of experience, and linguistic competence (Smith et al., 1994; also see the discussion of transmission deficit hypothesis, Chapter 9). Furthermore, this relationship may be complex and nonlinear, depending upon other factors such as age (cf. Gollan & Brown, 2006).

# ☐ Recency

Another dimension that might influence TOT incidence is how recently a particular target word has been encountered. A target word last retrieved 5 years ago may be more difficult to access than one produced last week, because its baseline activation level is lower. In their diary investigation, Burke et al. (1991) requested that for TOT on an acquaintance's name, participants should evaluate how recently they have had contact with that person. As one would expect, average recency decreased systematically across age group: 3 months ago for young; 5 months ago for midage; 4 years ago for older. Although informative with respect to age trends, these data are of limited usefulness in answering the recency question because no baseline information exists for names that participants successfully retrieve, those that did not elicit TOTs.

Using a different definition of recency, Bonin et al. (2008) compared name retrieval performance with how old the subjects were when they first learned the celebrity's name (age of acquisition, or AoA). One group of subjects attempted to name each celebrity, and another group rated AoA as before 5, 6–8, 9–11, 12–14, 15–17, 18–20, 21+. Bonin et al. (2008) found a significant positive correlation ($r = .55$) between AoA and TOTs, suggesting that names acquired early are associated with fewer TOTs. Although this superficially suggests that more recently acquired names are associated with more TOTs, other factors may be driving this relationship. Earlier-learned names may be encountered or rehearsed more often, making them relatively stronger, or recently acquired names may not be fully consolidated, making them more vulnerable to TOTs. In any event, the generality of this outcome may be limited by the restricted stimulus domain (French celebrities) and age or experiential range of subjects, given that Bonin et al. (2008) tested college students. AoA norms exist for English words, and it may be useful to see if this relates to TOT frequency using data on TOT rate across target words (Abrams, Trunk, & Margolin, 2007; Burke et al., 1991) (see Chapter 3).

An experimental approach has been used to manipulate target word recency using a priming paradigm. As described in Chapter 4, some of the target words are presented in a list immediately preceding the TOT task, making them uniformly higher in recency rather than the nonprimed set of target words. These results have consistently supported that recent experience of a target word reduces TOT incidence. Rastle and Burke (1996) exposed subjects to half of the target words in a supposedly unrelated task preceding the TOT-eliciting session. Priming significantly reduced the number of TOTs for recently encountered target words, suggesting that TOTs are relatively more likely for less recently encountered words. Cleary and colleagues (Cleary, 2006; Cleary & Reyes, 2009; Cleary & Speckler, 2007) have also found that recent exposure to a target word can reduce TOT incidence on general information (Cleary, 2006), famous faces (Cleary & Speckler, 2007), and famous structures (Cleary & Reyes, 2009).

The empirical results generally support that recent exposure to a target word reduces TOT probability. Bonin et al. (2008) provide evidence against a recency hypothesis for target word activation, but other factors could easily mitigate this outcome as it is derived from correlational data. Note that the concept of recency plays a theoretically central role tied to TOT probability in transmission deficit theory, a point covered more thoroughly in Chapter 9.

# ☐ Word Type

## Diary TOTs

A consistent aspect of naturally occurring TOTs is the prominence of proper name targets. Burke et al. (1991) found proper names to be the most common type of target word (62%) in their diary study, with the remaining TOTs involving object names (12%) and abstract words (23%) such as "idiomatic" and "consensus." Most of the proper-name TOTs involved acquaintances (27%), with the remainder on famous persons (18%), places (11%), and movie/TV/book titles (9%) (Burke et al., 1991). Schwartz's (2001a) diary study replicated Burke et al. (1991) with 68% of TOTs involving proper nouns (32% acquaintances, 19% famous persons, 7% places, 7% book titles, and 3% music groups), 16% object names, 10% abstract nouns, and 6% adjectives/verbs/adverbs.

Participants in Cohen and Faulkner's (1986) diary study were asked to record only proper-name TOTs, and acquaintances comprised 69%, famous persons 17%, and places 7%. Consistent across all of the above studies, the highest proportion of proper-name TOTs involve acquaintance names. The highest rate of proper-name TOTs on acquaintances in the above studies (Burke et al., 1991; Schwartz, 2001a; Cohen & Faulkner, 1986) suggests that TOTs may occur for relatively stronger targets, but Cohen and Faulkner (1986) point out that this could result from more retrieval attempts on names accessed more often (acquaintances). Thus, the higher frequency of reported TOTs may reduce to a relatively low percentage when adjusted for usage.

Interestingly, this elevated rate for proper-name TOTs may only apply to monolingual individuals. In their diary study, Gollan et al. (2005) confirm that proper names account for the majority of TOTs (52%) in monolinguals. However, bilinguals show quite a different pattern, with proper-name TOTs accounting for only 17%, a rate significantly below monolinguals. Ecke (1997; 2004) found a similar outcome for bilinguals in his diary study. Considering only TOTs in the bilinguals' primary language, Ecke (1997) discovered that 33% were on proper names, 45% on common nouns, 7% on verbs, and 11% on adjectives (4% other). In a subsequent investigation, Ecke (2004) again found a relatively low percentage of TOTs on proper names (19%) for bilinguals. It appears that facility in two languages may reduce the likelihood of TOTs on proper names, although this drop in relative percentage may instead be caused by an absolute TOT rate increase for nonproper names among bilinguals.

A problem with interpreting variations across target word categories in diary TOTs is that it is difficult to pinpoint the causes of such differences.

Do more TOTs occur for proper names because they are more likely to trigger TOTs, or do proper-name TOTs create a stronger memorial impression when they occur (embarrassment?) making them more likely to be remembered, or do relatively more retrieval efforts occur for proper names, thus inflating their TOT frequency? Also, a proper name rarely has a synonym to substitute, whereas many common nouns do. A TOT on the word *kiss* can be quickly remedied by substituting *smooch, osculate,* or *peck on the cheek.* However, a TOT for the *Eiffel Tower* cannot be so easily sidestepped.

## Laboratory TOTs

Do target word differences in naturally occurring TOTs replicate in the lab? Evrard (2002) found a striking and significant difference between proper names (13%) and common nouns (1%), but this outcome is an exception. For the most part, investigations have demonstrated modestly but consistently higher rates for proper names. Burke et al. (1991) designed a more precise comparison with diary findings by using an equal number of target words from five different categories. Similar to their diary outcome, proper names elicited the highest rate of TOTs: famous people (15%), places (9%), objects (13%), nonobject nouns (10%), and adjective/verb (10%). Again, Rastle and Burke (1996, Experiment 1) found a higher percentage of TOTs on proper (14%) than common (8%) nouns (values estimated from their Figure 3, p. 592). Experiment 2 replicated this ordinal difference between proper (10%) versus common (9%) nouns, although the magnitude was considerably reduced. In their Experiment 3, TOTs for proper names (8%) were marginally, but significantly, greater than common nouns (6%). Rastle and Burke (1996) suggest a reliably higher proportion of TOTs occur on proper nouns, but that this difference is not as dramatic as with natural TOTs.

Gollan et al. (2005, Experiment 2) conducted a laboratory study to experimentally verify the diary findings regarding the predominance of acquaintance TOTs within the proper name category (Burke et al., 1991; Cohen & Faulkner, 1986; Schwartz, 2001a). They asked subjects to try to retrieve a common set of 46 famous names, and then to recall the names of 46 people they knew personally (mainly former school teachers). Unlike the diary outcomes, more TOTs occurred for famous names (36%) than personal acquaintances (30%).

Some laboratory investigations capitalize on the high TOT rate with proper names by using these exclusively as targets (Brédart & Valentine, 1998; Cross & Burke, 2004; Finley & Sharp, 1989; Gollan et al., 2005, Experiment 2; Maylor, 1990b). Brédart and Valentine (1998) propose that proper names elicit more TOTs because most are arbitrary and without direct reference to any physical property or characteristic of the person. They tested this speculation with cartoon characters, comparing three different categories of name–character connection. Category A included names directly descriptive of the individual, such as Snow White and Scrooge. Category B involved names that were common nouns or adjectives, but not descriptive of any dimension of the individual, such as Pif (nose) and Ric Hochet (rebound) (study conducted in French). Category C involved words that were not common nouns or adjectives, and without descriptive connection to any aspect of the character (Mary Poppins, Pocahontas). Fewer TOTs (and more correct retrievals) occurred for names in Category A than for either Categories B or C, supporting their conjecture.

As a footnote on this topic of word type, Gruneberg et al. (1973) had subjects prospect for TOTs (no cues given) during a laboratory study. Confirming diary outcomes, the most common category searched "spontaneously" in these self-directed searches was personal acquaintances, and there were more TOTs with personal acquaintances (51%) than all other categories combined. However, Gruneberg et al. (1973) caution that this may have been biased by the instructions, which included a personal name example to launch them.

# ☐ Neighborhood Density

The collection of words that resemble one another on a particular structural dimension is referred to as a linguistic *neighborhood*, and the number of words in a particular neighborhood is referred to as the *density*. Using a phonological definition of word neighborhood, Harley and Bown (1998, Experiment 1) found significantly fewer TOTs for words from high-density (HD; related to many other words) compared to low-density (LD) neighborhoods. A problem with this outcome, as noted by Harley and Bown (1998), is that the pool of words used in the study confounded word length with density. More TOTs occurred with longer (versus shorter) target words, and LD words were longer on the average than HD words. Thus, the TOT elevation could be due to longer words instead of lower density. In Experiment 2, Harley and Bown (1998) controlled word length across LD and HD targets and replicated Experiment 1, with more TOTs for LD than HD target words.

Another structural dimension, aside from length, that was correlated with neighborhood density in the target word set tested in Harley and Bown (1998) is number of syllables. To address this, Vitevitch and Sommers (2003) refined Harley and Bown's (1998) materials by controlling for both syllable number and word length when examining the effects of neighborhood density on TOTs. Another change is that Vitevitch and Sommers (2003) used orthographical, rather than phonological, similarity to define word neighborhood. Employing only one-syllable words, they manipulated both neighborhood density (number of orthographically similar words) and neighborhood frequency (average background frequency of neighborhood words). Experiment 1 revealed significantly more TOTs for LD than HD on orthography, but no difference for background frequency. However, Experiment 2 showed no difference for either neighborhood density or frequency. This Vitevitch and Sommers (2003) investigation may not be the definitive test of the neighborhood density question because TOT rates were unusually low at 2% to 3% across conditions, which may have been due to the relatively simple one-syllable target words. In summary, there is some support for TOTs being more likely on words from less dense neighborhoods. This topic needs more exploration with a variety of different neighborhood definitions, and expanding experimentation with the types of target word characteristics that alter TOT probability could represent an important contribution to our understanding of TOTs.

# ☐ Other Word Characteristics

## Name Imagery

In a study by Bonin et al. (2008), separate groups of subjects rated a set of celebrities on each of three different dimensions. Two related to imagery: face agreement and distinctiveness of the imaged face. For face agreement ratings, subjects formed a mental image of the celebrity's face when shown the name. The actual face then appeared, and the subject rated how closely the presented face matched his or her mental image (low to high agreement). This rating was negatively related to TOTs (–.59) derived from another group of subjects, suggesting that TOTs are more likely on celebrities whose faces are harder to imagine visually.

For the other image rating task, Bonin et al. (2008) had subjects generate distinctiveness scores for each celebrity by a two-step process: first, forming a mental image of the celebrity and second, evaluating this image on distinctiveness or how easy or hard it would be to spot this face. Distinctiveness was also negatively correlated with TOTs (–.67), indicating that these two imagery-related dimensions both showed that poorer image quality is more likely to evoke a TOT. Also related to imagery, Astell and Harley (1996) found a negative relationship between TOTs and word *imageability*: the mean imageability of target words inducing TOTs was significantly lower than that for target words that elicited no TOTs. Again, lower imageability appears to relate to higher TOT probability.

# Naming Consistency

A third group of raters in Bonin et al. (2008) derived a name agreement measure for celebrities. This was indexed by the consistency with which the same name was used for a celebrity across all subjects. Name agreement also correlated negatively with TOTs (–.75), indicating that more variability in name use is related to more TOTs. Mitchell (1989) found something similar using line drawing stimuli from Snodgrass and Vanderwart (1980) with low codability pictures resulting in more TOTs than high codability pictures. A low codability picture cue has multiple possible names: a pictured beetle may also be called bug, insect, or roach. In contrast, a high codability picture usually has one name: a pictured kangaroo has no alternative names (cf. Snodgrass & Vanderwart, 1980).

# Target Length

Two studies have examined the relationship between target word length and TOTs, from very different perspectives. The first involved number of words used for a target, whereas the second looked at the number of phonemes comprising the single target word. Hanley and Chapman (2008) examined whether subjects knew the number of words comprising a celebrity's name during a TOT, a dimension similar to syllabic length information (see Chapter 5). More TOTs were associated with three-word (Catherine Zeta Jones) than two-word (Clint Eastwood) celebrity names, and this difference replicated for both high familiar (20% versus 13%) and low familiar (22% versus 16%) celebrities. This difference could be due to more opportunities for retrieval problems when attempting to recall three versus two words. Hanley and Chapman's (2008) outcome is congruent with the phonological activation model of TOTs, discussed in Chapter 9, which postulates that TOTs result from deficient transmission of activation from semantic to phonological nodes. With three names, there are simply more nodes to activate, which may create an increase in the likelihood of retrieval failures. Interestingly, the ratio of TOT percentages on three- versus two-name celebrities is roughly 3 to 2, or 21% to 15%.

In the second study, Hanly and Vandenberg (2010) compared long and short target words as defined by number of phonemes. Long targets had six or more phonemes, whereas short words had four or fewer phonemes. Significantly more TOTs were elicited by long (2.8) than short (2.1) words, and this difference was greater with low- compared to high-frequency target words. Although intriguing, these results should be cautiously interpreted because a relatively small sample of words was used (about 35) in each of the four cells of the design, and only young children (8–10 years old) were tested. Finally, half of the young subjects were dyslexic.

# ☐ Summary

It is commonly assumed that TOTs occur primarily for low-frequency, or uncommon, words. A moderate amount of data from both diary and laboratory research supports this assumption, although the subjective impression of TOT diarists is the opposite, that TOT-eliciting words tend to be more common than rare. There is consistent evidence that TOTs are more likely with proper names, relative to common nouns, verbs, adjectives, and so on, in both diary and laboratory studies. Within the broad category of proper names, acquaintances seem most likely to elicit natural TOTs, but lab research has yet to confirm this. Neighborhood density may also influence TOTs, with words from low-density neighborhoods, defined either phonologically or orthographically, eliciting more TOTs than words from high-density neighborhoods. There is some indication that name imagery and consistency are negatively related to TOTs, and that name length is positively related to TOTs, although these relationships await further verification. More research is needed addressing the range of different word properties that might relate to TOT probability. Given the difficulty in creating sets of words that are manipulated on one variable and successfully controlled on potentially confounding word dimensions, it may be more expeditious to use a multivariate analytical approach on a large pool of words to identify those word dimensions that differentiate high from low TOT-eliciting potency.

CHAPTER 7

# Interlopers

On August 13, 2002, a contestant on the TV game show *Jeopardy!* buzzed in to answer an item requesting the name of the character in a fictional story who was in love with Roxanne, but was too shy to talk to her. When host Alex Trebek asked the contestant to provide her question, she said that the name was on the tip of her tongue. Asked to give a guess anyway, she said "Cicero" (the correct answer is "Cyrano").

Incorrect words often intrude during our TOT experiences. Some are related to the target in a meaningful or semantic way, such as *vibrator* for blender (Burke et al., 1991). Others have a structural relationship based upon orthographical or phonological similarities, such as *charity* for chastity (Burke et al., 1991), *flame* for flamboyant (Burke et al., 1991), or *intemperance* for deliverance (Reason & Lucas, 1984). A few share both semantic and structural elements, such as *Rock Hudson* for Rex Harrison (Schachter, 1988). Such intruding words have been variously referred to as associates (Ecke, 2004), candidates (Cohen & Faulkner, 1986), relatives (Astell & Harley, 1996), blocking intermediates (Reason & Lucas, 1984), interloper intruders (Schwartz, 1994), ugly stepsisters (Reason & Lucas, 1984), and persistent alternatives (Burke et al., 1991; Heine et al., 1999; White & Abrams, 2002). The term *interloper* (Jones, 1989) is used here because it is relatively neutral.

There are several distinctly different interpretations of the significance of interlopers (cf. Perfect & Hanley, 1992). Perhaps such words are simply a reflection of the generic nature of retrieval. When one reaches the phonological or semantic neighborhood of the missing target word, words nearby also become inadvertently activated due to a spillover from an attempt to identify the target word. With this perspective, interlopers are simply a by-product of a word retrieval attempt and play no role in causing or resolving the experience (Cross & Burke, 2004). Supporting such an interpretation, Kohn et al. (1987) found that the presence or absence of interlopers did not appear to be related to successful TOT resolution.

From a second perspective, interlopers play a part in *causing* TOTs. The inadvertent activation of such words hinders progress toward successful retrieval of the target (Anderson, Bjork, & Bjork, 1994; Brown, 1991; Jones, 1989; Jones & Langford, 1987; Reason & Lucas, 1984; Schacter, 1999). This interpretation is a key component of the blocking theory of TOTs, covered later in Chapter 9. Reason and Lucas (1984) provide a particularly colorful analogy regarding interlopers, likening them to the pushy stepsisters in the Cinderella fairy tale who attempted to usurp the prince's search for Cinderella. In this analogy, the prince embodies the memory search, Cinderella stands for the target word, and the ugly stepsisters are the interlopers who actively interfere with and divert the hunt for the target word.

A third perspective turns the blocking position around, and views interlopers as facilitating TOT resolution.

> … whenever an SS word (such as *secant*) includes middle letters that are matched in the faintly entered section of the target then those faintly entered letters become accessible. The match brings out the missing parts the way heat brings out anything written in lemon juice. In other words, when secant is retrieved the target entry grows from Se*x tan*T to SE*x* tANT." (Brown & McNeill, 1966, p. 335)

Cohen and Faulkner (1986) similarly suggest that interlopers sharpen the specification of the missing target word, making it more identifiable and accessible.

Smith (1994) proposes that interlopers may play both positive and negative roles in TOT resolution, and that a distinction should be made between *blocked* TOTs where interlopers hinder retrieval, and *mediated* TOTs where interlopers facilitate target word access. He further suggests that the negative function relates to insight problems, whereas the positive function resembles noninsight problems.

# ☐ Demand Characteristics

Instructions may influence the type or number of interlopers reported (Brown, 1991). Brown and McNeill (1966) took a rather strident position, informing subjects that "… words … related to the target word do almost always come to mind" (p. 327). Koriat and Lieblich (1974) used a similarly strong statement which perhaps accounts for a large number of SS words reported on both TOT and DK trials (Koriat & Lieblich, 1975). Subsequent research does not support the notion that interlopers are a necessary part of TOTs. In fact, their incidence varies considerably from study to study (see below), and interlopers are reported on only about half of all TOTs.

Brown and McNeill (1966) assumed that interlopers could be dichotomized into ones that resemble the target by sharing either a similar sound (SS) or similar meaning (SM), and asked their subjects to classify each of their own interlopers as one or the other as they were reported. This technique has been used in some subsequent investigations, although it is more routine for the experimenters to do this type of sorting later. It is important to note that Brown and McNeill's (1966) questionnaire, which subjects filled out on each TOT, may have influenced the quality as well as the quantity of interlopers reported. More specifically, Yarmey (1973) suggests that Brown and McNeill's (1966) subjects may have been biased toward noticing, and reporting, acoustically related interlopers and ignoring semantically related interlopers (cf. Norman, 1969; Dale & McGlaughlin, 1971). A blank for similar sounding interlopers was listed first, before the blank for words of similar meaning, and subjects were instructed that after writing down multiple SS words to "…look again at the words you have listed as 'Words of similar sound.' If possible, rank these…in terms of the degree of their seeming resemblance to the target" (Brown & McNeill, 1966, p. 327). The implication is that multiple SS interlopers are more likely than multiple SM interlopers.

Incidentally, Widner et al. (1996) found that manipulating the perceived difficulty of the target words influenced the number of interlopers reported. When subjects thought that the targets were relatively easy (high demand), interlopers accompanied 5.6% of TOTs. However, when target words were perceived as difficult (low demand), interloper incidence increased to 7.1% of TOTs. Although this difference is small and nonsignificant, it suggests that target word attributions might influence the number of interlopers experienced.

# ☐ Incidence

The data from *diary* investigations are very clear that interlopers accompany TOTs. This is consistent across studies, and at somewhere between half to three quarters of reported TOTs: 45% (White & Abrams, 2002), 50% (Cohen & Faulkner, 1986), 58% (Burke et al., 1991, Study 1), 62% (Reason & Lucas, 1984), and 69% (Heine et al., 1999, Experiment 2). Reason and Lucas (1984) note that subjects rate their diary TOT interlopers as more frequently occurring and recently used (or both), compared to the intended target word, for more than three quarters (77%) of TOTs. Finally, Gollan et al. (2005, Experiment 1) report that for diary TOTs involving nonproper name target words, all of the monolinguals' TOTs were accompanied by interlopers, as well as 77% of TOTs reported by bilinguals.

With laboratory research, interloper incidence is lower than with diary studies. With the same group of subjects in each condition, the percentage of TOTs with interlopers was about a third lower in a laboratory (41%) than diary (58%) study (Burke et al., 1991). In line with Burke et al. (1991), most laboratory studies also find that about a third to half of TOTs are accompanied by interlopers: 35% (Harley & Bown, 1998, Experiment 1), 44% (Harley & Bown, 1998, Experiment 2), 56% (Astell & Harley, 1996), and 58% (Brown & Nix, 1996). Brown and McNeill (1966) report that an average of 1.4 interlopers were reported per TOT, but this incidence may be atypically high because they informed subjects that interlopers routinely accompany TOTs. A considerably lower incidence is found in Riefer et al. (1995; 17%) and Riefer (2000; 13%), but Riefer et al. (1995) suggest that this is due to the nature of TV show name targets. Show titles are relatively long and with few potentially competing alternatives, compared to the usual category of target words in TOT research. In addition, interloper scoring may be problematic because of multiple target words in most TV show titles.

Regardless of whether interlopers are viewed as a cause or by-product of TOTs, their presence appears to interfere with target word access (Burke et al., 1991). At the least, they momentarily command attention and direct it away from the target word search, as well as being difficult to get out of mind (Brown, 1991; Reason & Lucas, 1984). As Woodworth (1938) cogently pointed out, "the wrong name recalled acquires a recency value and blocks the correct name" (p. 38). Although it is immediately apparent that an interloper hampers retrieval (Reason & Lucas, 1984), most individuals experiencing one may find it difficult to let go of it because the word generates a sense of closeness to the target that motivates a continuation of the search (Brown, 1991). Interlopers might also discourage a continued hunt for the target word because of a feeling of being stuck and frustrated in the wrong linguistic "location." However, Burke et al. (1991) found no difference in one's confidence of eventual target word retrieval between TOTs with and without interlopers, which fails to support either speculation.

# ☐ Categorizing Interlopers

Clues about the target word may be derived by the interloper–target resemblance on meaning (semantics), structure (phonology, orthography), and linguistic usage (syntax). Woodworth (1929) speculated that "the initial sound of the true name is likely to be present in the recalled name, though not always in the first position. The number of syllables and the accent are usually preserved" (p. 100). Subsequent data suggest that this conjecture may be inaccurate, and that interlopers are more likely to resemble the target word's meaning than structure. However, this finding may be strongly related to the use of linguistic (definition) cues that contain other words related to the target.

As touched upon earlier, Brown and McNeill (1966) distinguished between interlopers that share a similar sound (SS) or similar meaning (SM) with the target word. SS interlopers for *sampan* include *sarong*, *Siam*, and *Cheyenne*, and SM interlopers include *barge*, *houseboat*, and *junk*. In Brown and McNeill (1966), 70% of interlopers were SS and 30% were SM. In contrast to this, most subsequent research making such a differentiation finds more SM than SS interlopers (respectively): 100% versus 0% (Astell & Harley, 1996), 80% versus 20% (Bak, 1987), 43% versus 26% (Cohen & Faulkner, 1986), 49% versus 25% (Ecke, 1997), 42% versus 38% (Ecke, 2001), 68% versus 5% (Harley & Bown, 1998), and 72% versus 6% (Riefer et al., 1995).

Many experimenters do not differentiate between SM and SS interlopers, partly because such classification is ambiguous. For example, the interloper *charity* for the target word *chastity* could be classified as either SS or SM or both (SS + SM). To handle such ambiguity, Harley and Bown (1998) used unclassified (U) for interlopers that did not fall neatly into either SS or SM, and U accounted for 20% of their interlopers. This SS + SM category of mixed or ambiguous target-word resemblance accounts for a reasonable percentage of interlopers in other investigations: 8% (Harley & Bown, 1998), 19% (Ecke, 2001), 25% (Ecke, 1997), and 30% (Cohen & Faulkner, 1986).

The atypical SS/SM ratio found by Brown and McNeill (1966) may reflect their emphasis on reporting structural features of the missing target word. It is ironic that Brown and McNeill (1966) stated that they expected more SM than SS interlopers because of the semantic context set up by their definition cues. More specifically, their definition of sampan—"a small boat, not the junk, used in the river and harbor traffic of China and Japan" (cf. Rubin, 1975)—provides sufficient semantic information to generate other possible water vehicles (canoe, rowboat, kayak), but no structural information to prime SS interlopers.

Most research since Brown and McNeill (1966) has not attempted to differentiate between SS and SM interlopers, focusing primarily on numbers. However, the interloper–target relationship can provide clues to the nature of lexical storage and retrieval. Schachter (1988) analyzed this extensively with a large collection of about 600 TOTs accompanied by interlopers. Numerous examples illustrate a number of different target–interloper resemblances. Unlike the data summarized above, phonology tends to predominate. Also, examples are presented where orthography can be separated from phonology (e.g., *Ptolemy* for Pompeii; *Phyllis* for Peg), and morphological resemblance separated from phonology. Syntactic, phrase structure, and semantic relationships are carefully explained by Schachter (1988), as well as indirect relations such as *Helen George* for Olivia Newton-John: both have a man's first name as their last name. Schachter (1988) does a thorough job of detailing this topic, as well as the difficulty involved with disentangling the overlap among phonology, morphology, and orthography.

## Syntactic Class

A strong and consistent finding is that most interlopers share the same syntactic class (e.g., noun, adjective, verb, adverb) as the target (cf. Schachter, 1988). Nearly all interlopers in Burke et al.'s (1991) diary study (87%) were from the same syntactic class as the target, and there was a similarly high correspondence in their lab study (78%). This high congruence between interloper and target has been found repeatedly in other investigations: 82% (Browman, 1978); 90% (Ecke, 1997); 77% (Ecke, 2001); 88% (Harley & Bown, 1998). This outcome supports speculation by Burke et al. (1991) and findings by Abrams, Trunk, & Merrill (2007; see Chapter 8) that the presence of an interloper syntactically related to the target can interfere with retrieval, whereas one from a different syntactic class is less likely to do so.

## Letter Matches

As discussed earlier in Chapter 5, several investigations have evaluated interloper–target structural relationships for clues on what dimensions of the target word may be accessible during TOTs. This exploration is based on the assumption that word retrieval is a sequential activation of semantic to phonological components, and that the correct target word results from the focused activation of the phonological nodes for that particular word. When multiple words are closely related to the semantic or phonological aspects of the target word, then a related (but incorrect) word may receive indirect activation, along with the target word. Thus fragments of the intended target that overlap with interlopers can provide insight into what phonological, orthographical, or semantic elements of the target word are activated in the absence of whole word access (cf. Burke et al., 1991).

Brown and McNeill's (1966) analysis of letter overlap between SS interlopers and associated targets revealed a U-shaped curve, with higher matches at the beginning and end positions (see Figure 7.1). The probability

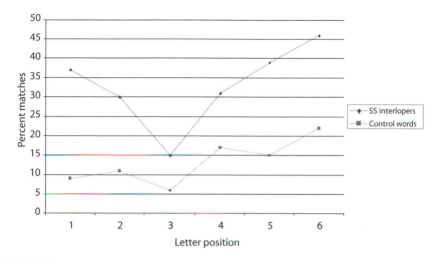

**FIGURE 7.1**    SS interloper match to target.

of a *first* letter match between target and SS interloper was 48% (approxi-mated from their Figure 1, p. 330), well above the 8% found with SM inter-lopers (Brown & McNeill, 1966). Reanalyzing TOT data from Koriat and Lieblich (1974), Koriat and Lieblich (1975) similarly found a U-shaped cor-respondence between SS interloper and target across six letter positions, with the strongest match for the first letter, a modest elevation for the last two positions, and a flat function for the other three positions.

Rubin (1975) also found that 35% of SS interlopers matched the target on the first letter, and 21% for the second letter. In addition, Browman (1978, cited in Vihman, 1980) found that 58% of interlopers duplicated the target's initial letter, and 51% had the same first phoneme. With celebrity names, SS words are highly likely to match on the first letter of the target for both the first name (83%) and last name (77%), although chance levels are difficult to determine for proper names (Yarmey, 1973). Finally, Burke et al. (1991) found 36% first letter interloper–target matches in diary TOTs (Study 1) and 19% in laboratory TOTs (Study 2) TOTs, both significantly above their determination of chance (6%).

In summary, the structural resemblance between interloper and intended target words is clear, and more so at the beginning than the end of the word. Some selective bias exists in such comparisons, especially when only SS interlopers have been culled from the larger set of all inter-lopers (SS, SM, and U), as these have already been sorted by structural resemblance to the target word. However, the correspondence remains impressively above chance even when all interlopers are included for such comparisons (Burke et al., 1991).

## Syllabic Matches

Syllabic match between interloper and target was covered already in Chapter 5 as indirect evidence for target word syllable access, and this is briefly summarized again here. Brown and McNeill (1966) compared SS interlopers and targets on both syllable *number* and *stress*. For the syllable number, the target word matched 48% of SS interlopers compared to 20% of SM interlopers. As noted above, the circularity of defining SS interlopers by structural resemblance clouds an interpretation of this difference. Burke et al. (1991) were nonselective, including all interlopers in their analysis. In their diary study (Experiment 1), the 43% correspondence was significantly above the chance level that they calculated to be between 21 and 25%. This difference was replicated in their laboratory study (Experiment 2), with the 35% correspondence again significantly above their chance level established at 26%. Thus, there is solid evidence of an interloper/target resemblance on number of syllables.

For syllabic stress comparisons, Brown and McNeill (1966) considered only multisyllabic SS interlopers with the same number of syllables as the target word. For targets with a first-syllable stress, 81% of SS interlopers matched; for targets with a second-syllable stress, 67% of SS interlopers matched (overall correspondence of 76%). Whereas subjects appear to have knowledge of stress patterns during TOTs, as reflected in interlopers generated, Brown and McNeill (1966) were not highly confident in this conclusion because of the data restriction.

## Closeness to Target

As part of the questionnaire filled out during the TOT experience, Brown and McNeill (1966) instructed subjects that when they happened to generate two (or more) SS words for a given target, they were to indicate how closely each SS interloper resembled the target word in sound. A point system (0 to 3) was used later to score the resemblance between SS interloper, with one point each given for matching on syllable, initial letter, and final letter. Keeping in mind that only 6% of TOTs were accompanied by multiple SS interlopers, the interloper ranked by subjects as closer to the target had significantly more points than the one ranked farther. Although subjects do seem to be able to judge correctly which interloper is closer to the target word in sound, this conclusion is very tentative. A better approach would be to use a controlled procedure where a pair of SS interlopers is constructed for each target word, and have subjects rank these on degree of target word correspondence when in a TOT.

# ☐ Malapropisms

When an interloper comes to mind during a TOT, we can immediately identify it as incorrect. During routine conversation, something similar occurs where "interlopers" are produced but go undetected: "He had to use biceps to deliver the baby" (Brandreth, 1980, p. 131). Malapropisms, or slips of the tongue (SOT; cf. Tweney et al., 1975), differ from TOT interlopers only in level of awareness. An SOT is a retrieval failure accompanied by monitoring failure, whereas a TOT is a retrieval failure accompanied by successful monitoring (Brown, 1991; see Ellis, 1985, for additional discussion of this point). Another difference is that most SOTs occur during routine speech generation when we may be only partially attentive to word generation, whereas most TOTs (and interlopers) happen during a focused retrieval effort directed at some discrete piece of information (e.g., personal name).

Data on malapropisms are gathered from a variety of different sources of speech errors, including transcripts (Fay & Cutler, 1977; Zwicky, 1982), personal diaries (Tweney et al., 1975), and literary records such as those summarized by Freud (1960; cf. Tweney et al., 1975). Fay and Cutler (1977) found that 99% of SOTs match the target word on grammatical category, 87% on syllable number, and 89% for syllabic stress. Similarly, Zwicky (1982) found correspondence of 91% on grammatical category, 71% for syllable number, and 93% on syllabic stress. In addition, Zwicky (1982) also found high agreement on initial vowel (79%), initial consonant (77%), and vowel with primary stress (70%). Additional analysis of Fay and Cutler's (1977) SOTs by Vitevitch (1997) uncovered that a malapropism is usually higher frequency than the intended target. Furthermore, most of these higher-frequency malapropisms come from dense neighborhoods (see Chapter 6), whereas most of the (less-common) lower-frequency malapropisms come from sparse neighborhoods.

As noted earlier, Brown and McNeill (1966) were surprised to find such a high level of availability of structural features for target words during TOTs (see Chapter 5). Tweney et al.'s (1975) concern that this finding may pertain only to low-frequency words motivated them to examine a broader frequency range of SOTs to clarify whether such information was also available with higher-frequency words. Their SOTs were comprised of 86% SS and 14% SM, a split similar to Brown and McNeill's (1966; SS = 70%; SM = 30%) but different from the modal finding of more SM than SS interlopers (see earlier, this chapter).

The correspondence between SS SOT and target on number of syllables was impressive at 80%, and higher than the 53% found for SM SOTs. Furthermore, Tweney et al. (1975) discovered that SS SOTs matched the target word letters more often at the two ends (initial = 52%; final = 77%) than one letter in (second = 49%; second to last = 62%). In contrast, SM SOT to target letter matches were much lower, ranging from 20 to 31% across these same four positions. Note that Tweney et al.'s (1975) SS SOTs were matched to the target more closely in the final two positions (70%) than in the initial two positions (51%), a difference similar to the letter match percentages found for the final two letters (42%) than the initial two letters (34%) among interloper–target matches (Brown & McNeill, 1966; Koriat & Lieblich, 1974; Rubin, 1975).

## Slip of the Pen

Another language production error could be considered the written equivalent of the oral SOTs. A slip of the pen, or SOP (Brown, 1991) involves an inadvertent substitution in written word production. Comparing SOP and intended target, Wing and Baddeley (1980) found a high level of correspondence across five letter positions (70 to 90%) with the highest matches for the first (89%) and last (90%) positions. High match probabilities between SOP and intended target for first (93%) and final (89%) letters was also found by Hotopf (1980; estimated from his Figure 1, p. 302, by Brown, 1991). Thus, unnoticed oral and written production errors both show a structural resemblance to the target word that is similar to that found with interlopers during TOTs.

In assessing parallels between SOT/SOP errors and TOT interlopers, an important caveat is in order. An SOT or SOP only occurs when the error goes undetected. Logically, the closer the structural resemblance (orthography, phonology) to the intended target word, the less likely that the error will be noticed. Thus, a high degree of structural resemblance may not be so surprising. An interesting, but perhaps difficult to test, question is at what point does the generation error capture one's attention, and perhaps morph into a TOT? That is, when does a discrepancy between the intended and produced word cross an attentional threshold to capture our awareness, and initiate a corrective re-retrieval?

## ☐ General Caution

Evidence suggests that most interlopers are semantically, structurally, or syntactically similar to the intended target word. However, this correspondence may be less informative than it superficially appears, especially given the clues present in the definitional. Often, one can produce a variety of synonyms for a defined target. For the target word *sampan*—"a small boat, not the junk, used in the river and harbor traffic of China and Japan" (Brown & McNeill, 1966; Rubin, 1975)—one could easily produce SM words such as ship, riverboat, or canoe based upon this information (see earlier point in this chapter). It is also clear that a *noun* is being defined, not a verb or adjective. Thus, a tuned-in subject is likely to stay within these bounds, producing words only from the same semantic and syntactic category.

Strangely, Brown and McNeill (1966) give *boat* and *junk* as examples of SM interlopers produced by their subjects for the target word sampan, but these words actually appear in their definition (see above)! Given an oral presentation of the cue, these just-activated words may be produced because the subject is distracted by the search for the target, and the definitional word(s) is still in working memory. Thus, an SM interloper may occasionally result from unconscious plagiarism (cryptomnesia) of information processed moments earlier in the cue (Brown & Murphy, 1989). SS interlopers may be more informative because target word cues (definitions, pictures) usually lack hints about the sound or structure of the intended target word.

# □ Summary

TOTs are often accompanied by nontarget words, or interlopers, that are related to the target either semantically (SM) or phonologically (SS). These extraneous words have been variously viewed as (a) causing TOTs, (b) a by-product of the experience, or (c) facilitating resolution by sharpening the search process. Whereas interlopers occur on about half to three quarters of natural TOTs, they are less common in laboratory studies occurring on about a third to half of TOTs. Similar-meaning (SM) interlopers are generally more common than similar-sound (SS) interlopers. Malapropisms (SOTs) may represent undetected interlopers, and a more systematic investigation of these speech errors could benefit our understanding of TOTs. Unlike TOT interlopers, SS words predominate over SM words with SOTs. Findings on interlopers must be interpreted with caution because instructions to subjects may influence the type and frequency of interlopers reported, and classification of interloper as SS or SM is often ambiguous.

# 8

# Resolving TOTs

One of the few cognitive experiences that elicits an immediate sense of delight and relief is when a sought-after TOT target word finally comes to mind. The process whereby TOTs are resolved is one of the more important questions in this literature. Given that a defining feature of TOTs is unresolved retrieval, aspects of the resolution process potentially hold valuable clues to the cause of a TOT. Curiously, Brown and McNeill (1966) ignored this topic in their ground-breaking work, simply noting that some TOTs were resolved and others were not.

## ☐ Resolution Probability

### Diary Studies

In diary investigations, one might expect a relatively high resolution probability for several reasons. First, there is no implied time pressure, similar to that present in a laboratory investigation. Thus, the effort to resolve a TOT can extend over considerable periods of time, ending when one is no longer motivated to search. Second, naturally occurring TOTs that are resolved may be more memorable than ones that are not, and this would make them more likely to be recorded later in the diary (Schwartz, 1999; Smith, 1994). Finally, one's motivation to resolve a natural TOT is probably much higher than for laboratory TOTs. The personal investment is much greater for resolving a TOT connected to one's life, such as remembering a friend's name or a past vacation spot, compared to a TOT on information in which one may not be particularly invested (capital of Brazil, a doctor's instrument for listening to the heart).

All diary studies report high TOT resolution probabilities, with most above 90%: 95% (Burke et al., 1991); 78% (Cohen & Faulkner, 1986), 97% (Ecke, 2004), 95% (Heine et al., 1999), and 89% (Schwartz, 2001a). Research by Linton (1996) deserves special note (see earlier discussion in Chapter 3) because she documented her own retrieval efforts for taxonomic plant names over 8 years. The number of her TOT resolutions was 47%, and this may be a more accurate indication of a naturalistic resolution rate given that her study was not subject to the potential selective reporting biases in diary reports, as described earlier. However, this evidence is based on a limited category of information (Latin names for plants), and Linton may not have been as invested in resolving her TOTs as would someone experiencing more personally relevant TOTs (e.g., a friend's name). Burke et al. (1991) asked participants for retrospective estimates of resolution percentage for everyday TOTs, and the 89% estimate is close to the actual resolution percentage reported in the diary study. The retrospective query was conducted prior to the diary study, so that estimates were not biased by the diary outcome.

# Laboratory Studies

A summary of TOT resolution probabilities from 23 laboratory studies appears in Table 8.1, in increasing order. These data represent averages in studies with multiple age groups (Brown & Nix, 1996; Burke et al., 1991; Dahlgren, 1998; Heine et al., 1999), multiple experiments (e.g., Caramazza & Miozzo, 1997), or multiple language groups (Faust et al., 1997, 2003; Faust & Sharfstein-Friedman, 2003; Gollan & Acenas, 2004, Gollan & Silverberg, 2001), and some resolution rates are estimated from figures (Burke et al., 1991; Lawless & Engen, 1977; see Brown, 1991). Also note that Faust et al.'s (2003) resolution probabilities may be unusually high because they combine resolutions both before and following a target word cue (Faust and Sharfstein-Friedman, 2003, report these resolution rates separately). Finally, there is considerable variation in the time period allowed for TOT resolution, ranging from 10 seconds in Heine et al. (1999), to 90 seconds in Jönsson and Olsson (2003), to 2 to 3 minutes in Finley and Sharp (1989), to the entire investigation in Brédart and Valentine (1998).

The mean resolution probability is 39% (median = 38%), with an interquartile range of 24 to 50%. Although the immediate resolution probability in laboratory studies can be highly sensitive to instructions, type of material, and time allowed, a reasonable estimate is that more than a third of TOTs are resolved relatively soon after the initiation of the experience.

Beattie and Coughlan (1999) report a 66% resolution rate within 45 s, but provide the first letter of the missing target word after 30 s if no response has been given. They do not separately report resolutions prior to versus

---

**TABLE 8.1** Immediate Resolution
Probabilities in Laboratory Studies

2% Frick-Horbury & Guttentag (1998)
11% Heine et al. (1999)
13% Gollan & Acenas (2004)
14% Choi & Smith (2005)
22% Faust & Sharfstein-Friedman (2003)
22% Brown & Nix (1996)
24% Jönsson & Olsson (2003)
30% Abrams, Trunk, & Merrill (2007)
31% Caramazza & Miozzo (1997)
34% Warriner & Humphreys (2008)
36% Burke et al. (1991 )
38% Lawless & Engen (1977)
38% Riefer et al. (1995)
42% Faust et al. (1997)
43% Vitevitch & Sommers (2003)
44% Harley & Bown (1998)
48% Finley & Sharp (1989)
50% Faust et al. (2003)
50% Gollan & Silverberg (2001)
54% Brédart & Valentine (1998)
66% Beattie & Coughlan (1999)
68% Gruneberg et al. (1973)
90% Dahlgren (1998)

---

after the cue, so that it is difficult to get a pure (unaided) estimate of resolution likelihood. Abrams and Rodriguez (2005) also report resolution
rates following cues related to the target on both orthography and part
of speech (26%), related on orthography but not part of speech (37%), and
unrelated to the target (25%). The resolution interval used in this study
appears to be relatively short (between 15 and 30 s) so these rates may be
lower because of a time limitation. Also consider that a neutral (unrelated)
cue condition might not be a good baseline, because subjects may mistakenly attempt to use this word to guide target word retrieval.

## TOTs Versus Non-TOT Trials

Is one more likely to retrieve a target word when experiencing a TOT, versus when not experiencing a TOT? This would be our expectation, and the
data convincingly show this to be the case (Burke et al., 1991; James & Burke,
2000; Kozlowski, 1977; Schwartz, 1998, 2001b; Schwartz & Smith, 1997;

Schwartz et al., 2000; Smith et al., 1994). Similarly, target word recognition is higher for TOT than non-TOT trials. Schwartz's (2002b) examination of 14 outcomes comparing recognition probabilities for TOTs versus non-TOTs (his Table 3.2, p. 54) reveals much higher recognition rates for TOTs (60%) than non-TOTs (36%) (Kozlowski, 1977; Schwartz, 1998, 2001b; Schwartz & Smith, 1997; Schwartz et al., 2000; Smith et al., 1994).

But is this outcome particularly surprising or noteworthy? Perhaps not, given the complex set of factors that may elicit a TOT. Is it possible that being closer to retrieving the target word makes a TOT report more likely? Does experiencing a TOT propel one to search longer or with more effort and persistence? Or is greater knowledge about a certain category of information more likely to lead to both TOTs and retrieval/recognition success?

# ☐ Resolution Time

## Diary Studies

Participants are asked to keep track of TOT resolution times in some diary studies. Burke et al. (1991) present a cumulative plot of reported resolution times, but only include TOTs resolved by pop-ups (see later discussion in this chapter) which comprised about half of all resolutions. The time span was very broad, ranging from 20 s to several days. Burke et al.'s (1991) summary of this information in their Figure 3 (p. 560) suggests that 20 to 30% of TOTs are resolved within 1 min, and most are resolved within 10 min. In dramatic contrast to this, a mean resolution time of 8 hr was reported by Heine et al. (1999, Experiment 2). However, because resolution times are a positively skewed distribution, Heine et al.'s (1999) mean may be highly distorted by extreme scores.

In an attempt to make their report comparable to Burke et al., Heine et al. (1999) computed another mean for only pop-up resolutions. They found no difference between the outcome considering all resolutions and pop-up resolutions, suggesting that the data from Burke et al. may generalize to all resolutions. Cohen and Faulkner (1986) found somewhat longer average resolution times than Burke et al. (1991), with 49% occurring within one hour, but they considered only proper names TOT targets whereas Burke et al. (1991) were not selective. Finally, Schwartz (2001a) broke down TOT resolutions into initially resolved (76% of the total) and later resolved (13% of the total). Mean resolution time was 19 min for initially resolved TOTs, and 32 hr for later resolved TOTs. Separated by type of resolution (see below), Schwartz (2001a) found 15 min for pop-ups, 15 min for deliberate search, 10 min for recognition (someone else said it), and 36 min for consulting a resource.

It is difficult to draw clear conclusions from these data on diary resolution times because each study uses a different approach. Furthermore, personal time estimates are rough, especially at longer intervals. However, it seems safe to say that the majority of diary TOT resolutions occur within 20 min. Given the recent developments in portable electronic technology, future data collection could be easier, more immediate, and more precise.

## Laboratory Studies

In most laboratory investigations, a TOT experience halts the trial procedure (whether individual or group) to allow documenting the details about the missing target word. Targets accessed within this window are referred to as *immediate* (usually within 1 min). Some have tracked TOT resolutions that occur either later during the study (Brown & Nix, 1996) or after the laboratory session (Gruneberg et al., 1973), but these percentages are generally small. Brown and Nix (1996) discovered that 17% of TOT resolutions occurred later in the study, whereas Gruneberg et al. (1973) found an additional 6% resolved within several hours of leaving the lab.

Resolution times have rarely been reported, mainly because the amount of time allowed for resolution is limited by the length of the individual trial. Several studies report relatively short resolution times of approximately 7 seconds. (Heine et al., 1999, Experiment 1; Riefer et al., 1995, for 68% of resolved TOTs), although Brown and Nix (1996) found a somewhat longer average resolution time of 17 seconds (range = 5 to 56 s, interquartile range = 11 to 19 s). The most systematic exploration of resolution time ranges, by Gruneberg et al. (1973), employed an audio record of the entire 30-minute session. The full range was 2 to 135 seconds with a median of 17 seconds, similar to Brown and Nix (1996). Just over a third were recovered within the first 10 seconds (35%), with another 18% resolved in 11 to 20 seconds, 24% between 21 to 40 seconds, and 24% in 41 seconds or longer. After the lab session, Gruneberg et al. (1973) contacted subjects between 2 to 9 hours later (mean = 4 hr) and of those TOTs not resolved during the lab session, 6% had come to mind during the intervening interval, and 21% were resolved when re-cued by the experimenter. Interestingly, about half of these later recoveries were associated with TOTs where the search was abandoned early, within 10 seconds. As a rough summary, it appears that most lab TOTs are resolved within 20 to 30 seconds after the original experience.

## Brief TOTs

Some TOTs appear to be resolved very quickly (see Chapter 2), within a few seconds. Gruneberg et al. (1973) referred to such TOTs as "fleeting," and preferred to define TOTs as episodes that "lasted at least 2 s" (p. 190; cf. Burke et al., 1991). Similarly, Hamberger and Seidel (2003) defined a TOT as a retrieval effort lasting at least 2 or more seconds after the definition, citing Goodglass et al.'s (1984) distinction between two stages of retrieval, the first being *automatic* (up to 1500 ms) and the second *effortful* (after 1500 ms) (cf. Kikyo et al., 2001).

Such brief TOTs are generally ignored in the TOT literature and counted as correct, primarily because subjects may not choose to mention it inasmuch as resolution is so swift. A few experimenters, however, state that they intentionally discount immediately resolved (brief, by their definition) TOTs and lump them in with correct retrievals. Caramazza and Miozzo (1997) reclassified as correct 15% of all TOTs reported in Experiment 1, and 33% of Experiment 2 TOTs. Using the same rationale, Miozzo and Caramazza (1997) reclassified 11% of TOTs in Experiment 1 and 25% of TOTs in Experiment 2 as correct. Finally, Biedermann et al. (2008) recoded TOTs resolved within 15 s as correct, but did not report the number of such items. The central goal in both Caramazza and Miozzo (1997) and Miozzo and Caramazza (1997) was to assess peripheral information availability and cue efficacy during TOTs, and quickly resolved TOTs made such data difficult to gather.

One could argue that this "shorting" of the total TOT count is relatively trivial, as they do not comprise a large percentage of all TOT experiences. However, this ambiguity relates to a broader measurement issue in TOT research: is there a minimum duration for a TOT? Later in this chapter, I argue that TOT research would be better served if we legitimized quickly resolved TOTs (cf. Gruneberg et al., 1973; Schwartz, 2001b). Although fleeting, the mechanisms underlying these may be similar to more extended TOTs lasting 15 s or 15 min, and potentially could contribute to our understanding of the phenomenon.

These brief, or mini-TOTs, were first discussed by Schwartz (2001b, Experiment 4). Following each correct response, subjects were instructed that: "... you may have momentarily experienced a TOT just in advance of retrieving the word. The TOT may have only lasted an instant, but may have been felt prior to the retrieval of the answer" (p. 123). These brief TOTs were found to precede 22% of correct responses, or 9% of all trials. Their brevity makes them easy to overlook or ignore, and precludes collecting data on peripheral information or interlopers. However, such brief TOTs are TOT+ trials where the target word is simply recovered faster than usual.

We conducted an investigation specifically focused on brief TOTs here at Southern Methodist University (SMU) with the assistance of Jill Gregory and Christine Kendrick. We used picture cues and tested subjects individually. The experimenter differentiated correct responses produced immediately and without hesitation, within 2 seconds (78% of correct retrievals), and those given after a brief pause of 2 seconds or more (22% of correct retrievals). On the correct trials with a delayed response, subjects were then asked whether they had experienced a brief TOT. These delayed correct responses were comprised of 9% brief TOTs and 13% non-TOTs. Considering all items, brief TOTs comprised 5% of the total. Although this rate was lower than in Schwartz (2001b), both our and his outcomes suggest that a reasonable number of TOTs may be missed with an extended retrieval criterion. Linton (1996) also thought that it would be worthwhile to distinguish between correct retrievals given at "criterion speed" (39%) from those that took longer to produce (25%). Although not further specified by Linton, these slow retrievals were probably equivalent to our brief TOTs.

## Persistent Subthreshold Activation

A particularly fascinating and elusive aspect of TOTs involves the cognitive processes associated with experience. During the TOT, it feels as if an intense mental search effort is being undertaken just behind a mental veil. The nature of our cognitive efforts defies easy description. Related to this is the issue of whether some residual mental search persists after the initial TOT experience, one that is outside our awareness. Such speculation has been fueled by the personal experience of pop-ups, where the TOT target word appears to suddenly come to mind, on its own accord, intrusively inserting itself into our ongoing mental activities.

Ryan et al. (1982) reasoned that if a TOT puts such demands on cognitive resources, then performance on a working memory task (number probe) should be diminished immediately following a TOT because some cognitive capacity is siphoned off to search for the missing target word. Evaluating this speculation, Ryan et al. (1982) had subjects initially learn a list of word–word pairs. Subsequently, on each test trial subjects were presented the stimulus and immediately evaluated the probability of providing the response *before* actually giving it: yes, TOT, and DK. Following this rating, subjects performed a number probe task for 20 seconds and then attempted to recall the response term. Correct number probe responses were lower on TOT (7.00) compared to yes (7.07) and DK (7.19) trials, and Ryan et al. (1982) proposed that the diminished performance on TOTs reflects surreptitious retrieval activity. However, these differences are rather small, especially between the TOT and yes trials.

Yaniv and Meyer (1987) also evaluated "… when and how the memory trace of a currently inaccessible item may be at least partially primed for a period of time after information is processed from an initial probe question … ." (p. 188). In Experiment 1, on each trial where the correct answer to a general information question was not retrieved (TOT, DK), a lexical decision (LD) task was presented requiring a rapid word/nonword decision and the target word was occasionally presented in this series. Following a TOT, the lexical decisions to the target word were significantly faster than to nontarget words, whereas there was no difference between target and nontarget words following non-TOT trials. Separating the definition and lexical decision tasks by about 1 minute (Experiment 2) replicated Experiment 1, although the difference between target and nontarget words was diminished. Yaniv and Meyer (1987) suggest that target word identification is faster after a TOT because even though it is not accessed, the target word node is in a heightened state of activation which facilitates the identification response.

There is, however, an alternative explanation for Yaniv and Meyer's (1987) finding. Connor, Balota, and Neely (1992) hypothesized that individuals discriminate between their high- and low-knowledge areas, and that such evaluations drive both TOT assessments (greater probability) and lexical decisions (faster times). For instance, if I know more about chemistry than history, I will be more likely to (a) experience a TOT to a chemistry question than to a history question, and (b) identify chemistry words faster than history words. To test this, Connor et al. (1992) separated the definition and lexical decision tasks by 1 week to eliminate the possibility of any remaining subthreshold activation. Similar to Yaniv and Meyer (1987), they found faster lexical decisions for previous TOT target words than for control words, with no target-control latency difference for words following non-TOT trials. This outcome clearly supports their alternative interpretation because the same results were found without any possible subthreshold activation.

Naito and Komatsu (1989) put forth a similar reinterpretation of Yaniv and Meyer (1987) but used an approach different from Connor et al. (1992). After each of 50 definitions, subjects either generated the target word, a *yes* FOK (which Naito and Komatsu, 1989, define as a TOT), or a *no* FOK. After all retrieval attempts and a 2-min distractor task, a perceptual identification (PI) test was given where subjects attempted to identify briefly flashed words, presented at near-threshold levels. PI rate was significantly higher for words successfully retrieved earlier, with no difference among TOT, non-TOT, and filler words (all lower than correct words). Naito and Komatsu (1989) concluded that a TOT is not accompanied by increased target word activation, although this may not be a definitive test because the long interval (about 10 min) between TOT and the PI tasks may have allowed activation to dissipate.

# ☐ Resolution Processes

When confronted with an inability to access a word that you are positive that you know, how do you try to get at the target word? Approaches loosely fall into four categories. The first is an effortful and consciously directed mental search during the "active" initial phase of the TOT experience (within a minute or so). The second type of resolution effort involves research, where external resources are consulted: dictionary, Internet, friend. The third and somewhat controversial route to TOT resolution involves pop-ups, where the target word comes to mind seemingly on its own. A fourth process is incidental cueing, involving an inadvertent encounter with a word, object, or person, that cues the missing word.

## Mental Search

The most direct TOT resolution technique is a focused mental search, and this can involve a variety of different cues (Cohen & Faulkner, 1986; Finley & Sharp, 1989; Reason & Lucas, 1984; Yarmey, 1973). Perhaps the most widely used personal strategy is an alphabet search, where one systematically goes through the letters one at a time. This process is based on the assumption that when one hits the first letter of the target word, it will trigger retrieval (Cohen & Faulkner, 1986; Finley & Sharp, 1989; Reason & Lucas, 1984). Focused mental imagery has also been used, where various aspects of the missing object or person are visualized (Finley & Sharp, 1989). Finally, a contextual association strategy has been described, such as thinking about a past encounter with a person (where, when) to help retrieve an acquaintance name (Cohen & Faulkner, 1986).

Across six diary investigations, 24% of resolutions are via mental search procedures: 12% (Heine et al., 1999, Experiment 2), 20% (Burke et al., 1991), 21% (Schwartz, 2001a; dubbed "deliberate search"), 26% (Cohen & Faulkner, 1986), 26% (Ecke, 1997), and 39% (Reason & Lucas, 1984). Read and Bruce (1982) found that this "subject-generated recall" was associated with 61% of their laboratory study TOT resolutions. As part of their instructions, Finley and Sharp (1989) recommended several types of mental search strategies to their subjects as possible aids to TOT resolution. With this bias in mind, visualization (generate a mental picture the person/place) accounted for 10% of resolutions, an association strategy was used for 26%, and an alphabet search helped resolve 27%. Combined, these three mental search strategies accounted for 63% of TOT resolutions in Finley and Sharp (1989), an outcome similar to Read and Bruce (1982).

Yarmey (1973) evaluated the order in which subjects select to sort through categories of information about a missing famous name, in the process of attempting to resolve a TOT. Typically, subjects first identify the *profession*, then *where* they last saw this person, and finally *when* they last encountered this individual. Phonemic information was searched after these contextual categories, starting first with initial letter and then progressing to number of syllables and similar sounding names. Relevant to subjects' choice of a context-first retrieval strategy, Cook, Marsh, and Hicks (2006) suggest that TOTs may actually be precipitated by occasions where contextual cues become available in the absence of name recall. This speculation stemmed from Cook et al.'s (2006) finding that subjects who could not remember a target word could still identify contextual features about it (cf. Cleary, 2006).

## Research

A second technique used to resolve TOTs is research using external resources, such as reference books, websites, friends, and so on. Averaged across five diary investigations, research accounted for 28% of successful TOT resolutions: 20% (Schwartz, 2001a), 22% (Cohen & Faulkner, 1986), 29% (Burke et al., 1991), 35% (Heine et al., 1999, Experiment 2), and 33% (Ecke, 1997). External research strategies accounted for 29% of diary TOTs resolutions in Reason and Lucas (1984), but this category was combined with the strategies of asking somebody and looking it up, plus accidentally seeing or hearing it (the fourth resolution strategy; see below). In general, the percentage of TOTs resolved by research is about the same as for mental search, and both together account for about half of TOT resolutions.

## Pop-Ups

… after vain efforts to remember a date or name, we give it up, but when thinking of other things, it suddenly pops up, so to speak, in consciousness. It is possible, that in our casting about for the desired memory, we have started a train of association which has run its course in the organic dispositions, and terminated successfully. (Baldwin, 1889, p. 166)

These colorful quotes illustrate personal experiences with pop-up resolutions, where the TOT target word appears to come to mind spontaneously when attention is directed elsewhere (Norman & Bobrow, 1976; Pillsbury, 1939; Reason & Mycielska, 1982; Wood, 1983). The word feels as if it is automatically generated, and it is tempting to speculate that subconscious mechanisms are involved in tracking down the missing target word: "sometimes the answer seems to come to us spontaneously, after some 'incubation' time" (Hintzman, 1978, p. 307).

The surprising nature of this experience has captured the imagination for over a century (e.g., Baldwin, 1889) and some speculate that pop-ups are a routine part of TOT resolution (Reed, 1974). Gruneberg et al. (1973)

even instructed their subjects that "sometimes the word just pops up after a time" (p. 188). Interestingly, in spite of their biasing instructions, they found *no* pop-up resolutions occurred for those TOTs experienced in the lab.

The preferred choice to resolve natural TOTs appears to be pop-ups. In other words, ignore it and the word will come back to you. Although there is a wide variation, this strategy accounts for 36% of TOT resolutions across diary studies: 17% (Cohen & Faulkner, 1986), 20% (Ecke, 1997), 32% (Reason & Lucas, 1984), 42% (Schwartz, 2001a), 50% (Heine et al., 1999, Experiment 2), and 53% (Burke et al., 1991, Study 1). Pop-ups account for more TOT resolutions than any other strategy for Burke et al. (1991), Heine et al. (1999), and Schwartz (2001a). Furthermore, this was consistent in each of three age groups in both Burke et al. (1991) and in Heine et al. (1999). When Burke et al. (1991) asked for retrospective estimates of TOT resolution strategies, pop-up was the clear favorite: 65% said that they would "relax and direct attention elsewhere."

In stark contrast to the relatively high percentage of pop-up resolutions in diary investigations, the incidence is considerably lower in the lab: 2% (Read & Bruce, 1982), 20% (Brown & Nix, 1996), and 37% (Finley & Sharp, 1989). Read and Bruce (1982) found such a miniscule proportion of TOTs resolved through "spontaneous retrieval" that they suggest that it is "practically nonexistent" and that prior research has exaggerated the frequency because pop-ups are so striking and hence memorable.

## Incidental Cueing

Target word retrieval may occasionally be cued by some information that is encountered following the TOT, such as hearing a word with sounds similar to the target, or seeing a physical object that is related to the target. We may not consciously recognize the cue when we see or hear it, and misattribute the sudden retrieval as a pop-up.

> A person who had blocked on the name of Al Capp's heroine went for a bike ride several days later. He thought to himself how wonderful it was to ride during "days in May" and then suddenly recalled the blocked name: Daisy Mae. In the excitement of resolving a TOT, it would be easy to overlook or forget the cue that triggered recovery, thus producing inflated estimates of how often "spontaneous" pop-ups are observed. (Schacter, 2001, p. 78)

Burke et al. (1991) provide a similar anecdote involving inadvertent cueing. Frustrated by a TOT for the name of the California town "Ojai," the person exclaimed, "Oh hell," at which point the resolution occurred via the phonological resemblance.

Abrams et al. (2003) speculate that pop-ups may result from overt speech (or thought) priming, when words have a first syllable in common with the target. Various phonological components of the missing target word shared with words in conversations may boost target word activation, thus pushing it over the threshold (James & Burke, 2000; Seifert, Meyer, Davidson, Patalano, & Yaniv, 1995; Yaniv & Meyer, 1987). Such indirect activation may be more likely from silent (reading; thinking) than oral (conversation) formats, given Abrams et al.'s (2003) finding that post-TOT cue words were more likely to prime target word retrieval when processed silently than out loud.

Kleinbard describes other nonlinguistic "environmental recognitions" where cues experienced after an experimental session trigger names of simple line drawings that were not retrieved during the laboratory test where he was the subject:

> ...feather – I was returning home from the lab on the first day of the experiment when I saw a feather lying on the ground and suddenly recognized it as one of the picture items; telephone – during the very same trip, I recognized "telephone" as an item upon seeing a pay-phone in a subway station ...key – particularly interesting is that I recovered this item via an auditory recognition; specifically, I heard the jingle of some keys and recognized "key" as a picture item. (Erdelyi & Kleinbard, 1978, p. 280)

Schwartz (2001a) found that "recognized when somebody else said the word" accounted for 14% of diary TOT resolutions. Reason and Lucas (1984) presented accidentally seeing or hearing the target word as one possible TOT resolution strategy to their subjects, but unfortunately reported this incidence in combination with several other strategies (asking somebody, looking it up). Gathering hard evidence of such resolutions may be very difficult. Aside from the problem of explaining to subjects how to go about being attentive to such subtle evidence, many of these occasions would probably still slip away without notice. In summary, it seems very reasonable that incidental cueing does account for a number of TOT resolutions, and provides a reasonable account for pop-ups.

# Influence of Interlopers

When interlopers occur during a TOT, does this influence one's ability to access the target word? Some suggest that an interloper interferes with TOT resolution, in that TOTs with (versus without) interlopers (a) are less likely to be resolved (Burke et al., 1991; González, 1996) and (b) take longer be resolved (Burke et al., 1991). Burke et al. (1991) found that TOTs with interlopers took two to three times longer to resolve compared to TOTs without interlopers, and that interlopers drastically reduced TOT resolution probability from 46% without to 11% with. These findings suggest that interlopers are not neutral in the TOT resolution process but may stick in one's mind because their lexical nodes are more active than the target's to the detriment of TOT resolution (Burke et al., 1991).

Another way that interlopers may hamper TOT resolution is by strategy disruption. We may interpret an interloper as a signal that we are closing in on the TOT target word and about to resolve it (Schacter, 2001). Thus, we carefully scrutinize the interloper for clues that might lead in the direction of the target word. Paradoxically, this prolongs the TOT by strengthening one's focus in the wrong direction, on the interloper.

# ☐ Re-Cueing and Resolution

In some TOT laboratory investigations, the target word cue is presented a second time during the same session. This repetition may be immediate, a minute after the original cue, or at the end after all items have been tested. Most use this avenue to evaluate whether unresolved TOTs can be resolved on a second try (Schwartz et al., 2000), assuming that the TOT represents a negative cognitive state(s) that dissipates over time.

Four studies repeat the cue within a short time following the original cue. Diaz et al. (2007) re-presented the same face cue after a brief delay (5–10 s), during which time participants pronounced three words, one of which was related to the target. Following the repeated cue, 35% of formerly unresolved TOTs were resolved. Galdo-Alvarez et al. (2009a) used this same procedure and found similar resolution rates for their younger (39%) and older (35%) groups. However, in both of these investigations, the influence of the re-cue alone cannot be separated from any effects (positive or negative) of the related words presented in the interim. Both studies lacked a control comparison condition with no intervening cue words.

Two studies by Brennen employed an immediate re-cuing procedure for proper name targets, as a control comparison for resolution probabilities elicited by the addition of face cues (Brennen et al., 1990) and first letter cues (Brennen et al., 2007). Brennen et al. (1990, Experiment 1) discovered that 15% of TOTs were resolved by re-cueing, whereas Brennen et al. (2007) found a somewhat higher level of 27%, across two outcomes (Experiments 2 and 3). The problem with each of the above investigations is the lack of a control condition to determine the additional resolutions that one would naturally expect to occur over additional time.

A longer delay has been used in several studies, where the unresolved TOTs are re-cued at the end of the experimental procedure, following completion of all initial cue trials. These re-cueing intervals vary considerably, depending upon where the TOT item is on the original list, but generally ranges between 15 and 30 min. This procedure has yielded remarkably consistent resolution rates for prior TOTs: 15% (Brown & Nix, 1996), 12% (Schwartz, 1998, Experiment 2), and 13% (Schwartz et al., 2000). Choi and Smith (2005) compared re-cuing either immediately, 20 s after the original cue, or after the end of the procedure (see above). Significantly more TOTs were resolved after the longer (28%) than the shorter (14%) re-cue delays, suggesting some dissipation of the negative set that caused the TOT or positive encounter with other cues (words) related to the target.

It is difficult to draw any clear conclusions from these re-cueing outcomes. The short-term studies show that a substantial number of TOTs are resolved upon second cueing, but it is hard to tell whether this would occur with additional time, in the absence of cue repetition. A comparison group is needed where the extended time course of target word retrievals is mapped. With longer-term recueing, there is also evidence of a reasonable (if smaller) percentage of additional TOT resolutions. However, it is again hard to interpret in the absence of an extended retrieval opportunity without re-cueing. Also, there may have been other cues (words) encountered on intervening trials that helped trigger the target word.

## ☐ Recurring TOTs

The above research tackles the short-term issue of TOT resolutions occurring shortly after the original experience. However, a more important question has barely been addressed: what is the probability that a TOT will reoccur on the same item on the next attempt days, weeks, or months later? This issue connects to the larger question concerning the very nature of a TOT. A TOT might reflect a momentary deflection of a normally stable retrieval function. This perturbation is conceptualized as a relatively random process, with an equal probability of affecting any of a vulnerable subset of words at any given point in time. On the other hand, there may be characteristics of particular words that make them more likely than others to have repeated TOTs.

The most straightforward way to address this issue is to present the same set of target words on separate occasions and track the reliability of TOTs by items. One case study relevant to this issue of TOT fluctuation and consistency is Linton's (1996) 17-year investigation into the maintenance of knowledge (MOK) (described earlier) where she used herself as the subject. Of 477 different botanical terms tested, 23% elicited no TOTs, 20% triggered 1 TOT, and over half (57%) elicited multiple TOTs ranging from 2 to 11. This seems to provide a straightforward answer to the above question: some words are more vulnerable than others to TOTs, and these are likely to recur.

The 14 most TOT-prone target words (3%) accounted for 11% of all TOTs. Linton (1996) speculated that the lack of resolution on one occasion increases the likelihood of a similar outcome—an unresolved TOT—on the next encounter. However, she did not test this speculation. Although Linton's data are intriguing, there is no documentation of a specific nature of TOT fluctuations across repeated trials. We don't know the pattern of successful and unsuccessful (TOT or DK) retrievals. When a TOT was experienced, had that item ever been successfully retrieved on an earlier attempt? When an item elicits multiple TOTs, did correct retrievals ever intervene? And more critically, did resolving a TOT reduce the likelihood of another TOT? In short, there are many possible patterns of retrieval success and TOTs, and it would be helpful to examine how these patterns connect to specific types of words.

A design to address this question would involve two separate sessions cueing the same items, and tracking the fate of each item (K, TOT, DK) from the first to the second attempt. In the previous section on "Re-cueing and Resolution," only the percentage of initial TOTs that changed to Ks were tracked. In a more complete mapping of such item fluctuations, Schwartz (1998, Experiment 2) repeated the cueing procedure for all items, one immediately after the other, and reported the second attempt for first-trial TOTs or DKs. Of trial-one TOTs, 52% remained TOTs on the second trial, 12% were resolved (see above), and 36% changed to DKs. For DKs at trial one, 84% remained DKs, 9% were resolved, and 7% morphed into TOTs. This is an important first demonstration that TOTs emerge from DKs, and TOTs changing to DKs. However, a complete evaluation should include the fate of K items from test to test, as well as inserting a much longer interval between cue sessions to allow for the dissipation of short-term retrieval activation (or inhibition).

Recently, Warriner and Humphreys (2008) published such an investigation, with a 2-day intersession interval and a complete accounting of all types of item fluctuations. They were motivated by anecdotal reports that people seem to get repeatedly stuck on the same words. Their intriguing hypothesis is that a TOT is like experiencing an error trial in a learning paradigm, which increases the likelihood of making that same error on the next retrieval attempt. The alternative associative-learning position suggests that activating any components of the target word during a TOT (semantic node, some phonological nodes) should incrementally strengthen that word's retrieval success on the next try.

Subjects were allowed either 10 or 30 seconds to attempt to retrieve the missing target word during a TOT, prior to being supplied the correct answer. If error learning is occurring, the likelihood of a repeat TOT should be greater for the long interval (cf. Tomlinson, Huber, Rieth, & Davelaar,

2009). However, if associative learning is occurring, then a repeat TOT should be less likely with the long interval. Several outcomes support the error-learning hypothesis for TOTs. First, for unresolved TOTs in session 1, another TOT on session 2 (2 days later) was more likely for items in the 30 seconds (37%) than in the 10 seconds (25%) condition. Second, considering only resolved session 1 TOTs, a session 2 TOT was more likely (30%) if the resolution took a longer (>10 s) than a shorter (≤10 s) (8%) amount of time. As a comparison, there was no difference in the likelihood of a DK turning into a TOT on the second try comparing the 30 seconds (6%) and 10 seconds (8%) feedback conditions. Thus, the delay of feedback was not related to TOT probability on session 2 for non-TOTs. Also important for our purposes is that 3% of the Ks on session 1 turned into TOTs on session 2. Thus, TOTs can emerge later for items either high (K) or low (DK) in accessibility on the initial retrieval attempt.

The Warriner and Humphreys (2008) study suggests that more research on TOT stability would be very useful. The switch from DK to TOT is less surprising, as the TOT may simply reflect a relatively weak item and that correct feedback enhances the strength of a DK sufficiently to cross the TOT threshold at a later attempt. A more interesting finding is that a small percentage of K items shift to TOTs on the second try. This type of retest paradigm needs to be extended to longer re-test delays (weeks) that more closely resemble what one experiences in everyday life.

In summary, when a retest is given several days later, 30% of TOTs recur even when the target word is provided or retrieved. This presents clear evidence of the persistence of TOTs for certain words, and suggests that item-specific factors apart from strength and recency of experience influence the etiology of TOTs. Furthermore, second-try TOTs happen for both formerly K (3%) and DK (7%) items. These DK to TOT shifts may be due to enhanced fluency, where familiarity for the question which is generated by simply experiencing it in session 1 may be mistaken for familiarity for the answer at session 2. This inference may push one toward a TOT assessment for the item. Shifts from K to TOT are even more interesting, showing that momentary retrieval access is probabilistic.

# ☐ Manipulating Resolution

Chapter 4 evaluated attempts to manipulate the likelihood of *precipitating* a TOT. Moving the time frame forward, a closely related question is whether we can influence the probability of *resolving* a TOT. Investigations have explored this topic in two ways: through manipulating how readily the target word could be made available, or by providing cues related to the missing target word.

# Approaches to Resolution

Schwartz (2002a) compared different preferences for gaining access to a missing target word, including both DKs and TOTs. In natural settings, we have two choices: either we persist and keep searching, or give up and go about our lives. Using this as a starting point, Schwartz (2002a) decided to give subjects three different options for TOT decisions. One option was *directed search*, where the question was presented again and subjects simply continued with the search for the missing target word. This resembles choice one, noted above. The second option was that subjects could choose to turn away from the search at that moment, and have the cue presented again at a later time. This *delayed search* option resembles the second one noted above, but had the added benefit of the cue being given again. Finally, subjects could choose to have the correct answer simply provided for them, thus immediately ending the search effort. This *consultation* condition is one not usually available to us for everyday TOTs.

Subjects were divided into two groups, varying in whether they were assigned or allowed to choose the manner in which the search would (or would not) continue. In the metacognitive control condition (MCC), Schwartz (2002a) subjects could choose which resolution strategy to use on each failed-retrieval trial (TOTs and DKs). In contrast, subjects in the no-control condition (NCC) were assigned one of these three strategies, equally distributed across TOTs and across DKs. MCC choices for TOT versus DK trials (respectively) were directed search (20% versus 10%), delayed search (58% versus 32%), and consultation (22% versus 58%).

Schwartz (2002a) suggests that a TOT informs subjects that the answer is available, leading those in the MCC group predominantly to select search again either now (directed) or later (delayed). In contrast, DK trials do not give subjects an indication that the answer is available, so subjects predominantly select consultation. More TOT resolutions occurred in the MCC (65%) than NCC (43%) group, suggesting that control over retrieval strategy leads to higher TOT resolution probability (Schwartz, 2002a). MCC subjects selected search (now or later) for 78% of TOTs, whereas NCC subjects were assigned search on 67% of trials. Thus, there were fewer search opportunities for NCC subjects, but this is insufficient to account for the entire difference in TOT resolution probability.

# Target Word Information

Can resolution probability be enhanced by experiencing related words or structural features of the missing target during a TOT? As noted with TOT priming studies (see Chapter 4), when related information is provided in an obscured manner, it is difficult to determine the extent to which subjects become aware of the relationship between cue and target. Even if they become aware, how well can they use such information to influence the target word search success? Although occasionally assessed via postexperiment questionnaires (Abrams et al., 2003), this problem is more often ignored.

Whereas the intent of post-TOT cueing is either to facilitate or not affect TOT resolution, this procedure may occasionally be detrimental to retrieval. Furthermore, when given following DKs, postdefinitional cues may cause additional TOTs. Heine et al.'s (1999) study illustrates this point. Presenting related words (or first-letter cues) following nonretrieval trials elicited both additional TOTs on don't know trials and additional resolutions on TOT trials (see fuller explication below).

## Opaque Cueing

The research summarized in this section involves cueing procedures intended to be opaque to participants. More specifically, the cue–target relationship is designed to be not readily apparent, yet capable of boosting activation of the target word (Abrams et al., 2003; Abrams & Rodriguez, 2005; James & Burke, 2000; White & Abrams, 2002). As discussed earlier (see Chapter 4), James and Burke (2000 Experiment 1) initially used phonetic primes to influence TOT probability, and followed this up in Experiment 2 with a parallel cueing study. All TOTs and DKs were followed by the same type of 10-word sets used in their Experiment 1. To review, in related sets, 5 of 10 words share a phonological feature with the target word (first, middle, or last sound), whereas in unrelated sets none of the 10 words shares any phonological components with the target. More TOTs were resolved following related (72%) than unrelated (53%) cue sets, leading James and Burke (2000) to conclude that the related words collectively boost phonetic activation of the unretrieved target to overcome the TOT (see discussion of the transmission deficit theory; Chapter 9).

Although James and Burke (2000) demonstrated that phonological activation assists TOT resolution, their results do not specify which portion of the word (first, middle, or last) is important to facilitation because each set of cue words was mixed with respect to shared components (first, middle, last sound). So White and Abrams (2002) tried to clear this up with a modification of James and Burke's (2000) design. They used homogeneous sets of cue words where each related set had 3 words (out of 10), all of which shared only one syllable (first, middle, or last) with the target word. Thus, three different syllable sets were created for each target word. To illustrate, for the target word "abdicate" the first-syllable set included aberrant, abacus, and abdomen; the middle-syllable cue set consisted of indigent, handicap, and tradition; the last-syllable set was comprised of educate, duplicate, and fabricate.

As in James and Burke (2000), the other 7 words in each set were unrelated to the target on any syllable. To reiterate, diluting each set with unrelated words was designed to prevent subjects from detecting the relationship. As before, in the unrelated sets none of the words was related to the target on any syllable. Despite their efforts to mask this, White and Abrams (2002) found that quite a few subjects detected the cue–target relationship. Those who were aware and used this to guide retrieval were excluded from the analyses. Those who were aware yet did not use the information to inform retrieval, as well as those unaware of the relationship, were retained in the analyses. The first-syllable sets led to significantly more resolutions (50%) than middle (29%) and last (34%) sets, with no difference among middle, last, and unrelated (28%) sets. Although this outcome was compromised by dropping nearly half of the subjects, it still suggests that first-syllable activation may enhance TOT resolution.

Using this same type of approach to cueing, Abrams et al. (2003, Experiment 2) followed up White and Abrams (2002) to determine what aspect of the initial syllable was most important for activating the target word. In Experiment 1, DKs and TOTs were followed by 7 words that were either all unrelated to the target, or where 3 of 7 words shared the same first letter with the target. The first letter had no effect on TOT resolutions, with 45% resolved after related versus 40% after unrelated sets. Apparently a single letter does not supply enough activation to overcome the phonological insufficiency, so Experiment 2 used cue words that shared either the first, middle, last, or no syllable with the target word. The cue word sets were increased from 7 to 10 words, and in related lists 3 words shared a syllable with the target word. TOT resolution probability was significantly greater following first (50%) than either middle (33%), last (23%), or unrelated (25%) sets. The implication from this finding is that TOT resolution requires the entire first syllable, and not simply the first letter.

Whereas this outcome demonstrates that a multiletter unit aids resolution, it is unclear whether this is based on syllable or sound (phoneme). To separate these, Abrams et al. (2003, Experiment 3) compared cue words sharing a common first syllable versus first phoneme with the target. As in Experiment 2, the cue list remained at 10 words, but to reduce the likelihood of subjects detecting the cue–target relationship, the number of related words was decreased from 3 to 2. When subjects read the cue words aloud, there was no difference in TOT resolutions across first syllable (36%), first phoneme (30%), and unrelated (32%) sets. However, when subjects read the cue words silently, the first syllable elicited significantly more TOT resolutions (50%) than either first phoneme (32%) or unrelated (23%) sets, with no difference between the latter.

Thus, the first syllable significantly improved TOT resolution over the first phoneme and unrelated sets, but curiously this only happened in the silent condition. Abrams et al. (2003) speculate that the null effect in the aloud group may be due to subjects' occasional mispronunciations of the target words, which diluted the manipulation potency. The first syllable is clearly the most important component of target word activation. The ineffectiveness of the first phoneme may be due to its activation of a larger set of phonological nodes beyond the first syllable, thus diffusing the effect so that no one node receives sufficient activation to make a difference.

Taking this cue-word set design in a different direction, Abrams and Rodriguez (2005) examined the influence of a syntactic correspondence between cue and target word on TOT resolution. Within five-word cue sets, one shared the first phoneme and syntactic class with the target, or one had the same initial phoneme but came from a different syntactic class, or no word shared either first phoneme or syntactic class. For the target word *rosary*, examples of each cue type (respectively) are *robot*, *robust*, and *fever*. Abrams and Rodriguez (2005) discovered that a shared first phoneme facilitated TOT resolution, but only if the word was from a different syntactic category from the target. Cue words sharing the same syntactic class as the target word yielded the same TOT resolution probabilities as the unrelated cue.

Burke et al. (1991) suggest that if two words share the same phonology and syntactic class, they compete for activation. Only one or the other can be activated, but not both together. Thus, a post-TOT cue word sharing both phonology and syntax with the target word prevents target activation. However, a word from a different syntactic class can activate the phonology of the target word without blocking access. This theory was further clarified by examining the relationship between the cue word background frequency and the TOT resolution probability (Abrams & Rodriguez, 2005). With different syntactic class cues, the correlation was positive, suggesting that higher-frequency cue words provide a stronger level of activation leading to higher TOT resolution. In contrast, for the same syntactic class cues the correlation was negative: greater cue word activation reduces target word accessibility. This hypothesis fits nicely with the finding that most reported interlopers share a common syntactic class with the target (see Chapter 7).

Abrams, Trunk, and Merrill (2007) demonstrated that Abrams and Rodriguez's (2005) finding—different-syntax cues facilitate TOT resolution; same-syntax cue words don't—replicated for both young and young–old adults. Again disguising the cue word in a five-word list presented after a TOT or DK response, cue words phonologically related to the target word (same first syllable) increased TOT resolution, but only if the syntactic class differed from the target. The same syntactic class led to a resolution probability no different from an unrelated prime word. However, this outcome was not found with old–old (80+ years) adults, which suggests that the phonological deficit faced by these individuals may be too great to overcome via cueing.

Kozlowski (1977) used another variety of phonetic cueing procedure to influence TOT resolution, although the cue technique may be only partially opaque. In Experiment 1, following the target word definition subjects heard either the target or an unrelated word spoken to them. All such cue words were passed through a low-frequency filter, distorting the auditory details. The word was generally unrecognizable but retained its general rhythm and sound. TOT resolution was greater after hearing the garbled target versus the unrelated word. In Experiment 2, TOT target word recovery was again enhanced (relative to an unrelated word) after hearing a clearly pronounced word or word pair (*tall conifer*) that was related to the target word (*Excalibur*) in syllable number and stress.

Diaz et al. (2007) used a similar partially opaque cue word procedure. Following each TOT, three words were presented, one of which shared two of the following with the target: first syllable, last syllable, syllable number, syllable stress, or terminal vowel rhyme. The other two words were unrelated to the target. A re-presentation of the same face cue following these words resulted in a resolution of about a third (35%) of the TOTs, but the absence of a control condition with no cue words (only a second presentation of the face cue) makes it uncertain whether these resolutions resulted from the post-TOT cue word or would have occurred naturally with more time.

# Transparent Cueing

The prior section summarized results from cue-word studies where the connection between cue and target was intentionally obscured in some way. Other research has attempted to influence TOT resolution through cues that are related to the sought-after target word and provided to the subject expressly to aid retrieval. For example, Lawless and Engen (1977) provided a hint from the dictionary definition of an odor name during a TOT, and this resulted in a 70% resolution rate, although a DK trial comparison was not provided.

Most of the transparent cueing studies focus on the utility of the first letter in resolving TOTs. For instance, Brennen et al. (1990, Experiment 2) demonstrated that orthographic cues about a famous name (initials) facilitated TOT resolution (47%) to a greater degree than either semantic cues about the person (face) (11%) or repeating the original semantic cue (15%; the latter two conditions did not differ). They replicated this finding with famous landmarks: initials of a famous landmark (e.g., ET for Eiffel Tower) were significantly more effective in facilitating TOT resolution (44%)

compared to both repeating the original cue (14%) or showing a picture (22%) which did not differ (Brennen et al., 1990, Experiment 3).

A later study by Brennen et al. (2007, Experiment 3) also found a substantial positive effect of an initial letter cue on TOT resolution. Compared to a baseline resolution probability following simple re-presentation of the definition (21%), the famous person's initial letters substantially increased the probability of resolution (68%). Interestingly, this difference was also found among individuals whom they defined as illiterate: 32% of TOTs were resolved after the definition was repeated, whereas 72% were resolved when the person's initials were provided.

Using a sequential cueing procedure, Heine et al. (1999) first provided subjects with the target word definition (*chameleon*), and if the target word was not retrieved within 10 seconds they were shown either a semantic (related word or adjective, *salamander*) or orthographic (first letter plus dashes, *c* _ _ _ _ _ _ _ _) cue for 2 seconds. Then, the subjects were shown the definition again for 5 seconds. If the target word was still unavailable, the other cue was provided for 2 seconds. TOT resolutions were much higher following orthographic (34%) than semantic (9%) cues. However, it is unclear how much the word-length information in the form of number of dashes (one per missing letter) contributed to resolution success, beyond that from just the first letter. Interestingly, additional TOTs were elicited after both orthographic (3%) and semantic (2%) cues, suggesting that greater cue specificity may have the potential to move a target word access (strength of activation) from DK to TOT.

Given the consistent evidence concerning availability of the target word's first letter during TOTs, it is not especially surprising that Brennen et al. (1990; 2007) and Heine et al. (1999) found first-letter cues to be potent aids in TOT resolution. However, one interpretive problem with all of these investigations is the absence of a non-TOT comparison. Is the first letter cue efficacy limited to only TOTs, or is this information also useful when the subject is not experiencing a TOT?

To address this, Brown and Burrows (2009) provided letter cues on all trials where the target word was not initially retrieved, which subjects identified as unfamiliar, vaguely familiar, moderately familiar, or TOT. First-letter information was clearly available during TOTs, as reflected in a selection accuracy of 67% which was well above chance (33%; see Chapter 5) and the average rating for the three non-TOT categories. Aside from identification, the subjects' selection of the correct first letter automatically triggered the target word on 25% of TOTs, and significantly above the rate (7%), for non-TOT trials.

There appears to be solid evidence that providing or selecting the target word's first letter can be effective in facilitating TOT resolution (Brennen et al., 1990, 2007; Brown & Burrows, 2009; Heine et al., 1999). This rate is above that found with semantic cues (Brennen et al., 1990; Heine et al.,

1999) and repeating the original target word cue (Brennen et al., 1990, 2007). Furthermore, this also occurs at a substantial level even when the correct first letter is subject selected rather than experimenter presented (Brown & Burrows, 2009).

These findings seem to support the efficacy of the alphabet-scan TOT resolution strategy, noted in numerous diary studies (Burke et al., 1991; Cohen & Faulkner, 1986; Finley & Sharp, 1989; Reason & Lucas, 1984). Alphabet scan involves going through the alphabet, one letter at a time, until hitting upon the correct letter which often triggers target word retrieval. Despite this strong evidence, one negative outcome needs to be mentioned. Gollan and Silverberg (2001) provided the letters of the missing target, one at a time, starting with the first one. They found 4% of TOTs were resolved prior to and 6% following letter cues, a minimal and nonsignificant difference.

# ☐ Gestures

One of the more unusual manipulations used in an attempt to facilitate TOT resolution involves body movements. The literature suggests that physical gestures have a functional value in lexical access (Butterworth & Beattie, 1978), and Beattie and Coughlan (1999) extended this logic to evaluate whether such movements influence TOT resolution. Subjects in one group were allowed to gesture freely during retrieval efforts, whereas subjects in the other group folded their arms to eliminate spontaneous arm or hand gestures. Rather than directly asking subjects whether they were experiencing TOTs, Beattie and Coughlan (1999) inferred this from verbal reactions, facial expressions, and body movements (see Chapter 2).

TOT rate was greater in the gesture-allowed (15%) compared to the gesture-restricted (10%) group. Although they do not address it, this TOT rate difference is puzzling and in the wrong direction, because if gestures facilitate lexical access then TOTs should be reduced when gestures are allowed. But turning to their TOT resolution data, which is the focus of the investigation, the outcome was in line with their predictions: more TOTs were resolved in the gesture (71%) than in the no-gesture (58%) group. Although resolutions support gesture-facilitated lexical access, the overall retrieval success does not. Total target word retrieval, combining both correct retrieval and successfully resolved TOTs, did not differ between groups. In a supplemental inspection of the gesture group's data, Beattie and Coughlan (1999) found no difference in TOT resolution probability when TOTs were (69%) versus were not (73%) accompanied by spontaneous gestures, raising some doubt about the strength of the connection between gesture and lexical access.

Another investigation on gesturing and TOTs expanded this gesture restriction procedure to include both hands and feet. Frick-Horbury and Guttentag's (1998) restricted-gesture subjects were required both to hold a rod in their hands and depress a foot pedal during word retrieval efforts. They found no difference in either TOT rate or TOT resolution probability between restricted and unrestricted groups. However, within the unrestricted group they discovered that gestures accompanied a higher percentage of TOTs than non-TOTs. However, this outcome fails to demonstrate a causal connection from gesturing to TOT, it does suggest that TOTs may have compelled subjects to become more animated.

This gesture-restriction approach has also been used by Pine et al. (2007) with children. All subjects participated in both a gesture-restricted and a gesture-allowed condition. For gesture-restricted, subjects put their hands in a pair of mittens which were anchored (with Velcro) on a board in front of them. No special instructions accompanied the gesture-allowed condition. Using picture cues, there was no significant difference in the number of TOTs between the two conditions. However, there was a significant difference in the resolution success: more TOTs were resolved in the gesture-allowed (75%) compared to the gesture-restricted (46%) condition. Incidentally, the children also had more correct retrievals when gestures were allowed (86%) versus restricted (80%). Finally, in the gesture-allowed condition the children exhibited more than twice as many gestures when experiencing a TOT compared to when not. Thus, a number of different measures all point to the conclusion that gesturing facilitates lexical access.

Another study on this topic took an active (stimulate) rather than passive (restriction) approach. Rather than using forced restriction of gesturing, Ravizza (2003) tried forced activation. More specifically, subjects in the activity group were instructed to tap the index fingers of both hands (at their own pace) or keep absolutely still during their retrieval attempts. Tapping enhanced TOT resolutions (51%) relative to the no-activity control (27%) group (estimated from their Figure 1). Target retrieval for DK items was similarly higher in the gesture (26%) compared to the no-gesture (10%) group, so retrieval enhancement through forced activity may not be specific to TOTs.

The impact of gesturing on retrieval, in general, and TOTs, in particular, is mixed. If gesturing facilitates retrieval, then the impact should be demonstrated in three ways: increased correct retrievals, decreased TOTs, and increased TOT resolution. In the four studies presented, there is moderate support for this hypothesis but a number of outcomes are inconsistent with the interpretation. Schwartz (2002b) suggests that certain gestures associated with target words may be stored along with the semantic and syntactic representation of that word. Thus, gesturing has the potential to boost activation of the semantic representation, but it is unclear whether this would increase TOTs (pushing some DK into TOTs) or decrease them (by moving some TOTs to K). The only unambiguous prediction is that the likelihood of correct retrieval should increase when gesturing is encouraged (and decrease when gesturing is discouraged). An inferential interpretation related to gesture effects is that perhaps gesturing leads one to feel closer to retrieving the target word, and thus more likely to experience a TOT (Schwartz, 2002b). An alternative is that gestures are more likely to occur when one is aroused or more engaged in the retrieval effort, such that gesturing results from rather than causes TOTs.

# ☐ Imagery

The use of mental imagery as an intentional resolution strategy to resolve diary TOTs was discussed earlier in this chapter. Interestingly, fMRI data (Maril et al., 2005) reveal that areas related to visual–spatial processing (right inferior prefrontal cortex) as well as visual imagery (posterior medial parietal region) are selectively activated during TOTs. Maril et al. (2001) report that a few of their subjects reported relying on visual imagery to recover missing target words: "…they tried to 'keep looking' at the face of the person whose name escaped them, or that they attempted to 'read' the name of an author from an imagined book cover" (p. 658).

May and Clayton (1973) note that when they attempt to recall an acquaintance's name, they created a face image to facilitate this. Image construction also occurs with other categories of imageable nouns such as famous edifices, flowers, and birds, and "the phenomenon seemed sufficiently frequent in ourselves to encourage us to think it may be common to others" (p. 683; cf. Yarmey, 1973). Also relevant is Kleinbard's colorful description of TOT experiences while attempting to retrieve names of earlier-presented line drawings:

> By far, the most interesting subjective experience was getting a general "visual feeling" in my mind for a particular shape such as a length or roundness. I remember seeing a vague, oblong shape in my mind from which I was able to extract such items as gun, broom, and baseball bat; from an oval shape – football and pineapple… . I often experienced what might best be described as a "tip-of-the-eye" (TOE) phenomenon, in which I was certain a particular item was on the verge of recovery but which would take its time before suddenly coalescing into an image in consciousness. (Erdelyi & Kleinbard, 1978, p. 280)

A similar experience was described by other subjects in their follow-up study (Experiment 2): "The image of a small, furry creature kept popping up in my mind, but it was sort of unclear. I thought it might be a cat or a dog but somehow knew that this wasn't right. Finally, I tried 'rat' and poof! I knew it was the one" (Erdelyi & Kleinbard, 1978, p. 283).

Both descriptions suggest that the mental image is out of focus (Brown, 1991) or won't jell, in spite of high confidence in target word availability. Incorrect images resemble the target object in shape, similar to how interlopers share parts of the target word's orthography or phonology (see Chapter 7). These descriptions suggest that what Kleinbard describes as a TOE relates more to the semantic or first stage of word retrieval where the meaning representation of the target word is not fully formed. The typical TOT is generally conceived of as a later-stage retrieval problem where the semantic representation is clear, but the phonological form is not.

The evidence for the involvement of visual imagery in TOT resolution is intriguing and compelling, but it is primarily anecdotal and needs laboratory verification. Also of interest would be the involvement of other types of imagery in resolving TOTs, such as the voice of a celebrity (auditory) or the gait of a friend (kinesthetic). (cf., Lovelace, 1987.)

# ☐ Vocabulary

Does vocabulary size influence TOT resolution probability? This seems to follow logically, because broader verbal skills provide more resources to assist one in mentally hunting down the target word. Abrams et al. (2003) did find a significant positive correlation between vocabulary and TOT resolution probability with first-syllable cues (.32), but not with first phoneme (.12) or unrelated (−.06) cues. Perhaps people with high verbal skills can use the cue syllables more effectively because they have a wider range of words connected to various syllables. Alternatively, people with lower vocabularies may have more false TOTs, an interpretation supported by a negative correlation between vocabulary level and positive TOTs (−.30; Abrams et al., 2003). The unrelated cue condition, however, suggests there is no relationship between TOT resolution probability and vocabulary. This seems puzzling because one would expect some advantage, however slight, of verbal ability in word access. A problem with evaluating this speculation is that most TOT research involves samples of high-verbal subjects (college students), which presents a serious restriction on the range of vocabulary variability.

# ☐ Memory for Retrieved TOT Targets

What is the fate of the successfully retrieved target words associated with TOTs? One might expect these to be better recalled later, due to the deeper processing and greater effort expended on retrieving them. In Gardiner et al. (1973), subjects retrieved target words from definitions. When unsuccessful, they were provided the target word. After the last trial, subjects took an unexpected free recall test. In their pilot study, 76% of TOT targets successfully retrieved were recalled, a level substantially above the 44% average for all retrievals. In the main experiment, the outcome was ambiguous because target word recall (59%) was combined for strong FOKs (rating 3) and TOTs (rating 4; 59%) to compare with weak FOKs (ratings 1 and 2) (27%). Thus, the rate for TOTs was not presented by itself. Assuming that TOT targets were recalled better in both pilot and main study, what specific factors led to this enhancement: longer initial retrieval time, greater retrieval effort, or distinctive cues associated with the experience (cf. Brown, 1991)? Incidentally, Frick-Horbury and Guttentag (1998) also used a final recall test for all retrieved target words, but given that only 2% of TOTs were resolved the pool of successfully retrieved targets was too small to be meaningful.

# ☐ Retrieval Control Function of TOTs

Schwartz (2002b) suggests that rather than simply reflecting a memory state, TOT's function is to actively regulate, energize, or extend retrieval efforts. More specifically, a TOT state serves as a cognitive regulatory process extending our retrieval efforts because this signals that we are close to success. Just a bit more effort may pay off. Such TOT control functions were further subdivided into four processes (Schwartz, 2002b): retrieval time, enhanced processing, motivation, and social lubrication. With respect to retrieval time, TOTs push us to search for missing words longer than when we are not having a TOT. Subjects devote more time attempting to retrieve target words given high FOK ratings (Barnes et al., 1999; Nelson et al., 1984) and Schwartz (2002b) argues that these data can be similarly applied to TOTs. Supporting this speculation, Schwartz (2001b) found that across four experiments, subjects spent more time on TOTs than DKs prior to giving up and asking for the answer. There was one qualifier on this outcome, however: extended retrieval time was associated only with TOTs rated as emotional, and not for TOTs rated as non-emotional. Given that these data are correlational, the causality may actually run in the opposite direction (Schwartz, 2002b). A long retrieval effort may convince subjects that they are having a TOT, or familiarity with a domain of knowledge may lead to both longer searches and higher TOT probabilities.

A second control function of TOTs, suggested by Schwartz (2002b), is that because of our prior experience on such occasions, we are likely to expend more time and effort on TOTs just because the retrieval success is more problematical and the target more likely to be forgotten. From this perspective, the TOT process is a way to ensure that the associated target word will become more distinctive and retrievable, and thus reduce the likelihood of another TOT on that particular word in the future. Schwartz (2002b) supports this speculation by pointing to Gardiner et al. (1973): items associated with TOTs show higher final recall probability than those not associated with a TOT. However, as pointed out above, Gardiner et al. (1973) combined TOTs with high FOK items in their main experiment, so we can only conclude that high FOKs and TOTs improve later recall.

It should be noted that this finding only confirms a possible short-term benefit of deeper processing, rather than demonstrating a reduced likelihood of retrieval difficulties recurring days or weeks later. A finding problematic for a self-correcting interpretation of TOTs is Linton's (1996) outcome that many target words have a tendency to elicit TOTs on repeated retrieval attempts (cf. Warriner & Humphreys, 2008). It may be valuable to separate those TOTs that are resolved from those that are not when making such comparisons. More specifically, a resolved TOT may reduce the likelihood of a subsequent retrieval problem, but an unresolved TOT may actually increase the probability of another TOT later (cf. Linton, 1996). This question can be easily addressed in a design similar to Warriner and Humphreys' (2008) where the target word is not provided to subjects for unresolved TOTs that occur during the first session.

A third possible control function for TOTs is supplying the motivation to continue and persist in a current retrieval effort. To support this view, Schwartz (2002b) points to Ryan et al. (1982) who found more errors when subjects performed a secondary number-probe immediately after declaring a TOT, compared to following non-TOTs. Schwartz (2002b) interprets this as evidence that TOTs generate goal-directed activation connected with the target word search, and such cognitive effort diminishes the resources available for performing another, secondary, task.

Finally, Schwartz (2002b) proposes that there is a social function of TOTs. A TOT can provide a graceful way out of an awkward social situation. If unable to recall an acquaintance's name when running into her, admitting to a TOT can smooth this over and make her feel more positively about you. To admit that somebody's name is on the brink of being remembered makes for a better impression than acknowledging that you have drawn a blank. As suggested by Skinner and Vaughan (1983), in the face of a TOT when meeting an old acquaintance, one should tell him that you always tend to get stuck on the names of the people most important to you (cf. Brown, 1989).

# ☐ Summary

TOTs are more likely to be resolved than non-TOTs, perhaps suggesting that TOTs may function to energize and guide resolution processes. More than a third of laboratory TOTs are resolved, with the majority occurring within 10 to 20 s. Diary TOTs are much more likely to be resolved (90%), and most resolutions occur within 10 to 15 min. Brief TOTs are quickly resolved (several seconds) and occur with reasonable frequency (about 5% of retrievals) but are routinely ignored by the published reports and routinely combined with correct retrievals. Brief TOTs could provide a valuable addition to TOT studies, although measuring these would require modifying standard laboratory procedures. The possibility of subthreshold activation during TOTs has been examined, but appears to be an artifact of knowledge level of the target word's topic area. TOT resolutions may occur through a variety of different processes, including mental search, reference checking, pop-ups, or inadvertent cueing. It is likely that many resolutions labeled as pop-ups actually result from inadvertent cues, processed below one's conscious level of awareness.

It appears that TOT resolutions can be aided by structural, but not semantic, information about the target. Indirect cueing can facilitate TOT resolution by activating the initial syllable, via related words sharing that feature. Direct cueing with initial letter cues also increases TOT resolutions. When a TOT target is tested again in an experimental session, about 15% of unresolved TOTs become resolved. TOTs are more likely to recur on prior TOTs, compared to prior know (K) or don't-know (DK) trials. Further research on repeated TOTs for the same word would be worthwhile, for two reasons. First, it would help empirically confirm (or contradict) anecdotal reports of the phenomenon. Second, there is no current theoretical perspective that easily accounts for this possibility (assuming the target word was initially recovered). Physical gestures may play a role in TOT probability and resolution, but more research is needed before firm conclusions can be drawn. Anecdotal reports connect imagery with both the experience and resolution of TOTs, but this also lacks empirical verification.

# 9
CHAPTER

# Etiology

Speculation about the cause of TOTs was slow to evolve, although commentary concerning this experience stretches far back into the 18th century. Early interpretations were rather dramatic, painting possible connections between TOTs and deep psychological disturbances.

> I know my friend's middle name perfectly well, and yet when asked for it a moment ago, I could not command it. Some momentary stoppage of the associated pathways in the cortex checked the attempt at recall. Many of the most serious disorders of insanity involve this kind of disconnection and disintegration among ideas, of course much exaggerated. (Angell, 1908, p. 231)

Such pathological and psychodynamic perspectives gained little traction in the scientific literature (Morgan & Gilliland, 1939). However, more reasonable explanations took much longer to emerge, and were based upon more sophisticated theoretical developments in memory and language processing.

Most explanations of TOTs fall into two broad categories: direct access and inferential. Under direct access, a TOT reflects partial activation of information stored in memory. Direct access positions are based upon common-sense logic, given that both recall and recognition are consistently higher for target words associated with TOT compared to non-TOT states (Schwartz, 1999). Furthermore, partial target word information is often available during TOTs (see Chapter 5). As Schwartz (2002b) points out, direct access interpretations are preferred by psychologists and nonpsychologists alike, and have some intuitive appeal.

The other interpretation of TOT causality is inferential, that TOTs reflect our judgments about our knowledge (metamemory) rather than the actual contents of memory. We convince ourselves that we are having a TOT because of what words we believe we know or should know. Schwartz

(1994) presents a comprehensive summary and comparison of both categories of interpretation. He favors the inferential position but is careful to note that both target activation and inferential factors may contribute to TOTs. Smith (1994) similarly cautions that TOTs should not be considered a unitary phenomenon with a single cause, characterized by common features, and resolved by one process.

# ☐ Direct Access

Three direct access interpretations of TOTs have been proposed. *Generic recall* is global and somewhat sketchy, and assumes that TOTs reflect one of several stages in the general progression toward target word access. The second direct-access interpretation is *blocking*, which posits that retrieval has been inhibited or interfered with by another word. The primary support for blocking is the frequent report that interlopers crop up during a TOT. The third position, *transmission deficit,* is a more sophisticated and thoroughly developed interpretation, based upon theoretical mechanisms of language production.

## Generic Recall

In their ground-breaking study on TOTs, Brown and McNeill (1966) suggested that word retrieval involves generic recall, where one first sorts through subgroups of words sharing characteristics common to the target, prior to reaching the sought-after word. These generic word clusters coalesce on either common meaning or phonology (neighborhoods; see Chapter 6). Brown and McNeill's (1966) speculation was strongly influenced by the presence of interlopers during TOTs that were related to the target word (Chapter 7). For the target word "sextant," they noted that some interlopers reside in a semantic cluster with the target—*astrolabe, compass, dividers, protractor*—whereas others share space in a phonetic cluster, *secant, sextet, sexton.* Brown and McNeill's (1966) lengthy discussion about lexical organization and retrieval involves a computer punch-card analogy, with some punch-holes common to interloper and target word (aligned) and others not (misaligned). When our initial effort to access the target word encounters an incomplete or indistinct entry (Brown, 1991), the fragmentary information that is available may be sufficient to activate a related grouping of words, which then helps pull out the elusive target. Thus, there are two stages in the progress toward word retrieval. The word form access comes first, and if this fails a second stage involves activating related information which is then used to facilitate retrieval.

A similar idea was introduced earlier by Wenzl (1932, cited in Woodworth, 1938), who likened word retrieval to a mental funnel, proceeding from the general to the specific. Brown (1970) later expanded upon this, emphasizing that words are not fully processed when first accessed, thus accounting for the availability of fragments of the target word, as well as related words, during TOTs. To test this idea that we progressively "close in" upon the target word node, Kohn et al. (1987) hypothesized that target word information accessibility should follow a consistent sequence, with each successive piece being closer to the missing target word. But a careful examination of subjects' output order of information reported during TOTs revealed virtually no support for a systematic progression through successively more informative layers of partial information. However, Kohn et al.'s (1987) negative evaluation may be premature because it is based on the unverified assumptions that subjects report (a) everything that comes to mind and (b) in the order that it becomes available (Brown, 1991).

The idea of nonspecific generic recall has been embraced by others (Reed, 1974; Schachter, 1988; Yarmey, 1973; cf. Brown, 1991). Yarmey (1973) suggests that the concept be expanded beyond a verbal framework to encompass word imagery as well, and Roediger and Neely (1982) propose a position close to generic recall that could be relabeled active generic recall. Despite some affirmation, the concept of generic recall presented by Brown and McNeill (1966) did not capture the imagination of most researchers and has had little impact on subsequent empirical or theoretical speculation about TOTs. Aside from their dated punch-card analogy, the model did not explain why retrieval stopped short of completion. Did the retrieval effort simply "run out of steam," or perhaps get diverted in the wrong direction? Subsequent direct access theorizing has taken this next step.

# Blocking

The first rigorous and scientifically oriented explanation of TOTs is that some form of retrieval inhibition blocks access to the target word. This explanation has deep historical roots (Wenzl, 1932, 1936). Woodworth (1929; 1938; 1940) suggested that TOTs might occur because words similar to the target block its access, and that "… one seems to start towards the goal but to stray into a blind alley" (Woodworth, 1940, p. 127). "When we have run off the track in trying to remember a name, the wrong name recalled acquires a recency value and blocks the correct name …" (Woodworth, 1938, p. 38).

> This mutual interference of associates is probably the explanation of many cases of mental blocking. Often when one is trying to recall a perfectly familiar fact, it refuses to return… . It is probable that

the cue was associated with several ideas, and that they mutually prevented the return of any one. (Pillsbury, 1939, p. 265–266)

Freud (1901, cited in Reason & Lucas, 1984) also notes that when we try to access an elusive word during a TOT, we tend to bring to mind words that "although immediately recognized as false, nevertheless obtrude themselves with great tenacity" (p. 189).

Many studies use *retrieval block* as synonymous with TOT (e.g., Cohen & Faulkner, 1986; Jones & Langford, 1987; Linton, 1996; cf. Brown, 1991). For example, Gruneberg et al. (1973) instructed subjects that while prospecting for their own TOTs, "as soon as you block please try to remember the unobtainable word ..." (p. 188), and Roediger and Neely (1982) suggested that TOTs are "the best known instance of retrieval blocks in semantic memory" (p. 231). Some studies also refer to interlopers as *blockers*, suggesting that they have a role in TOT incidence or resolution (Maylor, 1990a; Reason & Lucas, 1984).

Roediger (1974) took issue with Brown and McNeill's (1966) assertion that peripheral information about the target word reflects a positive progression toward the target, with the individual drifting into the general lexical neighborhood. Instead, he posed the question: with all this accessory information available, shouldn't the subject be more, rather than less, likely to retrieve the target word? Roediger (1974) suggested that something akin to output interference may occur (Tulving & Arbuckle, 1966), with information available during a TOT (first letter, number of syllables, interloper) competing with target word access, similar to how presenting some words from an episodic list can inhibit the recall of the remaining words. Others have likened the possible negative effects of interlopers to output interference (Dagenbach, Carr, & Barnhardt, 1990; la Heij, Starreveld, & Steehouwer, 1993; Roediger & Neely, 1982; Roediger, Neely, & Blaxton, 1983; Schacter, 1999; Schulkind, 2002), retrieval-induced forgetting (Anderson, Bjork, & Bjork, 1994, 2000), and center-surround mechanisms (Barnhardt, Glisky, Polster, & Elam, 1996).

In research motivated by this perspective, Brown (1979) found that if a definition cue for a target (*Braille*) was preceded by a word *semantically* related to the target (*shorthand*), this would decrease retrieval probability relative to an unrelated (*cantaloupe*) word prime. This outcome fueled speculation (similar to Roediger, 1974) that something similar to output interference from interlopers could initiate or maintain TOTs (Brown, 1979). Roediger et al. (1983) later demonstrated that a semantically related prime was inhibitory only when there was ambiguity about whether it could be the actual target. When subjects know that the target word will occasionally appear as a prime, semantic prime inhibition occurs; when subjects know that the correct word is never a prime, no inhibition is found (Bowles, 1989; Roediger et al., 1983). One could argue that the Brown's (1979) finding is more applicable to TOTs because during normal word retrieval, we expect the correct target to come to mind. More specifically, when an interloper comes to mind during an actual TOT, it may not be immediately discounted; when one is expecting the target word, each word that pops up must be seriously examined, if briefly.

Reason and Lucas (1984) speculate that on most occasions, the interloper presents a more compelling lexical entity than the target word because most are higher in frequency or recency than the sought-after target. They liken interlopers to the ugly stepsisters in *Cinderella* (see Chapter 7):

> ... to the extent that their attempts at deception delayed the happy reunion, it could be said that they acted as blockers in the search process. And they were not just passive impediments who simply happened to get in the way; they actively sought to usurp Cinderella's rightful place. Furthermore, although they differed from her in looks and temperament, the ugly sisters, by virtue of their family connection and the shared address, had numerous features in common with the object of the search. (p. 62)

The influence of interlopers on the elicitation and resolution of TOTs has been extensively evaluated, using related words presented prior to (priming) and following (cueing) the target word definition (Askari, 1999; Jones, 1989; Jones & Langford, 1987; Maylor, 1990a; Meyer & Bock, 1992; Perfect & Hanley, 1992; Reason & Lucas, 1984). Both sets of findings have been covered earlier (Chapters 4 and 8). Some evidence suggests that both semantically related (Meyer & Bock, 1992, Experiment 2) and phonologically related (Reason & Lucas, 1984) cue words can increase TOT rate. Burke et al. (1991) further note that phonological primes may shift subjects' threshold downward for interpreting the present retrieval difficulty as a TOT. That is, if pertinent phonological information is available about the target through the related word, then some DKs may seem to be TOTs.

Cross and Burke (2004) tested the blocking hypothesis using a "competitor priming" paradigm. Subjects first generated a prime name from a cue, which consisted of a famous character either related (Eliza Doolittle) or unrelated (Scarlett O'Hara) to the target actor cued soon afterward. In the related condition, the target actor (Audrey Hepburn) had actually played the part of the related prime character. No TOT difference was found for related versus unrelated prime name conditions, thus casting doubt on the blocking theory of TOTs. In contrast to this outcome, Smith (1994) found that a semantically related prime did increase TOTs. Presenting a word phonologically similar to the TOTimal target name increased recall without affecting TOTs, but one of the other TOTimal names which was (by definition) semantically related to the target TOTimal increased both recall and TOTs. This partially supports blocking, in that a semantically related word increases TOTs. However, Schwartz (1999) points out that there is ambiguity about whether the semantic cue in Smith (1994) provided facilitation or blocking (or both) because the semantic cue increased correct retrieval as well as TOTs.

To summarize, there is at best modest support for blocking (Meyer & Bock, 1992; Reason & Lucas, 1984). As noted earlier (Chapters 4 and 8), such research is hampered by the fact that prime/cue studies may evoke retrieval strategies not present during the usual TOT experience. More specifically, processing related words has the potential to either facilitate or impair retrieval during TOTs (cf. Meyer & Bock, 1992). Compounding this, cues or primes may influence both TOTs and correct retrievals, and comparing changes in both types of items is necessary to determine whether any manipulation has an effect, and in what direction.

Assuming the existence of three retrieval states—inaccessible (DK), partially accessible (TOT), and fully accessible (K)—facilitation by a related cue could shift items "up" from DK to TOT, and from TOT to K. On the other hand, inhibition from a related cue could reduce activation, shifting words from K down to TOT, as well as from TOT back to DK. Thus, a cue word manipulation could have either positive or negative effects on target word access, yet leave the absolute TOT rate unaffected. This ambiguity can be resolved simply by examining K items across different manipulation conditions. This should increase if related words boost activation, and decrease if related words hamper activation (Perfect & Hanley, 1992).

Aside from experimental manipulation of interlopers, another approach to evaluating the blocking hypothesis involves TOT resolutions. TOTs with interlopers have a lower resolution probability (Burke et al., 1991; González, 1996) and longer resolution time (Burke et al., 1991), compared to TOTs without interlopers (see Chapter 8). This could be viewed as evidence for blocking, but Burke et al. (1991) suggest that resolving TOTs with interlopers is more complex. They discovered that interlopers most often come from the same syntactic class as the target word. When two phonologically related words from the same syntactic class are both primed, only the one with the most priming can be activated. In contrast, when both interloper and target are from different syntactic classes, a phonologically related interloper can actually facilitate target word retrieval (Abrams & Rodriguez, 2005).

Choi and Smith (2005) compared immediate versus delayed target retrieval for TOTs with interlopers, reasoning that a second attempt immediately afterwards should be less successful than one after a delay, because a delay should allow any negative influence of the interloper to dissipate. Also, they reasoned that the blocking position would predict that the presence of an interloper should increase rated TOT strength, relative to a TOT without an interloper. Thus, the rated strength of a TOT accompanied by an interloper should decrease after a delay, as the influence of an interloper disappears (Choi & Smith, 2005). If activation fades over time, then both TOT resolution probability and rated strength should decrease.

More TOTs were resolved on the delayed than immediate retest, whereas TOT strength dropped at the delayed versus the immediate retest. Thus, Choi and Smith (2005) suggest that their outcome supports blocking over activation deficit or metacognitive control (see later discussion), because the latter two theories predict greater TOT resolution at the immediate than at the delayed retrieval attempt. It is important to add that Choi and Smith (2005) believe that interlopers are a fundamental part of TOTs, and that on some TOTs the interlopers may not be detected or reported. Thus, interference from interlopers can occur outside conscious awareness. Choi and Smith's (2005) outcome is intriguing, but it would be useful to replicate this investigation including an inquiry about interlopers, rather than inferring their presence.

Perhaps the strongest empirical evidence against blocking is that interlopers are reported on about half of TOTs. To accommodate this deficit, blocking theorists assume either that (a) blocking is an explanation for some but not all TOTs, or (b) interlopers are activated on all TOTs but are undetected (subliminal) on some TOTs (cf. Choi & Smith, 2005). Reason and Lucas (1984) suggest that related word activation is a normal part of the retrieval process, but sometimes we don't notice these extraneous words because we start closer to the target and bypass related word activation, or clearly inappropriate words that come to mind are quickly rejected and do not produce interference with target word retrieval (Brown, 1991). Speculation that implicitly activated words can interfere with target access when out of conscious awareness needs empirical verification (cf. Choi & Smith, 2005), perhaps using a subliminal priming procedure. Would subliminally presenting one (or more) words related to the target word immediately prior to the target increase TOT incidence, relative to an unrelated word?

Another finding that is problematic for blocking is the negative relationship between TOT incidence and interloper frequency across age. Older adults have more TOTs, but fewer interlopers (Burke et al., 1991). Under the blocking hypothesis, the proportion of TOTs with interlopers should be constant. Additional evidence against blocking is that TOTs are more likely for words with low, rather than high, neighborhood density. Harley and Bown (1998) boldly suggest that this outcome represents "...another nail in the coffin of the blocking hypothesis" (p. 164) because more TOTs should occur with words in high-density neighborhoods where more potential blockers surround the target.

Finally, James and Burke (2000) note that presenting phonological components of the target word embedded in other words, either as primes or cues, generally reduce the incidence of TOTs and aid resolution. This is difficult to reconcile with blocking (Abrams et al., 2003; Abrams & Rodriguez,

2005; James & Burke, 2000; Lesk & Womble, 2004; White & Abrams, 2002). However, such prime/cue words containing only fragments of the target word are distantly related, and thus may not provide the strong interference that words clearly related to the target word do.

In general, the evidence for blocking is unimpressive. However, a convincing test of the blocking hypothesis may not have been conducted: "despite the mixed evidence on blocking, it should remain a viable hypothesis. Indeed, it is a hypothesis waiting for a better, as yet undiscovered, methodology" (Schwartz, 1999, p. 386). Whether or not blocking causes TOTs, interlopers appear to have a negative effect on TOTs by increasing resolution time and decreasing resolution probability (Burke et al., 1991). Attention directed to the interloper enhances its activation, making it more difficult to ignore (Schvaneveldt, Durso & Mukherji, 1982). In line with such speculation, Kinoshita (2001; Kinoshita & Towgood, 2001) notes that a spontaneously recognized word attracts and holds attention while blocking the processing of competitors (e.g., target word), and Logan and Balota (2003) demonstrate word fragment completion for a word is impaired following the processing of a phonologically related prime word. Thus, some general word-finding difficulties may stem from an inability to suppress phonologically related competitors that are brought to mind by oneself or others (Brown, Zoccoli, & Leahy, 2005).

## Transmission Deficit

In contrast to the active impairment framed by the blocking hypothesis, perhaps a passive insufficiency accounts for TOTs: the momentary level of word activation is not high enough to support word production. In 1991, Burke, MacKay, Worthley, and Wade proposed a clearly articulated and thoroughly developed theoretical version of direct access, which has become the most influential theory on TOT etiology (cf. Burke & Shafto, 2004; Burke, MacKay, & James, 2000). Derived from node structure theory (NST; MacKay, 1987), this interpretation applies to a wide range of cognitive phenomena, including language production, attention, awareness, memory, and aging. At the heart of the model, word production involves a sequential activation process, originating with the semantic system, then progressing through the phonological system, and finally ending in word generation.

Burke et al. (1991) propose that TOTs occur when activation fails to be fully transmitted from the semantic to the phonological system. On these infrequent occasions, word meaning is fully activated but phonological activation is insufficient to enable complete word production. This deficit in transmission from the lexical to the phonological nodes is the central tenant of the transmission deficit hypothesis, or TDH (MacKay & Burke, 1990), and excellent visual diagrams of the structure can be found in Figure 1 of Burke (1991, p. 544) and Figure 1 of Rastle and Burke (1996, p. 589).

A deficit in transmission from the semantic to phonological modes is influenced by three variables, under NST: frequency of word use, recency of word use, and age. The connections between the semantic and phonological systems are relatively weaker when the history of prior activation is less frequent or less recent, and with increased age of the individual. The first two factors are relatively self-evident and based on principles of simple reinforcement, but the aging relationship requires clarification. Burke et al. (1991) suggest that the aging-related increase in transmission deficit difficulties may indirectly relate back to recency because, on average, it has been longer since an older adult has experienced (generated, heard, seen) any given vocabulary word. Cohen and Faulkner (1986) similarly speculate that the age-related increase in TOTs results from impairment in the "concept-to-name path" (p. 192), and Faust et al. (1997) suggest that the TOT experience embodies "the most dramatic reflection of the rift between the lemma and the lexeme levels" (p. 1028). Burke et al. (1991) also propose that the "gap" that James (1893) refers to in his oft-quoted TOT description (see Chapter 1) characterizes the disconnection between the semantic and phonological activation.

Abrams et al. (2003) make an additional distinction between node *priming*, which involves the spread of excitation from one node to another related node, and node *activation*, where the level of excitation found in a given node exceeds a certain threshold. For successful word retrieval, all constituent nodes comprising the target word must be activated simultaneously. Occasionally, only some nodes constituting a particular word (e.g., final phoneme; first letter) become activated, allowing these aspects to be identified during a TOT even when complete activation fails.

Several lines of evidence support TDH. One is the frequent availability of partial target word information during TOTs. As long as activation has been passed to some of the target word's phonological nodes or properties, retrieval of part of the word form can occur without activation of the entire word. TDH also accounts for interlopers during TOTs, under the assumption that phonological nodes may be shared by multiple words (e.g., "cha" is shared by "charity" and "chastity"). Activating a node shared between a target word and one related to it can fully activate this structurally related word, even when activation is insufficient to reach the threshold for the intended target word.

In addition, TDH is supported by the age-related decline in the availability of both interlopers (Burke et al., 1991; White & Abrams, 2002) and partial target word information (Brown & Nix, 1996; Burke et al, 1991; Heine et al., 1999; Rastle & Burke, 1996) during TOTs. Under TDH, the decreased phonological activation with age not only makes the first letter and other structural features less available (Heine et al., 1999), it also reduces the amount of backward transmission to related words, thus decreasing the likelihood of interloper activation. Alzheimer's patients experience even fewer interlopers during TOTs than do normal older controls (Astell & Harley, 1996), and if one interprets Alzheimer's as an advanced form of normal aging processes, this provides additional support for the mechanisms underlying the aging-decrement component of TDH. Finally, several investigations on brain function have pointed to a central role of the left insula in both phonological retrieval operations and TOT incidence (Shafto et al., 2007, 2010).

In support of the recency predictions from TDH, Rastle and Burke (1996, Experiment 1) showed that presenting target words in a prior prime list decreased TOTs for both older and younger adults. This outcome was qualified in a follow-up study (Experiment 2) because this reduction occurred only for older but not younger adults. Rastle and Burke (1996) suspected that young adults detected the prime–target connection in Experiment 2, and used this to guide their retrieval effort. When the percentage of primed targets was reduced to make the list relationships less obvious (Experiment 3), Rastle and Burke (1996) again found the recency prime reduction in TOTs for younger subjects. These outcomes point to recency of word experience as an important factor contributing to TOTs, in support of TDH: TOTs are less likely to occur on words that have been experienced more recently.

According to TDH, providing phonetic information about a target word can reduce TOT probability and facilitate TOT resolution (see Chapter 8). If the underactivation of target word phonological nodes leads to a TOT, then a phonological boost could push the word over the threshold of accessibility, thus reducing TOTs. Abrams et al. (2003) demonstrated that priming the target word's first syllable during a TOT by exposing subjects to other words related on this dimension resulted in significantly greater TOT resolution, compared to priming the middle syllable, last syllable, first phoneme, or first letter. White and Abrams (2002) also found the first syllable facilitation effect occurred for younger and young–old adults, but not for old–old adults. Apparently, both young and young–old can remedy their transmission deficits through indirect first-syllable activation, but the age-related deficit for old–old adults is simply too great for this boost to overcome.

Abrams et al. (2003) further suggest that first-phoneme and first-letter primes are not as successful as first-syllable primes because activation spreads to a larger pool of words that share this dimension, thus diluting the impact. The first syllable, in contrast, connects with a smaller set of words in the lexicon, providing a relatively stronger indirect boost for the target word activation. They further speculate that both middle- and last-syllable priming are ineffective because activation is sequential, progressing from the first to middle to last part of the word. Thus, if the first syllable has not been activated, it is much more difficult to activate the remaining syllables.

Although support is generally strong, some have pointed out evidence that they believe contradicts TDH. For example, Dahlgren (1998) notes that her positive relationship between vocabulary size and TOT incidence fails to support the notion that weak lexical to phonological links cause TOTs (cf. Schwartz, 2002b; Gollan & Brown, 2006). A higher vocabulary should involve a richer set of interconnections among words and greater phonological activation, resulting in fewer TOTs. However, this positive vocabulary–TOT relationship could be viewed as support of TDH if interpreted within the framework of the fan effect (Anderson, 1974). A fixed amount of activation is spread thinner with individuals who have a large vocabulary, because their more numerous lexical interconnections result in less phonological activation for any given word.

Another possible problem with TDH is that TOTs take longer to resolve when accompanied by interlopers (Burke et al., 1991). Resolution should be unaffected with a semantically related interloper, and shorter with a phonetically related interloper because of the added phonological activation provided (cf. Brown, 1991). Burke et al. (1991), however, counterargue that a same-syntax phonologically related interloper may hamper target activation (see earlier discussion in Chapter 7). In such cases, an interloper may simply create a distraction, rather than functionally altering the mechanics of TOT resolution.

In an effort to forge a compromise position, Smith (1994) proposes that both blocking and TDH may underlie TOTs. More specifically, every TOT may not have the same etiology "any more than recall or recognition of a word can be traced to a unitary cause" (p. 38). Whereas a phonetically related prime presented before a TOTimal cue decreased TOTs, in support of TDH, a semantically related prime (incorrect TOTimal name) increased TOTs, supporting blocking. Smith (1994) proposes an "incomplete storage" modification of Burke et al.'s (1991) theory. TOTs may occur either because the name is not completely/efficiently stored, or the phonological and semantic components of the word are not well integrated.

Should the age-related decrease in transmission of activation, proposed by TDH, result in both an increase in TOT probability and a decrease in TOT resolution? Burke et al. (1991) assert that older adults should have more TOTs, but make no prediction concerning resolution. Schwartz and Frazier (2005) point out that the same mechanisms that result in a decrement word activation logically should negatively affect TOT resolution, as well. They note that the data are ambiguous on this point. In diary studies, older adults report more TOTs but resolve fewer (Burke et al., 1991, Study 1; Cohen & Faulkner, 1986; Heine et al., 1999, Experiment 2). Laboratory outcomes, however, are mixed. Some find a higher resolution rate for older adults (Brown & Nix, 1996; Dahlgren, 1998; Vitevitch & Sommers, 2003) and others a higher rate for young adults (Burke et al., 1991, Study 1; Heine et al., 1999, Experiment 1).

As a final comment on direct access interpretations of TOTs, Schwartz (1999) summarizes several lines of support that are not specific to any particular subposition (generic recall, blocking, incomplete activation):

1. TOT targets are resolved at a higher rate than non-TOT targets (Smith, 1994; Schwartz, 1998).
2. Recognition of targets is higher for TOT than non-TOT target words (Kozlowski, 1977; Schwartz, 1998; Schwartz & Smith, 1997; Schwartz et al., 2000; Smith et al., 1994).
3. Partial information about the target word is available during a TOT experience at levels consistently above chance.

# ☐ Inferential Theories

From the inferential perspective, a TOT does not result from the sought-after word receiving some activation. Instead, our personal assessments of the cues and knowledge base associated with the retrieval experience determine whether we experience a TOT. In other words, how we interpret our retrieval activities is central to the TOT experience (cf. Schwartz, Benjamin, & Bjork, 1997, for a summary). Especially pertinent is our belief about our ability to access the missing target word. A retrieval failure is nothing extraordinary, but our intense sense of retrieval imminence associated with a TOT is driven by our expectations within the present context. Thus, a TOT is "often an illusion produced by a familiar retrieval cue" (Schacter, 1999, p. 70). A thorough explication of this position is provided by Schwartz (2002b), and the following is a summary of the major theoretical points and pertinent findings.

The view that TOTs are a result of inferences connects to research and speculation on FOKs, and whether a TOT is simply an extreme FOK or a separate cognitive experience (see Chapter 2). Ryan et al. (1982) borrow from Hart's (1965) research on FOKs, proposing that TOTs are a by-product of a larger memory control processing system, that (a) monitors the contents of memory and (b) requires some processing resources. They support such speculation with evidence that performance is poorer on an attention-demanding task immediately following a TOT, compared to after a non-TOT. Thus, when more processing capacity is directed toward a specific retrieval effort, we assess this as a TOT. It should be noted here that the causal direction could be in the reverse direction, with a TOT coming first and followed by increased demand for attention. An additional point made by Ryan et al. (1982), against the direct access and for the inferential position, is that TOTs do not appear to be driven by the strength of the inaccessible target word because relevant manipulations (varying target word study times) fail to influence TOT probability.

Two different versions of the inferential perspective on TOTs have been proposed. With *cue familiarity* (Metcalfe et al., 1993), TOT assessments are based on how familiar the cue is, either in the general domain (e.g., geography) or specific fact (e.g., capital of North Dakota). In general, the more knowledge one has in a particular subject area, the more likely a TOT. To test this notion through an instructional directive, Ravizza (2003) tried to eliminate TOTs by informing subjects that a TOT is "... not a feeling that one should know the word given one's familiarity with the subject area ..." (p. 611). Subjects still reported TOTs, and Ravizza (2003) interpreted this as evidence against the inferential position. However, a stronger test would involve varying the instructions between groups, or including a no-instruction control group.

The second metacognitive interpretation is based on an *accessibility heuristic*, where the by-products of the retrieval effort drive TOT assessments (Koriat, 1993, 1994). More specifically, TOTs are based on the amount of partial word information that comes to mind (first letter, interloper, syllables), whether or not these bits and pieces relate to the actual target word. Research by Koriat and Levy-Sadot (2001) suggests that both accessibility and cue familiarity influence TOT assessments, and are not mutually exclusive.

Apart from instigating TOTs, the inferential processes may motivate us to maintain the retrieval effort longer than with non-TOT trials (Schwartz, 1999, 2001b, 2002b, 2006). Referred to as *metacognitive control*, Schwartz argues that this is supported by (a) higher target word recall following TOT versus non-TOT trials, and (b) longer time spent searching for a target word during TOT than non-TOT trials (Baars, 1993; Schwartz, 2001b). Furthermore, when allowed to choose a resolution strategy, subjects assume that the missing word is more likely to come to mind during a TOT than a non-TOT trial, suggesting that TOTs control the retrieval strategy (Schwartz, 2002a).

Schwartz (2006) presents a number of arguments for considering TOTs as reflecting inferential judgments over direct access. First, the pervasiveness of the "tongue" metaphor in 90% of languages surveyed (Schwartz, 1999) suggests a predominance of the metacognitive feeling about the experience over sensations that emanate from lexical access (see Chapter 2). If the linguistic dimensions were predominant (e.g., target word phonology or orthography; interlopers), there would be a panoply of different terms used to describe TOTs.

The second argument by Schwartz (2006) is that individuals can differentiate various TOT "states," such as emotional versus nonemotional, strong versus weak, and imminent versus nonimminent. If direct access were the driving force, then the experience should be monolithic, rather than having such fine gradations. Schwartz (2006) also notes that TOTs drive certain retrieval behaviors. During TOTs, people try harder (longer) to retrieve the target word, as indicated by poorer secondary task performance during TOTs (Yaniv & Meyer, 1987). A counterargument to this point is that motivation to find the target word is greater when clear clues are available. Wouldn't one work longer to retrieve an author's last name when the first name is available (versus not), or a 12-letter crossword puzzle word when one has uncovered 7 rather than 2 of the letters?

Another reason Schwartz (2006) provides as support for inferential over direct access explanations is that retrieval of related information can affect the feeling of temporary inaccessibility, without affecting retrieval probability. If direct access were driving TOTs, having more information available should increase resolution likelihood rather than having no effect. Finally, Schwartz (2006) notes that neuroimaging studies show that brain areas active during TOTs are also those associated with memory monitoring and control, and differ from those brain areas typically active during routine word (non-TOT) retrievals (Maril et al., 2001, 2003, 2005).

Metcalfe et al. (1993, Experiment 3) took an experimental approach to differentiate among three different interpretations of TOT etiology: direct access (blocking) and the two inferential positions (cue familiarity and accessibility). They used a traditional paired-associate design consisting of the following types of stimulus-response pairings on two successively learned lists:

1. A-B, A-B: same stimulus-response pairings repeated on Lists 1 and 2
2. A-D, A-B: same stimuli, but paired with different responses on Lists 1 and 2
3. C-D, A-B: both stimulus and response terms differ on Lists 1 and 2

After learning both lists, subjects attempted to recall List 2 response terms when given the List 2 stimulus word. Under the blocking position, more TOTs should occur with paradigm 2 because the List 1 response should interfere with (block) the List 2 response (2 > 1 = 3). With respect to cue familiarity, more TOTs should occur in paradigms 1 and 2, where the stimulus (cue) term is stronger due to having been repeated (1 = 2 > 3). Finally, under the accessibility position, TOTs should be highest in paradigm 1, intermediate in 3, and lowest in 2 (1 > 3 > 2). Paradigm 1 should yield more TOTs than paradigm 3 because responses are repeated in 1 but not 3, making them stronger and more accessible. With respect to paradigm 2, the unlearning of List 1 responses that is required to learn List 2 responses would decrease response-to-stimulus associative strength, relative to paradigm 3. Metcalfe et al. (1993) found that TOT rate was ordered (high to low) by paradigm as 1 = 2 > 3, thus, supporting cue familiarity over either blocking or accessibility. Incidentally, a similar ordering (1 = 2 > 3) was found for FOK evaluations in Experiment 3, implying that TOTs and FOKs may be related and based on common mechanisms.

## Contrary Evidence

The inferential position of TOTs has drawn some criticism. Riefer (2002) argued that inferential theories should predict that the type of cue should influence TOT rates. More specifically, if TOTs are influenced by cue familiarity, then more familiar cue formats should increase TOT rates. Although there was a significant difference between correct recall of TV show titles with cast photo cues (59%) than with theme song cues (48%), there was no TOT difference between cast photo (25%) and theme song (21%). Riefer (2002) also cites Brown and Nix's (1996) outcome as further evidence against the inferential position: no significant TOT difference between picture cues (12%) and definition cues (15%), although correct retrieval was significantly higher with picture (76%) than definition (69%).

An outcome that Schwartz (2006) pointed to in favor of direct access over inferential positions is faster lexical decision times for nonretrieved targets on TOT than non-TOT trials (Yaniv & Meyer, 1987), which supposedly reflects the faster detection of a target word that is in a higher state of activation (compared to a non-TOT target word). However, given that Connor et al. (1992) replicated Yaniv and Meyer's findings at one week, when all activation had dissipated, a cue familiarity interpretation may be more likely: target words are more rapidly accessed from more-familiar than from less-familiar knowledge domains (see Chapter 8).

Under the accessibility position, increasing target word information should increase TOT probability. In partial support of accessibility, Schwartz and Smith (1997, Experiment 1) found more TOTs when subjects were given three or five target word cues at the time of retrieval, compared to two cues. However, Schwartz and Smith (1997) subsequently discovered (Experiments 2 and 3) that this difference was accounted for entirely by the picture cue, and that information beyond this had no additional impact.

Although Schwartz and Smith (1997) view this as inferential support, how the cue access occurs may be important. More specifically, actively retrieving the bits and pieces of information surrounding the target word may be different from having it passively provided by the experimenter. If the act of retrieval is an important component of any inferential evaluation, providing cue material for the subject would not provide an appropriate test. Related to this, a finding from Schwartz and Smith (1997) did not support the inferential hypothesis. There was no difference in number of TOTs for subjects who reported the availability of related information versus those who did not. The inferential hypothesis predicts a higher TOT rate for those who access peripheral information compared to those subjects who do not (Koriat, 1993).

In Experiments 2 and 3, Schwartz and Smith (1997) evaluated cue familiarity by priming some of the TOTimal's country names in a prior list (see Chapter 4). The inferential position would predict that cue priming should increase the cue's familiarity, thus increasing TOT rate. TOT rates were equivalent for primed and unprimed TOTimals in both experiments, thus failing to support cue familiarity. However, Schwartz and Smith (1997, Experiment 3) did salvage other support of cue familiarity, but only where target word information was relatively impoverished in their minimal cue (two pieces of information) condition.

One of the biggest issues in TOT research is the age-related increase in TOT rate (see Chapter 10), and Schwartz and Frazier (2005) suggest that the inferential position can account for this consistent finding. Older and younger adults monitor word accessibility equally well, but because older adults have had time to accumulate more target word information, the likelihood of bringing some aspect of the target word information to mind is greater, thus eliciting TOTs on more occasions (Schwartz, 2002b; Gollan & Brown, 2006). Gollan and Silverberg (2001) similarly suggest that metacognition may explain why bilinguals have more TOTs than monolinguals. Bilinguals can often retrieve the missing target in the noncued language, and this leads to an overestimate of its accessibility in the cued language (cf. Gollan & Acenas, 2004).

As noted earlier (see Chapter 2), Schwartz (1998) claims that illusory TOTs support the inferential position. TOTs associated with TOTimals without names and with fake trivia should both be impossible unless TOTs are inferential. Schwartz (1998) does acknowledge the possibility of alternative explanations for illusory TOTs, as suggested by Taylor and MacKay (2003): activation of a wrong answer, demand characteristics, and retrieval of related information. However, he considers none of these credible (cf. Schwartz & Frazier, 2005; see Chapter 2).

As a closing thought, it may be possible to evaluate the contribution of both cue familiarity and accessibility to TOTs through an instructional manipulation. One group is given standard instructions, a second group is instructed to avoid TOT assessments based on domain familiarity (Ravizza, 2003), and a third group is told not to allow the presence of partial information to influence their TOT assessment. If either cue familiarity or accessibility contribute to TOTs, then TOT probability should be lower in groups two and three where subjects are cautioned about using such information.

# ☐ **Summary**

The two general categories of TOT explanations are direct access and inferential processes. Direct access interpretations of TOTs involve the retrieval functions related to target word activation, and could consist of (a) *generic recall*, word retrieval search becomes "stalled" in the general vicinity of the target word; (b) *blocking*, target word access is hampered by the activation of a related word; or (c) *transmission deficit*, insufficient activation is passed from the word's semantic node to the component phonological nodes necessary for word production

Under the inferential interpretation, a TOT stems from a metamemory evaluation by the subject rather than partial activation of the word's representation. Two varieties of the inferential perspective include (a) *cue familiarity*, TOTs originate from one's familiarity with the target word cue; and (b) *accessibility*, the availability of fragmentary parts of words (e.g., first letter) lead one to declare a TOT. TOTs may also have a *metacognitive control* function, energizing and directing one's search for the missing target. Although multiple factors may lead to a TOT, the transmission deficit hypothesis has received more empirical support than any other interpretation.

The current TOT literature provides the strongest support for transmission deficit theory, although it is possible that additional factors could contribute to creating a TOT. As noted earlier, a more concerted effort at clarifying the basic functionalistic dimensions of the TOT experience (word characteristics, individual differences, situational variables, stress/emotional involvement, etc.) would provide a more solid basis for testing theoretical positions.

CHAPTER

# Individual Differences

The high degree of variability in TOT incidence across subjects (see Chapter 3) naturally begs the question of what factors contribute to such person-to-person differences. Why does one individual experience no TOTs in a particular investigation, whereas another experiences eight with the same set of 50 target words (Brown & McNeill, 1966)? And why does the incidence of natural TOTs vary from one every 2 weeks in some, to one every 2 days in others (Burke et al., 1991; Reason, 1984; Thompson & Corcoran, 1992)? The bulk of research on this topic has been devoted to age differences, but the association of linguistic competence (bilingualism) and specific neurological deficits to TOT rate has also been evaluated.

## ☐ Older Adults

Although semantic memory ability shows little change over the adult age span (Balota, Dolan, & Duchek, 2000), older adults commonly complain about their struggles with slow or problematic information access (Perlmutter, 1978), and inability to recall important names (cf. Cohen & Faulkner, 1986; Lovelace & Twohig, 1990). But how do these subjective evaluations correspond to the empirical findings?

### TOT Incidence

#### Diary studies

TOT incidence is significantly higher for the oldest versus youngest age group in every published diary investigation (Burke et al., 1991;

Cohen & Faulkner, 1986; Heine et al., 1999). Burke et al. (1991) found mean TOTs per month of 3.9 for young, 5.4 for midage, and 6.6 for older adults. The difference between young and both midage and older was significant, but difference between midage and older was not. A similar increase in monthly frequency was reported by Heine et al. (1999, Experiment 2): 5.2 for young to 6.6 for young–old to 9.3 for old–old. The old–old incidence was significantly above both young and young–old, with no difference between young and young–old. Finally, Cohen and Faulkner (1986) found no significant difference between young (8.2) and midage (7.9) adults, but both were significantly lower than older adults (16.1).

Thus, there is a reliable increase across age groups in all diary investigations, when comparing the oldest and youngest groups. Despite this consistent increase in reported diary TOTs, Burke et al. (1991) found no age-related difference in either of two retrospective estimates. A Likert-scale rating on TOT frequency (1 = never; 7 = very frequently) yielded an average of 4.4 for young, 4.0 for midage, and 4.4 for older adults, and estimates of actual TOT frequency per month were 3.0 for young, 3.2 for midage, and 3.2 for older age groups.

## Laboratory Studies

In 16 laboratory experiments with multiple age groups, 26 of 30 pairwise age group comparisons revealed a higher TOT incidence for the relatively older group (see Table 3.2), regardless of statistical significance (Brown & Nix, 1996; Burke et al., 1991, Study 2; Burke et al., 2004; Cross & Burke, 2004; Dahlgren, 1998; Evrard, 2002; Galdo-Alvarez et al., 2009b; Gollan & Brown, 2006; Heine et al., 1999; James, 2006; James & Burke, 2000; Mitchell, 1989; Rastle & Burke, 1996, Experiments 1 and 2; Shafto et al., 2010; White & Abrams, 2002; Vitevitch & Sommers, 2003). Thus, nearly all age comparisons in lab studies show that the relatively older group has more TOTs. Sampling across a broad age span (range = 19 to 88 years; mean = 56 years) rather than comparing discrete age groups, Burke, Stamatakis, Broderick, Finan, Shafto, Osborne, and Tyler (2005) found a significant positive correlation between age and both common-word TOTs (.51) and proper-name TOTs (.42; cf. Facal-Mayo, Juncos-Rabadán, Alvarez, Pereiro-Rozas, & Díaz-Fernández, 2006; Juncos-Rabadán, Facal, Álvarez, & Rodríguez, 2006). Finally, Maylor (1990a) discovered a significant increase in TOTs in samples of adults in their 50s, 60s, and 70s.

## Measurement Issues

Although this is apparently overwhelming confirmation of an age-related increase in TOTs, the picture is not so simple. First, diary studies are suspect because of a reporting bias. As Cohen and Faulkner (1986) note, older adults are generally more concerned about the possible onset of cognitive changes with age, which may make them more sensitive to the presence of TOTs, and likely to report a higher proportion of those that do occur. Supporting this speculation about a reporting bias, Burke et al. (1991) found that retrospective TOT incidence estimates were comparable across three age groups for two different estimates of TOT frequency (see above).

Laboratory studies present a different interpretive problem. Typically, a common set of target words is used for all age groups. Although this keeps testing conditions comparable, older groups consistently have higher standardized vocabulary scores (Abrams, Trunk, & Margolin, 2007; Brown & Nix, 1996; Burke et al., 1991; Dahlgren, 1998; Evrard, 2002; Heine et al., 1999; James & Burke, 2000; Rastle & Burke, 1996; Shafto et al., 2007; White & Abrams, 2002) and more formal education (Abrams, Trunk, & Margolin, 2007; Brown & Nix, 1996; Dahlgren, 1998; Evrard, 2002; Heine et al., 1999; James & Burke, 2000; Mitchell, 1989; Rastle & Burke, 1996; White & Abrams, 2002). Both vocabulary and education present fundamental measurement problems because older subjects typically retrieve a larger proportion of the target word set, leaving relatively fewer items for possible TOTs (cf. Abrams, Trunk, & Margolin, 2007; see Table 3.2).

If the incidence of TOTs is expressed relative to all noncorrect trials (cf. Brown, 1991), this usually shows a TOT increase with age. This adjustment was originally suggested as a way to correct for differences in TOT opportunities between groups. More specifically, you can't have a TOT if you get the item correct, so you express it relative to the set of all unsuccessful retrievals. However, the implicit assumption associated with this correction is that TOTs represent a form of retrieval failure, as TOTs are grouped together with DKs. An alternative view is that TOTs represent a partial retrieval success, given that the word exists in one's knowledge base, that one can often retrieve some information about it even absent the actual word. If one expresses TOTs relative to correct retrievals, this often reduces or eliminates the age difference in TOTs (Gollan & Brown, 2006). This issue is addressed in more detail later in this chapter.

## Exceptions to the Age Increase in TOTs

A handful of outcomes do not demonstrate the usual age-related increase in TOTs. More specifically, there was no significant correlation between age and TOTs in Riefer (2002; range = 20 to 74 years, mean = 39 years) or Maylor (1994; range = 25 to 78 years, mean = 47 years). However, Maylor's (1994) sample consisted of game show contestants who retrospectively identified TOTs by viewing videotapes of their own TV performance. In a reversed age trend, Gollan and Silverberg (2001) actually found more TOTs in young (12%) than older (7%) subjects when dividing their broad age sample at age 40. They speculate that TOT incidence may be a U-shaped function of age, with higher-frequency targets placing fewer words in the potential TOT range for older adults. Finally, White and Abrams (2002) found significantly more TOTs with younger (17%) compared to either young–old (14%) or old–old (13%) adults, with no difference between the latter groups. Despite these exceptions, the overwhelming majority of empirical outcomes points to older adults experiencing more TOTs.

# Other TOT Dimensions

## *Target Word Characteristics*

Aside from the consistently higher TOT frequency in older adults, are there age-related differences in other aspects of the TOT experience?

The age difference in TOT rate is especially pronounced with proper names (see Table 3.2). Older adults also report that remembering proper names is one of their most serious personal memory problems (Cohen & Faulkner, 1986; Lovelace & Twohig, 1990). Burke et al. (1991, Study 1) found proper-name proportion in diary TOTs higher for midage (69%) and older (69%), compared to young (58%) subjects. As experimental confirmation of this, Burke et al. (1991, Study 2) discovered a large (10%) young–older TOT difference for famous people, but minimal age differences (0% to 3%) across other target word categories. Their assertion is that age differences in TOTs are primarily driven by proper names, with other categories of target words showing little or no difference.

Additional laboratory confirmation comes from Evrard (2002), who found a dramatic age increase in proper-name TOTs from young (9%) to midage (13%) to older (18%) groups, in stark contrast to no TOT age difference with common nouns (1% to 2%) across the three age groups (cf. Maylor, 1990b). Finally, averaging across two experiments, Rastle and Burke (1996) found the age difference in TOTs to be over twice as large for proper names (young = 8%; older = 16%) compared to common nouns (young = 7%; older = 10%). Given these dramatic differences in TOTs for proper names in older adults, some researchers avoid proper names so as not to exaggerate group TOT differences (Dahlgren, 1998; Gollan & Brown, 2006) or use only proper names to capitalize upon it (Cohen & Faulkner, 1986; Delazer et al., 2003).

Given the importance of proper names in eliciting TOTs, Burke et al. (1991) examined various subcategories of proper names and discovered an age-related increase for both acquaintance and place TOTs, a marginal difference for famous person TOTs, and a decline for title TOTs (movie/TV/book). Similar to Burke et al. (1991), Cohen and Faulkner (1986) also found an age increase for friend TOTs, but unlike Burke et al. (1991) they found an age-related decrease for both famous person and place TOTs.

Burke et al. (1991) also had participants evaluate acquaintance TOTs (diary study) on how well they knew the specific target person. Young adults had known the reference individual an average of a year, contacted them 3 months ago, and knew them moderately well (3.4; 1–7 scale). Midage participants had known the person 4 years, contacted them 5 months ago, and knew them moderately well (4.1). For older adults, the acquaintance had been known 18 years, contacted 4 years ago, and was well known (4.8). These dramatic age-related upward shifts are as expected, and suggest that recency of experience may underlie the age-related increase in proper name TOTs. A comparison set of data for names that were successfully retrieved, although potentially difficult to gather, would provide a valuable comparison point for these intriguing data.

Burke et al. (2000) provide an extensive summary and discussion of this exaggerated age difference in TOT rate with proper names, and suggest that transmission deficit predicts this effect. Common nouns can summate priming across many different words, facilitating phonetic activation. In contrast, proper nouns have fewer shared phonological connections with other words, thus limiting the amount of possible summation (Dahlgren, 1998). Furthermore, older adults are especially vulnerable to the negative retrieval impact of these skimpy interconnections. Relevant to this speculation, Burke et al. (2004) found that older adults had substantially more famous name TOTs (21%) than younger adults (12%) in an unprimed condition. However, when the proper name (Brad Pitt) was phonologically primed by a related non-proper noun (cherry pit), TOTs were reduced more for older than younger adults, suggesting that older adults have an inordinately greater phonological transmission deficit to overcome, compared to young adults.

## Differential Familiarity Issue

A problem with using proper names in laboratory studies is assuring that age-group differences in name familiarity do not account for TOT differences. Cross and Burke (2004) addressed this uncontrolled familiarity problem by pretesting the famous names (TV/film stars) on the Media Savvy Test to equate age groups on familiarity level. A significant age effect still emerged for famous-name TOTs, suggesting that such differences cannot be written off to differential familiarity. Addressing this same issue in a different manner, James (2006) developed a procedure where both proper and non-proper names could be retrieved from the same set of cues. More specifically, when presented the target person's photograph, participants retrieved both the first and last name as well as the individual's profession. Thus, James (2006) controlled for familiarity by matching proper names and common nouns (profession) to a common cue source, contrasting to the usual procedure of using a separate control set of common nouns that cannot be directly matched with the proper names on familiarity (e.g., Evrard, 2002). This design yielded a significant age difference in proper name TOTs between young (10%) and older (17%) groups (values estimated from their Figure 1), but no age difference in biographical information TOTs between groups, supporting a differential age-related increase in TOTs for proper but not common names (James, 2006).

This problem of differential familiarity also applies to target words that are not proper names. It is simply more obvious with proper names because of differences in the era during which an individual achieved (and maintained) her celebrity. However, Abrams, Trunk, and Margolin (2007) point out that comparisons between young and older adult TOTs may be based upon different subsets of items. To illustrate this, they separate young and older group TOT rates on 135 target words, and these data are provided in the appendix to Chapter 3. They suggest that TOT research on age differences would be improved by selecting sets of target words where TOT rates are roughly in the same range.

However, when using these norms, one must be careful to adjust for group differences on correct retrieval for each item. As noted earlier (see Chapter 3), Gollan and Brown (2006) suggest that TOTs should be framed as a partial retrieval success, representing satisfactory semantic access but failed phonological activation. Given that both correct and TOT items involve successful semantic access, expressing TOT as a proportion of all words where the meaning was correctly accessed would provide the best index of retrieval performance, especially when making between-group comparisons.

The importance of this adjustment is evident in the first target word listed from Abrams, Trunk, and Margolin (2007) in the appendix to Chapter 3. Abacus would look like a good candidate for use in a study on aging because the TOT percentages are roughly comparable for young (28%) and older (26%) adults. However, many more older (66%) than younger (25%) adults correctly retrieved that word, making the adjusted TOT rate (TOT/TOT + correct) very different for young (53%) and older (28%) adults. The phonological access for that word is twice as problematic for young adults, suggesting that this word should not be used in age group comparisons. On the other hand, the word "anagram" appears at first glance to be unsuitable based upon the large young/ older TOT difference (14% versus 24%). But when expressed relative to correct responses, these TOT percentages are roughly comparable (54% versus 52%).

## Target Word Background Frequency

Analyzing the background frequency for words reported in their diary investigation, Burke et al. (1991, Study 1) found a dramatic age-related decrease. TOT target word frequency was lower for older than younger adults, and this pertained to both abstract-word and object-name TOTs. However, Burke et al. admit that this comparison was problematic because nearly half of the reported target words do not appear in the norms. Furthermore, the percentage of unlisted words was substantially larger for older than young adults. Turning to laboratory studies, Vitevitch and Sommers (2003) found young subjects had significantly more TOTs with low- than high-frequency words, whereas older adults showed no significant difference. However, Vitevitch and Sommers (2003) used relatively simple (monosyllabic) words.

Gollan and Brown (2006) addressed the topic of TOT target word frequency head-on with a broader range of targets, and discovered a more complex outcome. Older adults have more TOTs than young for both high- and low-frequency words. However, older adults' higher TOT rate for low-frequency words was directly related to their increased ability to access such words. When adjusted for differences in retrieval success, the age-related TOT difference on low-frequency targets disappeared. A different story emerges with high-frequency words. Older adults clearly have more problems with these than do younger adults, even after equating the groups for word access competence. This is an important topic for further exploration, given that TOT differences related to age may be attributed to different retrieval dynamics at the two ends of the word frequency spectrum. More specifically, TOT differences on infrequent target words may result from an age-related increase in vocabulary competence, whereas TOT differences on frequent words may result from an age-related increase in phonological activation difficulties.

## Peripheral Target Word Information

There is a substantial and reliable age-related decline in the presence of peripheral target word information during TOTs (Brown & Nix, 1996; Burke et al., 1991; Dahlgren, 1998; Heine et al., 1999; Cohen & Faulkner, 1986). This holds whether one measures the percentage of TOTs where any information is reported (Cohen & Faulkner, 1986: young = 68%; older = 33%), the average number of features reported per TOT (Burke et al., 1991: young = 2.0, older = 1.5), or individual features such as correct first-letter guesses (Brown & Nix, 1996: young = 15%; older = 5%). Maylor (1990a) found a significant negative correlation between age and number of target word dimensions available during TOTs (–.50), and this decline in semantic and phonological features available during TOTs was also found within a restricted age range of individuals in their 50s through 70s (Maylor, 1990b). Older adults' subjective descriptions of natural TOTs confirm the objective data, with comments such as "my mind was just a complete blank," or "an empty gap," or "nothing will come" (Cohen & Faulkner, 1986, p. 190).

## *Interlopers*

Similar to peripheral target word information, most diary and lab research studies show an age-related decline in the percentage of TOTs accompanied by interlopers. Across seven outcomes from five studies, interlopers were reported on 55% of TOTs for young adults and 40% of TOTs for older adults (Brown & Nix, 1996; Burke et al., 1991; Cohen & Faulkner, 1986; Heine et al., 1999; White & Abrams, 2002). Although frequency differs, Burke et al. (1991) discovered that the nature of the interloper–target relationship is consistent across age groups. More specifically, there is no age difference in the percentage of interlopers that sharing the same syntactic class, first letter, and number of syllables with the target word, and this held true in both diary and laboratory TOTs. In contrast with this, Cohen and Faulkner (1986) did find an age-related increase in SM interlopers, a decrease in SS + SM interlopers, and no age difference in SS interlopers.

Aside from frequency, there appears to be a dramatic age-related increase in the negative influence of interlopers on TOTs. Burke et al. (1991) discovered that the presence of interlopers increases TOT resolution time (compared to no interlopers), but this impact is far greater for older than younger adults. In their diary study (Burke et al., 1991, Study 1), interlopers increased resolution time (versus no interloper) by 9 min for young subjects (4 min without, 13 min with). However, this increase is four times greater with older adults: interlopers increased resolution time by 35 min (16 min without, 51 min with). In addition, in their lab study (Experiment 2), interlopers reduced the likelihood of TOT resolution to a greater degree in older adults (from 38 to 5%), compared to young subjects (from 54 to 16%).

## *Resolution Probability*

Although diary studies show a higher average resolution rate for older (93%) versus younger adults (88%), these differences are generally modest and never significant (Burke et al., 1991; Cohen & Faulkner, 1986; Heine et al., 1999). Laboratory studies also fail to show a strong or consistent difference in resolution probability. Whereas Burke et al. (1991, Study 2) showed an age-related decline in resolutions (cf. Maylor, 1990b), both Brown and Nix (1996) and Vitevitch and Sommers (2003) found the opposite, with resolutions increasing with age. Abrams, Trunk, and Merrill (2007) also found higher resolution probabilities for both young–old (37%) and old–old (36%), compared to young (25%), subjects. It is noteworthy that Burke et al.'s (1991) opposing outcomes in their diary and lab studies (see above) were found using the same participants. Schwartz (2002b) suggests that the time constraints generally imposed in laboratory research may put older adults at a disadvantage in resolving TOTs, whereas diary TOTs do not have such a limitation. Thus, any lab comparison may artificially lower the resolution rate for older, compared to younger, adults. In summary, there do not appear to be consistent or impressive differences in TOT resolution probability across age groups.

## Resolution Times

Several diary studies show an age-related increase in TOT resolution times. Examining Burke et al.'s (1991) cumulative plot of TOT times for pop-up resolutions, 30% occurred within 1 min for young adults compared to 20% for older adults (estimated from their Figure 3, p. 560). Also, the average (median) resolution time is about 4 min for young but 20 min for older adults (again estimated from their figure). Heine et al. (1999, Experiment 2) also found that mean resolution time for diary TOTs was nearly twice as long for older (8 hr) than young (4 hr) adults. Laboratory investigations paint a different picture, with both Brown and Nix (1996) and Heine et al. (1999, Experiment 1) reporting no age difference in TOT resolution times. However, this null finding may be due to the necessary time limit imposed in laboratory studies (cf. Abrams, Trunk, & Merrill, 2007). Related to this topic, one laboratory study examined TOT onset latency, but found no evidence of an age difference (Heine et al., 1999).

## Resolution Process

Do older and young adults approach resolving TOTs differently? Diary studies suggest no age-related change in the use of the mental search (Burke et al., 1991, Study 1; Heine et al., 1999, Experiment 2). However, there is an age-related *decline* in research (consulting external sources) from young (32%) to older (24%) adults (Burke et al., 1991, Study 1; Cohen & Faulkner, 1986; Heine et al., 1999, Experiment 2), and an age-related *increase* in pop-ups from young (34%) to older (47%) subjects (Burke et al., 1991, Study 1; Cohen & Faulkner, 1986; Heine et al., 1999, Experiment 2; average percentages across studies). Participants' retrospective evaluation of TOT resolution strategies confirmed that the pop-up approach grows more popular with age: the strategy of "relax and direct attention elsewhere" increased from young (56%) to midage (60%) to older (78%) subjects (Burke et al., 1991, Study 1). In short, age-span comparisons in TOT resolutions indicate that pop-ups increase, research decreases, and mental search does not change.

## Priming and Cueing

Research on prime and cue manipulations has not yielded meaningful or consistent age-related differences (Burke et al., 2004; Heine et al., 1999;

James & Burke, 2000; White & Abrams, 2002). Maylor (1990a) found the negative influence of phonologically related cues to be greater for young (50s) than older (70s) subjects. However, several outcomes have revealed that old–old subjects are especially insensitive to prime and cue manipulations. For example, White and Abrams (2002), discovered that first-syllable facilitation in TOT resolutions (versus middle, last, and no syllable cues) was greater for both young and young–old subjects, but not for old–old subjects. Apparently, the boost needed to overcome the phonological deficit in very old subjects is too great for priming to overcome. In addition, the TOT resolution benefits from cue words differing from (versus sharing) syntactic class with the target word was found for both young and young–old adults, but not for old–old (Abrams, Trunk, & Merrill, 2007). Thus, whereas prime/cue effects seem generally consistent across age, there is some evidence that phonological prime/cue effects are less likely to occur at the oldest end of the age spectrum.

## Vocabulary Issue

As discussed earlier, the most popular explanation for older adults' increased TOTs is that the amount of activation transmitted from semantic to phonological nodes during word production declines with age (Burke et al., 1991). Older adults know the meaning of target words as well as (or better than) younger adults, but experience a greater deficiency in phonological activation. It is also possible that vocabulary differences contribute to the age difference in TOTs (Dahlgren, 1998; Gollan & Brown, 2006; Schwartz, 2002b). In nearly all TOT studies comparing different age groups, older adults score higher on standardized vocabulary measures (Brown & Nix, 1996; Burke et al., 1991, 2004; Cohen & Faulkner, 1984; Cross & Burke, 2004; Dahlgren, 1998; Evrard, 2002; Gollan & Brown, 2006; Heine et al., 1999; James & Burke, 2000; Maylor, 1990a; Rastle & Burke, 1996; Shafto et al., 2007; White & Abrams, 2002).

This vocabulary issue is not an alternative to the increase in transmission deficit, but rather another process that may also contribute to the age-related increase in TOTs. Perhaps older adults have more opportunities for TOTs because they know more words. When TOT frequency is adjusted for vocabulary size, age differences may be reduced or eliminated (cf. Gollan & Brown, 2006). When Dahlgren (1998) divided participants into high versus low knowledge, combined across three age groups, the high group had significantly more TOTs than the low group. Perhaps more important, when knowledge level was covaried out, the age difference in TOTs disappeared.

However, in contrast to this, Heine et al. (1999) found that the positive correlation of age with TOT frequency remained significant when vocabulary size partialled out, in both their laboratory and diary studies. The vocabulary hypothesis also fails to gain consistent support from correlational comparisons, where vocabulary and TOT rate should be positively correlated. Most of these correlations are actually nonsignificant, or even negative (Brown & Nix, 1996; Burke et al., 1991; Cross & Burke, 2004; Shafto et al., 2007). There is a more complete discussion of this point later in this chapter (under Language Competence: Vocabulary), but Schwartz and Frazier (2005) suggest that establishing this relationship between vocabulary and TOTs is problematic due to ceiling effects in vocabulary that limit measurement sensitivity (e.g., Burke et al., 1991).

Burke et al. (1991) propose that interpreting vocabulary size as causal in TOTs is contradicted by TOTs being more likely with small classes of words such as proper names, compared to large classes of words, such as object names and abstract words (cf. Taylor & MacKay, 2003). However, there are several reasons why this argument may not be relevant. Actual usage may be higher for smaller (proper names; acquaintances) than larger (common nouns) classes of words. In addition, many physical objects and abstract concepts have multiple words that are equally applicable, allowing one to find substitute words and avoid TOTs. Finally, TOTs with proper names may not be more frequent but more noticeable or dramatic (diary studies).

As a final note, Schwartz (2002b) suggests two additional reasons why TOTs increase with age: higher stress levels, and greater social motivation spurred by self-perceived declines in cognitive functioning. Taylor and MacKay (2003), however, provide counterarguments for each of these explanations. First, stress should also hinder correct recall for older adults, but this does not happen: older adults consistently outperform young adults. Using the same logical counterargument, social motivation should decrease recognition performance for older adults, but this again is not found in TOT studies (Heine et al., 1999).

## Summary

As a general summary of age differences in TOTs, older adults have objectively more TOTs than young adults in both diary and laboratory investigations. This difference is even more dramatic with proper than with common names, and some suggest that this alone accounts for most (or all) of the age difference (Burke et al., 1991). The TOT age difference for infrequent words may be because older adults know more of them, but the older adults' higher TOT rate for high-frequency words clearly reflects age-related transmission deficits as suggested by Burke et al. (1991; cf. Gollan & Brown, 2006). Interlopers and peripheral target word information accompany TOTs less often for older adults. It is unclear whether age differences exist in either resolution probability or resolution time, but older adults do attempt research less often and rely more on pop-ups. There is some suggestion that a larger vocabulary may contribute to more TOTs in older adults, but this needs further verification. However, deficient transmission of semantic to phonological activation has been strongly supported as the primary cause in the empirical literature.

# ☐ Children

When are TOTs first experienced, and does this evolve in parallel with the acquisition of language competence? The youngest documented occurrence of a TOT was in Elbers' (1985) report of one in her 2½-year-old son. She describes three different conversations showing indications of nascent TOTs. In one, her son shows tenacity in searching for a missing target word, and rejects a suggested synonym substitute. He also generates other words (interlopers?) related to the target in syllable number, syllabic stress, and phonology, but recognizes that none is the sought-after word. Elbers' (1985) study suggests that TOT-like language difficulties can occur at a very early age. Perhaps we do not become fully aware of this retrieval problem until a developmental stage where we acquire a sense of academic competence connected to successful word generation.

Additional observational support for the emergence of TOTs comes from Wellman (1977). Spontaneous oral comments during word retrieval efforts among 5- to 8-year-olds include parts of the target word ("vi" for "violin"), rhyming words ("fumbler" for "funnel"), or words including part of the target ("thermostat" for "thermos"). In addition, the children expressed TOT-like certitude in word knowledge: "I know I know that" and "I know, I just can't remember" (p. 17). These partial production features were observed on slightly less than 1% of all retrieval efforts, and expressions of certain word knowledge occurred about 3% of the time. Wellman's (1977) outcome tentatively points to a developmental increase in TOTs, with third-graders "surprisingly often seized by apparent tip of the tongue experiences" (p. 19) whereas "kindergarteners were much less prey to these obvious tip of the tongue experiences" (p. 20).

Three published laboratory studies have evaluated TOTs in younger children (Faust et al., 1997, 2003; Faust & Sharfstein-Friedman, 2003). In each, Faust and colleagues compared learning different (LD) to normal children, and these group comparisons are detailed later in this chapter (Language Competence: Learning Differences). Normal samples of children yielded TOT rates comparable to those found with adults (see Table 3.2) for grades 2–3 (11%; Faust et al., 1997), grades 3–4 (19%; Faust et al., 2003), and grades 7–8 (7%; Faust & Sharfstein-Friedman, 2003).

## SMU Study

We conducted an investigation at Southern Methodist University evaluating TOTs in children aged 3 ($N$ = 13), 5 ($N$ = 15), and 7 ($N$ = 15), tested individually using object picture cues. Easy and difficult subsets of target words (15 items each) were generated for each age group. The difficult subset for 3-year-olds served as the easy set for the 5-year-olds, and the easy subset for 7-year-olds served as the hard set for the 5-year-olds. The success in equating difficulty level across age groups was supported by the comparability in correct retrieval rates of 70 to 73% across age groups.

TOT incidence differed significantly with age, $F$ (2, 40) = 5.73, $p$ < .01: 2% for 3-year-olds, 7% for 5-year-olds, and 9% for 7-year-olds. Post hoc comparisons revealed that 3-year-olds were significantly lower than both 5- and 7-year-olds, with no difference between the 5- and 7-year-olds ($p$ < .05). One difficulty with this cross-age comparison is that the number of children experiencing TOTs increased dramatically from 38% of 3-year-olds, to 93% of 5-year-olds, and 87% of 7-year-olds. Analyzing data only from those children who experience TOTs, the age difference disappears, $F$ (2, 29) = 1.03, $p$ > .05: 5% for 3-year-olds, 8% for 5-year-olds, and 10% for 7-year-olds. This lack of a difference may be due to insufficient power, given the substantial reduction in number of 3-year-olds included, but this finding tentatively suggests that a certain minimal level of language competence may be necessary to experience TOTs, and that TOT incidence is relatively consistent once this has been achieved. As a final note, there was no age difference in TOT resolution probability ($F$ < 1), with 71% for 3-year-olds, 83% for 5-year-olds, and 85% for 7-year-olds.

In general, more research would be useful with young children to clarify how the quantitative and qualitative aspects of TOTs change as language ability develops (cf. Brennen et al., 2007). This question could be indirectly addressed by assessing TOTs during the acquisition of a second language, using either diary or laboratory procedures with high school or college students in foreign language courses. This design could be either cross-sectional (different course levels) or longitudinal (same student across multiple semesters).

## ☐ Cultures

An earlier review (Brown, 1991) noted the paucity of TOT research across different languages and cultures. Two decades ago, only four studies existed: two in German (Priller & Mittenecker, 1988; Wenzl, 1932, cited in Blumenthal, 1977) and two in Japanese (Naito & Komatsu,

1989; Murakami, 1980). Since then, such research has dramatically expanded. Over two dozen additional investigations have extended our knowledge about TOTs well beyond the English language and culture:

American Sign Language (Thompson et al., 2005; Pyers et al., 2009)
Chinese (Sun, Vinson, & Vigliocco, 1998)
Farsi (Askari, 1999)
French (Bacon et al., 2006; Brédart & Valentine, 1998; Ferrand, 2001; Georgieff et al., 1998)
German (Biedermann et al., 2008, Experiment 2)
Hebrew (Faust et al., 2003; Faust & Sharfstein-Friedman, 2003; Faust et al., 1997; Gollan & Silverberg, 2001)
Italian (Caramazza & Miozzo, 1997; Lesk & Womble, 2004; Miozzo & Caramazza, 1997; Vigliocco et al., 1997)
Japanese (Kikyo et al., 2001)
Russian (Ecke, 1997)
Spanish (Ecke, 1997, 2004; Gollan & Acenas, 2004; Gollan et al., 2005; Gollan & Brown, 2006; González, 1996; Facal-Mayo et al., 2006; Juncos-Rabadán et al., 2006),
Polish (Bak, 1987)
Tagalog (Gollan & Acenas, 2004)

Most of this research can be classified into two varieties. One applies the basic English-language TOT questions to other languages and cultures (Bak, 1987; Brédart & Valentine, 1998; Caramazza & Miozzo, 1997; Faust et al., 2003; Faust & Sharfstein-Friedman, 2003; Faust et al., 1997; Ferrand, 2001; Georgieff et al., 1998; González, 1996; Kikyo et al., 2001; Lesk & Womble, 2004; Miozzo & Caramazza, 1997; Sun et al.,1998; Vigliocco et al., 1997). This includes extensions to language dimensions that don't exist in English, such as target word gender knowledge during TOTs (Caramazza & Miozzo, 1997; Ecke, 2004; Ferrand, 2001; Miozzo & Caramazza, 1997; Vigliocco et al., 1997; see Chapter 5). The incidence of TOTs among these non-English investigations is generally comparable to that found in English-language studies (see Table 3.2), supporting Schwartz's (1999) characterization of the TOT phenomenon as universal. A second group of studies focuses on bilingualism, and what effect possessing words in two different language systems has on the incidence and resolution of TOTs (Askari, 1999; Ecke, 1997, 2004; Gollan & Silverberg, 2001; Gollan & Acenas, 2004; Gollan et al., 2005; Gollan & Brown, 2006). These studies are addressed later in this chapter.

# ☐ Language Competence

## Vocabulary

Brown and McNeill (1966) suggest that the pool of words that elicit TOTs probably varies with age and education, such that less verbally sophisticated individuals might experience TOTs with relatively more frequent words. Dahlgren (1998) further proposes that greater verbal competence may have an ironic dark side, resulting in an increased propensity for TOTs. This idea was discussed earlier in this chapter as a possible mechanism underlying the TOT increase with age. Although debate continues (cf. Gollan & Brown, 2006), a separate (but related) question is whether a positive or negative relationship exists between TOTs and vocabulary within groups of subjects.

As noted earlier, Burke et al. (1991, Study 1) found no significant correlation between verbal ability and naturally occurring (diary) TOTs within either young or older age groups. With laboratory TOTs (Study 2), there was again no significant correlation within the younger group (–.07), but a surprising negative correlation for older participants (–.63), suggesting that more TOTs are associated with lower verbal capabilities. Similarly, Cross and Burke (2004) found a significant negative correlation between vocabulary and laboratory TOTs for older adults (–.44), but no correlation for younger adults. However, Brown and Nix (1996) found no significant correlation between verbal competency and lab TOTs within either younger (.07) or older (.01) subjects.

In addition to the above findings with age groups clearly defined, several investigations find no significant correlation of TOT rates with vocabulary ability across a broad age range (19 to 88 yrs; Burke et al., 2005; Shafto et al., 2007). Thus, there is little support for a positive relationship between vocabulary and TOTs, and even some evidence for a negative relationship in older adults (Burke et al., 1991; Cross & Burke, 2004).

Perhaps current TOT research designs are not sufficiently sensitive to address this question because substantial restrictions exist on both the range of subjects (well educated) and type of target words (relatively difficult; Schwartz & Frazier, 2005). Abrams et al. (2003) also point out that individuals with lower verbal skills may assess their TOTs less accurately than those with high verbal ability, given that they found the rate of negative TOTs (TOT–) was significantly negatively correlated with vocabulary size. Compared to high-verbal subjects, those with lower verbal skills are more likely to declare TOTs where the target word is not the one designated by the experimenter.

# Anomia

When observing aphasics' difficulty in language production, they appear to experience TOTs frequently (Barton, 1971; Beeson et al., 1997; Bruce & Howard, 1988; Ellis, 1985; Goodglass et al., 1976; Pease & Goodglass, 1978). In addition, the anomia associated with pathologies such as Parkinson's disease (Matison, Mayeux, Rosen, & Fahn, 1982) and prosopanomia (Geva et al., 1997) also appears to be associated with a high incidence of TOTs.

> It is tempting to assume that normal "tip-of-the-tongue" states are an analogous, albeit milder, form of the aphasic anomic deficit. As with the normal subject, the aphasic patient seems in some sense to "know" the word he is searching for and can often demonstrate this by pantomime or circumlocution; if the "missing" word is given by the examiner he will recognize that it is the required response. He will also be able to pick out the "missing" word from a list that the examiner offers. (Marshall, 1979, p. 257)

On the surface, it would seem that examining TOTs among individuals with such word retrieval problems could provide some insights into TOTs. However, Marshall (1979) notes that the realities are not so simple. Knowledge of partial word features is inconsistent across patients, and the nature of this word finding difficulty varies widely across different subtypes of anomics. Due in part to their high frequency of occurrence, the subjective nature of these TOT-like experiences is qualitatively different and less distinctive among anomics than among individuals with normal language function. Thus, a much looser definition of TOTs is often employed, such as trials where phonological cueing elicits target retrieval (Matison et al., 1982) or all trials where initial retrieval is unsuccessful (Goodglass et al., 1976).

To illustrate this quandary, Vigliocco et al. (1999) had to dilute the operational definition of TOTs when testing an anomic patient, defining TOTs as trials where the person failed to retrieve the target, responded to questions about it, and correctly recognized the target word. Absent the subjective TOT phenomenology found in normal adults, Vigliocco et al.'s (1999) ad hoc operational definition seems to resemble simple recall failure. This aside, their patient had a high rate of so-called "TOTs," ranging from 21 to 36% across five sets of items, and knew word attributes at a level comparable to subjects with normal language function.

As another example of the interpretive difficulty presented with research on such subjects, Ralph et al. (2000) reported an anomic patient who made "remarkable TOT-like comments about pictures that he was unable to name" (p. 193), and had a strange ability to assess dimensions of compound word targets, such as "star" as a component of the missing target word "starfish." Despite this, the patient could not guess the syllable length or first letter above chance, and Ralph et al. (2000) suggested separating anomics into those with phonetic versus semantic deficits as a fruitful direction for future research (cf. Bruce & Howard, 1988).

To determine if aphasics' word-finding difficulty is an exaggerated form of normal TOTs, Barton (1971) used Brown and McNeill's (1966) methodology and discovered some intriguing similarities: aphasics were correct on 62% of first letter guesses (57% in Brown and McNeill) and 72% of syllable number guesses (60% in Brown and McNeill). Furthermore, words of similar meaning were provided by 81% of subjects and words of similar sound by 56%. In short, aphasics appear to have a well-developed sense of generic recall as described by Brown and McNeill (1966), with relatively good access to the general form of the missing word.

Goodglass et al. (1976) requested initial letter and syllable-number guesses for all missing target words in four different types of aphasics. Conduction aphasics were more accurate for both syllable number and first letter than were Wernicke's aphasics and anomics, with the Broca's aphasics not differing from the others. However, guessing levels for all but the conduction aphasics were near chance, but the broad definition used by Goodglass et al. (1976; all nonretrievals) makes these findings of questionable relevance to interpreting TOTs.

These data on anomic patients, in general, have not played an important role in understanding TOTs. Although tantalizing similarities exist, the experiences described only modestly resemble typical TOT experiences. Brown (1991) pointed out that "simply establishing a parallel between the features of aphasic subjects' typical nonrecall state and the TOT experiences does not help clarify either phenomenon" (p. 218). And as Schwartz (2002b) notes, these studies infer the existence of TOTs from retrieval behaviors that resemble TOTs in normal individuals, but do not verify this by simply asking subjects whether they are experiencing a TOT. Although the published research is not very useful at the present time, there is some potential in pursuing this area of inquiry but with improved TOT verification procedures.

# Bilingualism

There has been considerable recent growth in research on bilingualism and the TOT experience. TOTs have been used as a crucible within which to examine important issues related to the difference between bilingual and monolingual language in the domains of word storage and retrieval. A central and consistent finding is that bilinguals have more TOTs than monolinguals (Gollan & Acenas, 2004; Gollan, Bonanni, & Montoya, 2005; Gollan & Silverberg, 2001; Gollan & Brown, 2006).

Gollan and colleagues have suggested a "relative deficit" account for this difference, which has intuitive appeal. Because bilinguals use two different languages, the words in both languages are on the average activated less often than the words in a monolingual's single linguistic base. Thus, the semantic-to-phonological connections are weaker for a bilingual because they are activated less frequently, given the larger number of such connections that they maintain. This, in turn, leads to a greater number of activation failures, resulting in a greater frequency of TOTs for bilinguals, compared to monolinguals.

Several diary studies have examined naturally occurring TOTs in bilinguals (Ecke, 1997, 2004). Among those relatively proficient in both languages, Ecke (1997) noted that 80% of TOTs were in the primary or dominant language, a finding consistent across English–Spanish, English–German, and Russian–English bilinguals. This outcome makes intuitive sense, assuming that bilinguals use their dominant language more often and will thus experience more errors with greater use. In a more specialized diary-study analysis involving TOT differences during the acquisition of a second language, Ecke (2004) separated English–Spanish bilinguals into *balanced* (proficient in both languages) and *weak* (beginning to learn a second language) subgroups. Weak bilinguals experienced more TOTs overall than balanced bilinguals, and weak bilinguals had a higher proportion of TOTs in their less-dominant language, the one that they were acquiring. This outcome is consistent with the semantic-to-phonological linkage being relatively weaker and more susceptible to breakdown in the language that is being acquired, thus resulting in more TOTs.

In another diary investigation, Gollan et al. (2005, Experiment 1) found that the total number of TOTs for English monolinguals was roughly the same as for English–Spanish bilinguals, but comparing proper-name and non-proper-name TOTs brought an interesting difference to light. Most TOTs for monolinguals were on proper names (52%), whereas bilinguals had only 17% on proper name targets, significantly below the level for monolinguals. Thus, bilinguals had more non-proper-name TOTs than monolinguals, and this group difference was not accounted for by non-dominant language target words for bilinguals because it remained significant when these words were removed from the analysis.

In the laboratory follow-up to their diary investigation, Gollan et al. (2005, Experiment 2) again found that bilinguals had more (dominant language) TOTs than monolinguals for non-proper names, but unlike the diary study there was no difference for proper names. Gollan et al. (2005) speculate that when a particular word (e.g., proper name) shares a common representation in both languages, this eliminates the bilingual "disadvantage" of more TOTs. Bilinguals only show increased TOTs for words that have distinctly different word forms in each language. Because proper names have the same word form in both languages, they do not fall prey to the "dilution of activation" associated with words that have different representations.

In a further dissection of word category differences for TOTs, Gollan and Acenas (2004, Experiment 1) and Gollan and Silverberg (2001) found that the monolingual–bilingual difference held only for noncognate target words, which have different forms in each language. In contrast, cognate words that share similar forms in both languages (e.g., adult–adulto; photo–foto) elicit comparable TOT rates in both monolingual and bilingual participants. No TOT difference was found for the most-translated target words, whereas bilinguals had significantly more TOTs (than monolinguals) for the least-translated words. This difference even pertains to bilinguals who rate their English proficiency as comparable to monolinguals, and for bilinguals who recognize as many words as monolinguals. Gollan and Acenas (2004, Experiment 2) replicated these findings with English–Tagalog bilinguals: monolinguals had significantly fewer TOTs than bilinguals, but this difference held true only for noncognate and for least-translated target words.

Gollan and Silverberg (2001) noted that the typical laboratory finding that bilinguals experience more TOTs than monolinguals (Gollan & Acenas, 2004; Gollan & Brown, 2006) disappears for the lowest-frequency target words, and propose a "frequency threshold" above which words elicit TOTs with equal frequency in both language groups, and below which words are challenging to bilinguals but not to monolinguals (Gollan & Brown, 2006). Incidentally, Gollan and Silverberg (2001) discovered no difference in the immediate resolution rate between monolinguals and bilinguals, indicating that even though the etiology may differ, the resolution mechanisms for TOTs are comparable.

Another linguistic question addressed in bilingual research is whether TOT differences can help distinguish between single-store and dual-store models of bilingualism. The single-store model for word meaning assumes that both languages share a common representation for a word, whereas the dual-store model posits that each word resides in two separate stores, one in each language. Askari (1999) employed a rather complex design to evaluate the single- versus dual-store positions, evaluating the effect of postdefinitional phonological cueing on TOT resolutions. With Farsi–English bilinguals, there was no difference in whether the cue was presented in the same language as the definition or a different language, supporting the single-store position. Unfortunately, there were dramatic differences in correct word retrieval success in the control (unrelated cue) condition: 50% of Farsi words, but only 15% of English words were retrieved. Thus, their native-speaking Farsi sample appears only marginally competent in English, making cross-language comparisons problematic. However, Schwartz (2002b) notes that at this point in the evolution of the literature, the data are not sufficiently clear to aid such a differentiation between single- and dual-store models.

Another possible reason why bilinguals experience an increased incidence of TOTs is that there may be difficulty in word production if the two language systems share some phonological features, and nearly all spoken languages have substantial overlap in the types of phonemes that provide the foundation of the spoken language. Pyers, Gollan, and Emmorey (2009) designed a clever way to eliminate this possible problem by comparing Spanish–English bilinguals, American Sign Language (ASL)–English bilinguals, and English monolinguals. Given that phonology is not a part of ASL, this source of interference cannot exist in ASL–English bilinguals. It turned out that both groups of bilinguals had more TOTs than monolinguals, demonstrating that phonological overlap cannot play a major causal role in the increased incidence of TOTs.

In general, the research on bilingualism confirms that they experience more TOTs than monolinguals, and that this probably results from a relatively deficient semantic access rather than differences in phonological activation (Gollan & Brown, 2006). However, this complex line of research is rapidly expanding and updating our knowledge about the details underlying TOTs.

## Learning Differences (LD)

Faust et al. (2003) propose that children with dyslexia or learning differences appear to be deficient in retrieving phonological, but not semantic, information about words, a situation superficially similar to what may cause TOTs in individuals with normal language processing. Supporting such speculation, Faust and colleagues have consistently found that LDs experience substantially more TOTs than age-comparable control children (respectively) in grades 2–3 (11% versus 30%; Faust et al., 1997), grades 3–4 (19% versus 34% Faust et al., 2003), and grades 7–8 (7% versus 13%; Faust & Sharfstein-Friedman, 2003). Thus, LDs experience about twice as many TOTs as control children, and also resolve fewer TOTs than controls (Faust et al., 1997, 2003). In addition, LDs have less phonological information available than controls about the missing target, but are comparable in providing semantic information (Faust et al., 1997, 2003; Faust & Sharfstein-Friedman, 2003). Finally, phonological cueing is less helpful in facilitating TOT resolution for LDs than controls. Taken together, these outcomes suggest that LDs are selectively impaired in accessing the phonological properties of words, a challenge that may underlie their higher TOT rate (Faust et al., 1997).

This phonological difficulty in word production was also confirmed by Hanly and Vandenberg (2010). In children 8 to 10 years old, dyslexics experienced significantly more TOTs than controls. When dissecting these data further using Gollan and Brown's (2006) two-step model, they found that the two groups were equivalent at the first (semantic) stage of word retrieval, but that dyslexics were significantly worse at the second (phonological) step in word generation. This difference was not driven by receptive vocabulary differences, as the significant difference remained even when vocabulary was equated across groups.

## Poets

Connecting TOT research to a question regarding language creativity and sensitivity, Kozlowski (1977) reasoned that poets supposedly have a greater awareness of word sound and rhythm, and this should make them more aware than nonpoets of the phonological dimensions of any inaccessible but partially activated target words during their TOTs. To test this, both poets and nonpoets listened to an auditorally distorted version of either the target or an unrelated word during each TOT (Experiment 1). Hearing the distorted target word resulted in more TOT resolutions than a distorted nontarget word, but this effect was comparable for poets and nonpoets. In Experiment 2, during TOTs subjects were instead given related but undistorted cue word(s) ("tall conifer") that rhymed with the target ("Excalibur"). Similar to Experiment 1, TOT resolution was facilitated with the related word compared to an unrelated word, and poets and nonpoets did not differ in the magnitude of this facilitation. Kozlowski's (1977) outcome does suggest that phonetic information about the missing target word can boost TOT resolution, but poets do not appear to have special access to word phonology arising from their specialized interests, aptitudes, or experiences.

# ☐ Neurological Functionality

## Alzheimer's Disease

Several studies have evaluated the incidence and nature of TOTs experienced by patients with various neurodegenerative diseases associated with diminished language competence. Beeson et al. (1997) speculate that early-stage patients with disease of the Alzheimer's type (or DAT) have a breakdown in late-stage word production involving phonology, which seems to resemble word production difficulties associated with TOTs. In contrast, late-stage DAT patients should exhibit deficiencies in early word production (semantic or lexical access), making them less unlikely to experience TOTs. However, Beeson et al. (1997) note that a serious problem with this research is that DAT patients may not be sufficiently in touch with their subjective experiences to be aware that they are experiencing a TOT. In light of this, Beeson et al. (1997) used a lax definition of TOTs as trials where the name is not recalled but is subsequently recognized. This overly inclusive definition precludes considering their results here as standard TOTs, but their speculation could help guide future research on language function differences to help differentiate early from late stages of DAT.

Astell and Harley (1996) found support for the above speculation in that there were significantly more TOTs (12%) for DAT patients than for age-matched controls (6%). However, the dramatic difference in correct retrieval between controls (80%) and DATs (46%) makes interpreting any difference in total number of TOTs problematic (cf. Schwartz, 2002b). Incidentally, DATs were less likely than controls to produce phonologically related interlopers, but equally likely to produce semantically related interlopers. When dissecting the type of target words that elicited TOTs, Astell and Harley (1996) discovered an interesting group difference. DATs had TOTs for both high- and low-frequency target words, whereas controls had TOTs only for low-frequency words, suggesting that DATs are challenged over a much broader range of words.

Looking only at proper name retrieval (face cues), Delazer et al. (2003) compared DATs to two different groups of older adults: one with mild cognitive impairment (MCI), and a normal control group. Although there was no difference in TOT rate (see Table 3.2), postdefinitional cue efficacy differed substantially across groups. First-letter cues were significantly more effective at facilitating TOT target word retrieval for controls than either MCIs or DATs. Also, semantic cues resulted in higher resolution probability for controls than DATs, but there was no difference between controls and MCIs. Finally, a first-name cue did not differentially affect resolution across groups.

Thus, there is some evidence of increased TOTs among DATs, but problems with language process and self-monitoring make this assessment difficult. More specifically, a benchmark of TOTs is self-evaluation of retrieval failure in the face of the certitude of imminent word access. With individuals experiencing cognitive degeneration, one (or both) of these processes may be compromised, making TOT verification problematic.

# Temporal Lobe Epilepsy

Several investigations document that individuals with temporal lobe epilepsy (TLE) report an elevated TOT rate (Bell et al., 2001; Langfitt & Rausch, 1996). Thompson and Corcoran (1992) asked large samples of both controls ($N = 146$) and epileptics ($N = 760$) for a retrospective rating of 18 different memory problems. TOT was the most frequent memory problem for TLEs, with 43% claiming that these occur daily. In contrast, only 14% of controls reported daily TOTs, and TOT was the third-ranked memory problem, tied with *forgetting names* (14%), and behind *going back to check* (21%) and *forgetting where you have put things* (19%).

Langfitt and Rausch (1996) also comment on the apparently higher TOT frequency among TLEs, but only provide data from TLEs who have undergone a surgical procedure. All of their TLEs had received a lobectomy a year earlier in an effort to alleviate severe seizure symptoms, and they report that one result of the surgical procedure is an "exacerbation of word finding difficulty … that can be characterized as an atypically high frequency of tip-of-the-tongue experiences" (p. 72). Rather than providing specific details on TOT incidence, Langfitt and Rausch (1996) document the types of errors made by these post-surgical TLEs in confrontation naming. It is also worth noting that Salas-Puig, Gil-Nagel, Serratosa, Sánchez-Álvarez, Elices, Villanueva, Carreño, Álvarez-Carriles, and Porcel (2009) also found TOTs to be the most common memory problem (64%) in their large sample of epileptics being treated with antiepileptic medication, but include no control comparisons.

Putting these self-report observations among TLEs to an experimental laboratory test, Hamberger and Seidel (2003) compared TLEs with ($N = 56$) and without ($N = 20$) medically intractable seizures to controls ($N = 100$) on TOT frequency. They used both auditory definition cues, as well as line drawing cues from Snodgrass and Vanderwart (1980). Although TOTs were twice as likely for TLEs than for controls, it is difficult to interpret Hamberger and Seidel's (2003) data because they used a nonstandard TOT definition: words retrieved between 2 to 20 s after the cue, or following a phonemic cue that was presented 20 s after the definition. Their outcome seems to confirm that TLEs are less efficient (slower) than controls in retrieving words, but any strong assertion that TLEs have more TOTs may not be justified given their selective definition.

# ☐ Psychological Factors

Georgieff et al. (1998) report that a frequent complaint of depressed individuals is that they experience word-finding difficulties, and suggest that a high TOT incidence may be associated with this clinical group. However, they found no difference in TOTs between two hospitalized groups: one depressed, and one nondepressed but with peripheral neuropathology. This is not a convincing test, for several reasons. Aside from the questionable appropriateness of Georgieff et al.'s (1998) hospital control group, the TOT incidence rate was unusually low (about 1%) in both groups and the number of subjects tested (11 per group) was quite small. Furthermore, fewer than half of the subjects in each group (5 control; 4 depressed) experienced any TOTs. The anecdotal reports of word-finding struggles (and TOTs) in depressed individuals deserves a more careful evaluation with larger samples, more potent TOT-eliciting materials and better control comparisons.

# ☐ Summary

Age is clearly and consistently related to TOT incidence, with older adults experiencing more TOTs than younger adults in both diary and lab studies. This age difference is especially pronounced for proper names, and older adults have less peripheral information accompanying their TOTs (i.e., first letter, interlopers). The age-related increase in TOTs is most likely due to a decline in phonological activation, although it may also be connected to greater verbal competence in older adults. More specifically, they have more TOT opportunities because they know more words. Interpretive problems arise with between-group comparison involving age or bilingualism when there are baseline differences in retrieval success, and group differences should be adjusted relative to retrieval success (as well as retrieval failure). Children have TOTs as young as age 2, and at a rate generally comparable to adults. A large body of research on TOTs in other languages and cultures (aside from English) confirm its generality. With respect to language function variables, bilinguals have more TOTs than monolinguals, and LDs experience substantially more TOTs than non-LD children. Alzheimer's patients appear to have increased TOT rates, although deficient self-monitoring among these patients makes such comparisons problematic. Higher TOT rates have been noted with epileptics, but evidence is based primarily on anecdote and self-report and needs experimental confirmation. Finally, routine word-finding problems among anomics (e.g., Parkinson's; aphasia) resemble TOTs, although methodological irregularities limit the value of this literature in clarifying TOT mechanisms.

11
CHAPTER

# Summary

The volume of published research on the TOT experience has grown threefold in the two decades since this topic was first reviewed (Brown, 1991), and our understanding has advanced considerably. This is mainly due to the infusion of research expanding the cultural breadth of research, development of ideas from other fields (linguistics, metamemory), and the introduction of sophisticated theories about TOT causation (transmission deficit hypothesis, or TDH). The first section of this summary presents findings that appear strong and reliable, followed in the second section by topics that are worth further examination in future research.

## ☐ Consistent Findings

TOTs are universal
   Across cultures, languages, ages, and individuals
Many cues can elicit TOTs
   Definitions, faces, drawings, odors, songs, TOTimals
Types of TOTs can be differentiated
   Strong/weak; nearer/farther; imminent/nonimminent
TOTs occur ...
   About once a week in everyday life
   On between 10 to 20% of lab stimuli
TOTs occur more frequently with ...
   Proper names (especially acquaintances)
   Older (versus young) adults
   Bilinguals (versus monolinguals)
   LDs (versus normal children)

Interlopers ...
   Accompany about half of TOTs: 60% in diary studies; 40% in lab studies
   Resemble the target word more often in sound than meaning
   Hamper TOT resolution
   Come primarily (80% ) from the same syntactic class as the target
During TOTs, information is available about the target word's ...
   First letter, about half of the time (and above DKs)
   Syllable number, over half of the time (and greater than chance)
   Gender, for most (3/4) targets
Resolutions occur for approximately ...
   90% of diary TOTs, although selective memory may inflate this rate
   40% of lab TOTs, although limited time may reduce this rate
Most TOT resolutions happen ...
   Within 20 seconds in lab studies
   Within 20 minutes in diary studies
   Via pop-ups, although accidental cueing may account for many of these
During TOTs, older adults experience ...
   Less target word information
   Fewer interlopers
Phonological cueing aids TOT resolution
   Mainly via first letter, phoneme, or syllable

# ☐ Directions for Future Research

## Acknowledging Brief TOTs

Some TOTs are quickly resolved, within several seconds of the original experience, and may account for a substantial proportion of items labeled correct (Schwartz, 2001b). Although gathering brief TOT data would increase research complexity, it could be important in two research topics. First, in physiological comparisons between TOTs and C items, separating brief TOTs from other C items would be an important refinement. More specifically, with brain imaging using fMRI (Maril et al., 2001, 2003, 2005) or event-related potentials (Díaz et al. (2007), C trials are sometimes used as a baseline comparison for TOTs. Extracting brief TOTs from Cs would increase the analytical sensitivity of such research.

   Another situation where separating brief TOTs from Cs would be valuable is in investigations involving experimental manipulations intended to increase TOT rate via instructions (Widner et al., 1996), cueing (Abrams et al., 2003; James & Burke, 2000), and priming (Burke et al., 2004; Cleary,

2006; Cleary & Speckler, 2007; Cleary & Reyes, 2009; Cleary et al., 2010; Cross & Burke, 2004). In such designs, including brief TOTs with standard prolonged TOTs might yield a more sensitive measure of the impact of such manipulations.

## Interdependence of TOTs with DK and K Items

Given that a *fixed* set of words is used in laboratory studies, an increase or decrease in TOTs must involve a simultaneous change (decrease/increase) in the number of DKs, Ks, or both. A complete display of item shifts to and from each category (DK, TOT, K) that result from manipulations designed to influence TOT rate would help elucidate the mechanisms underlying TOTs (Meyer & Bock, 1992). More specifically, each TOT outcome (increase, decrease, no change) could be associated with at least two different patterns of change in DK and K items.

To illustrate using Figure 11.1, assume that Panel 1 provides a baseline comparison for the other panels.

1. A *null effect* or no change in TOTs could be accompanied by an increase for K and decrease for DK (Panel 2), *or* an increase for DK and decrease for K (Panel 3).
2. An *increase* in TOTs could result from a decrease of DK with no change in K (Panel 4) *or* a decrease of K and no change in DK (Panel 5).
3. A *decrease* in TOTs could result from an increase of DK with no change in K (Panel 6) *or* an increase of K with no change in DK (Panel 7).

Thus, any study evaluating differences in number of TOTs across manipulation conditions should do so in conjunction with evaluating concurrent shifts in DK and K items. The causes of changes in both DK or K items are potentially complex, and possibly related to variables other than the one being manipulated, such as motivation, time constraints, and cue clarity. Analyses including all three categories of items may be particularly informative where null effects are found with TOTs. More specifically, even though the total number of TOTs might remain constant, between-category shifts may still give clues to the effects of the manipulation (DKs to TOTs or TOTs to Ks) (Cleary, 2006).

## Can Pop-Ups Be Modeled in the Lab?

Spontaneous retrievals, or pop-ups, have been documented in many laboratory and diary investigations. These experiences are compelling

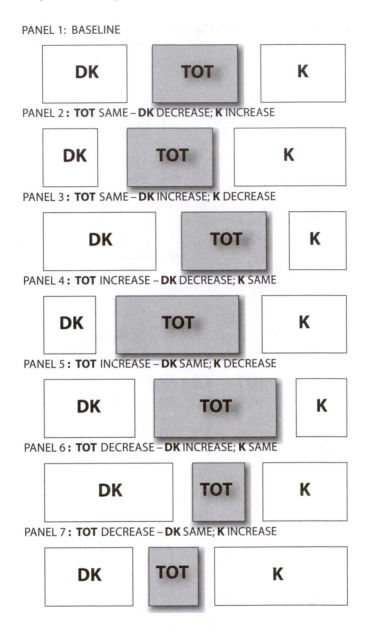

**FIGURE 11.1** Possible patterns of reciprocal item shifts across DK, TOT and K categories.

because the missing target feels as if it jumps into one's consciousness of its own accord. It is possible that unconscious mental search processes underlie this retrieval success, but it seems more likely that inadvertent cues from external (environment) or internal (rumination, implicit speech) sources trigger target word recovery (see Chapter 8; Burke et al., 1991; Schacter, 2001; Schwartz, 2001a). This explanation remains untested. One avenue is to have the subject perform a series of additional tasks following the TOT cue session that are supposedly unrelated to each other. One task could include the target (or related) words embedded in sentences or prose passages. Subjects would be given a general instruction to provide any of the unretrieved TOT target words, if they happen to come to mind. If successful, this hidden-cue task could be evaluated at different intervals after the original TOT task, to determine how long the target word node remained active or available.

## Connecting Gestures to TOTs

A number of studies have evaluated the functional connection between physical gestures and TOTs, including head, face, leg, and arm movements. Researchers have approached this topic from two directions. Some view these as integral to the TOT experience and a defining behavioral indicator (Beattie & Coughlan, 1999; Pine et al., 2007) that is potentially beyond the subjects' awareness (Schwartz, 2002b). From another perspective, gestures are a useful adjunct to facilitate word retrieval. Within this perspective, research is designed to influence TOT resolution probability through gesture manipulation (Beattie & Coughlan, 1999; Frick-Horbury & Guttentag, 1998; Pine et al., 2007; Ravizza, 2003). More specifically, restricting body gestures should decrease TOT resolution probability.

There is a substantial interest in this topic, as reflected in the amount of published research, but the outcomes do not paint a clear and consistent story. A more extensive observational and experimental evaluation of the gestures/expressions during TOTs (both verbal and physical) would be useful to resolve the two questions driving this body of research. First, are gestures an essential part of TOTs and, if so, what specific types are connected with the experience? Second, can various types of imposed restrictions or enhancements (bodily, verbal) influence TOT resolution probability?

## Closer Examination of TOT-Like Experiences

As described in Chapter 7, two language output errors bear a strong resemblance to TOTs: oral word substitution, or malapropism (Fay & Cutler, 1977; Tweney et al., 1975; Vitevitch, 1997; Zwicky, 1982), and written word substitution, or slip of the pen (Hotopf, 1980; Wing & Baddeley, 1980). Both resemble TOTs in that an interloper is produced without detection. These errors have been used to indirectly confirm some empirical and theoretical speculation concerning TOTs. However, the connection remains relatively undeveloped (cf. Vitevitch, 1997). The language production error databases used for these comparisons are relatively small (Fay & Cutler, 1977) and reused (Vitevitch, 1997). Thus, the corpus needs to be expanded, and Schachter (1988) provides an excellent example of how to gather and present a large corpus of such errors.

Two additional TOT-like experiences are also worthy of additional research, which involve symbol-based rather than word-based language systems. Thompson et al. (2005) has reported tip of the finger (TOF) experiences in sign language, where individuals get stuck on the precise gesture related to the semantic representation of the word. Also, a symbol production problem with Chinese characters was reported by Sun et al. (1998), which resembles TOT experiences.

## Examine Interloper–Target Closeness

Brown and McNeill (1966) first demonstrated that even when subjects cannot retrieve the target word, they can successfully discriminate between related words with respect to which one is relatively closer to the intended target. On those TOT trials where two (or more) SS interlopers came to mind, their subjects could identify which one more closely resembled the missing target word. However, these data were based on a very small number of TOTs (15, out of 223 total) where multiple SS interlopers were generated. This discrimination ability could be evaluated by providing 2 words structurally related to the target on TOT trials and have subjects evaluate which is closer to or farther from the target on sound, syllabic structure, etc.

## Increase TOT yield

A structural problem with TOT research is that it is inherently inefficient, given that TOTs occur on a small percentage of trials. Efforts to increase yield have involved instructions (Widner et al., 1996) and refining stimulus materials through pilot procedures (Brown & McNeill, 1966; Brown & Nix, 1996; Dahlgren, 1998; Frick-Horbury & Guttentag, 1998; Pine et al., 2007). Another way that might increase TOT yield would be retrieval under distraction, where subjects perform a secondary task (e.g., auditory or visual load) while retrieving target words. With slips of the pen (written errors), Hotopf (1980) found that the rate increases substantially when subjects are required to write quickly on a controversial topic in a noisy and distracting environment (cf. Brown, 1991).

Many believe that TOT probability is related to word background frequency, with TOTs more likely when retrieving rarer words (Brown & Nix, 1996; Dahlgren, 1998; Frick-Horbury & Guttentag, 1998; Pine et al., 2007), but empirical confirmation is lacking (see Chapter 6). It is obvious that some words are too simple and familiar to elicit any TOTs, and others are too rare, beyond a reasonable vocabulary range. But the frequency ranges between these extremes show considerable variability in TOT-eliciting probability, especially across groups differing in verbal competence (cf. Gollan & Brown, 2006). To further muddy this issue, in diary studies the target word is often evaluated as relatively familiar, even though many are so rare that they do not appear in frequency norms (cf. Burke et al., 1991).

A more thorough evaluation of possible links between TOT probability and word properties other than frequency would be very useful both practically (to increase yield) and theoretically (to understand the underlying TOT mechanism). The large corpus of target words and associated TOT rates provided by Abrams, Trunk, and Margolin (2007) and Burke et al. (1991) is a great start in this direction. And Linton's (1996) finding that certain words elicit TOTs repeatedly confirms the potential value of word characteristic evaluation. To move the field of TOT research toward more efficient designs, TOT probabilities for each target word used in published studies should be routinely reported in an appendix or compiled in an online database.

# Broaden Prime and Cue Designs

A number of TOT studies attempt to influence the incidence (by priming) and resolution (by cueing) of TOTs, most often using words related to the target either in meaning or phonology. These designs show modest priming with target word phonology on TOT probability (Burke et al., 2004), and these effects are most apparent with older adults. There is also evidence that phonologically related cues assist TOT resolution (Abrams et al., 2003; Abrams & Rodriguez, 2005; Burke et al., 2004; James & Burke, 2000; White & Abrams, 2002), although there are exceptions (Diaz et al., 2007). There is little evidence that semantically related words can influence TOT probability through priming (Cross & Burke, 2004; Meyer & Bock, 1992; Perfect & Hanley, 1992) or TOT resolution by cueing (Meyer & Bock, 1992; Perfect & Hanley, 1992).

A limitation on this research is the need to disguise the relationship between the prime and target words. This is generally accomplished by embedding prime/cue words in a larger set of unrelated words (Abrams et al., 2003; Abrams & Rodriguez, 2005; Diaz et al., 2007; James & Burke,

2000; White & Abrams, 2002), or employing a multistage trial design where the prime appears several steps prior to the target word cue (Burke et al., 2004; Cross & Burke, 2004). Despite such efforts, subjects may still detect this prime–target relationship (Abrams & Rodriguez, 2005), and this can be as high as a third of those tested in some investigations (e.g., Burke et al., 2004; White & Abrams, 2002).

This problem can be addressed by either transparent or subliminal priming. A good example of transparent priming is Cleary's (2006) extension of Rastle and Burke's (1996) examination of the influence of target word primes presented in a list preceding the target cuing session. Whereas Rastle and Burke (1996) tried to disguise the relationship between the preceding list and subsequent TOT session, Cleary (2006) made subjects aware by informing them that the prime list would contain some of the target words that would be cued in a later task (cf. Cleary & Speckler, 2007; Cleary & Reyes, 2009; Cleary et al., 2010). This transparent procedure reduces the likelihood of subject-to-subject variations in strategy or awareness, that become difficult to identify (or verify) after the fact. When the relationship between lists is opaque, subjects may devise a variety of hypotheses (correct and incorrect) about the connection between list items, and may or may not respond based on their hypotheses.

Subliminal priming, in contrast, makes use of brief prime or target word exposures. This approach would be most valuable in differentiating between varieties of incomplete activation. Under both inhibition and TDH versions of incomplete activation, subliminal target word exposure should decrease the probability of TOTs via activating the target word node prior to a retrieval attempt. The inferential view of TOTs should predict no difference between a repetition (identity) prime and no prime, unless this subliminal activation causes an increase in target word familiarity (which could also be assessed on each trial).

Having the target word (tornado) primed by a phonologically related word (tomato) should (a) *decrease* TOTs under TDH due to the boost in the phonological components of the target word, (b) *increase* TOTs under the inhibition position due to the competing activation of an incorrect word, and (c) *have no effect* on TOTs under the inferential position because a phonologically related prime word should not influence perceived accessibility of the target word. In contrast, a semantic prime (hurricane) presented subliminally should have no effect on TOTs under both the TDH position, because of the lack of phonological relationship between prime and target, and the inferential position, due to the semantic word being irrelevant to the target word accessibility. However, a semantically related prime should increase TOTs according to the blocking position, because of an inappropriate semantic activation that interferes with target word accessibility.

### Recency and TOTs

Extending the transparent priming procedure (described above) to longer intervals (days, weeks) between input list and TOT task could help evaluate how recent target word activation influences TOT probability. Such a design would model the temporal framework of our everyday language use (Burke et al., 1991). Presently, we know that recent exposure reduces TOT incidence, but this research has used relatively brief separations in the range of minutes between exposure and test (Cleary, 2006; Cleary & Reyes, 2009; Cleary & Speckler, 2007; Cleary et al., 2010; Rastle & Burke, 1996).

Defining recency more expansively, Bonin et al. (2008) found a negative effect when examining the connection between TOTs and age of acquisition (AoA) for celebrity names. More specifically, TOT rates were higher for celebrity names learned in the recent past compared to those learned long ago. This research on AoA is intriguing, and could be easily extended using AoA norms for a broader range of target words, or by relying on lists of persons (Butters & Albert, 1982) or events (Snow, 1992) that were in the public eye for a circumscribed period of time at different points in the past.

# Phonology and Resolution: Oral Versus Written Access and Cueing

A defining aspect of TOTs is reference to *oral* language production. The ubiquitous metaphor (cf. Schwartz, 1999) involves the act of saying the word aloud, using the tongue, rather than thinking about or writing the word. Given this oral framework of the phenomenon, it is odd that TOT research primarily involves written materials and testing procedures (Kohn et al., 1987). Dahlgren (1998) did address this by using oral responses, in the belief that these would aid TOT resolution. However, there was no written (control?) condition with which to compare this. Couldn't auditory cue presentation also influence TOT incidence, as well as resolution? Germane to this, Astell and Harley (1996) suggest that written response designs may actually inflate the rate of TOTs because subjects are more likely to lump high-FOK items in with TOTs.

As noted in Chapter 3, it would seem relatively straightforward to address this issue by comparing TOT etiology and resolution with oral versus written trial procedures, perhaps using a confidence scale to address Astell and Harley's (1996) concern. Given that the most influential theory on the etiology of TOTs involves a phonological system deficiency (Burke et al., 1991; see Chapter 9), comparisons of written versus oral presentation of the target word cue, and written versus oral responding, would seem relevant to better understand TOTs (Schwartz, 2002b). It should be noted that White and Abrams (2002) did find no difference between aloud versus silent processing conditions, but this manipulation was only used with the postdefinitional set of related words.

## Persistence of TOTs

If personal experience is at all a reliable indicator, TOTs seem to happen repeatedly for some specific words. Linton's (1996) findings on her personal TOTs confirm that TOTs happen over and over again on a subset of words in our vocabulary. Warriner and Humphreys (2008) published data indirectly related to this question. They assumed that repeated TOTs occur, but their question involved whether this likelihood was related to the length of time spent searching for the target word during the TOT. Their findings support an "error learning" explanation of repeated TOTs: when more time is allowed for working on resolving a TOT, there is a greater likelihood of experiencing another TOT on that same word at a later time. In the real world, we often have days or weeks between repeated retrieval efforts, so that an evaluation of their error learning theory with a longer intersession interval would establish more verisimilitude: does a long interval allow inappropriate learning to dissipate or extinguish, decreasing the probability of repeat TOTs?

While examining persistent or repeat TOTs, it would be worthwhile to examine test-to-test patterns for all three categories: DK, TOT, and K. Aside from TOTs changing to Ks (which is what most would expect), how many TOTs change to DKs, and how many former DKs and Ks change to TOTs? Warriner and Humphreys (2008) present evidence on the frequencies of such fluctuations: of initial TOTs, 61% shift to K but 23% remain TOTs and 15% change to DKs; 3% of initial Ks and 7% of DKs change to TOTs on the second try. Warriner and Humphreys (2008) did not present an in-depth analysis of these changes because this was not the focus of their paper, but these findings raise tantalizing questions regarding the lability of our retrieval processes.

## TOTs and Language Competence

Adults with normal-range language function have been the focus of most TOT research, whereas TOTs experienced by children have been only superficially examined. The three experimental reports (Faust et al., 1997, 2003; Faust & Sharfstein-Friedman, 2003) primarily focus on LD children, using normal control children for comparison. There is a need to evaluate how the TOT experience changes with increasing language competence. At what age does an adultlike awareness of a TOT emerge, how do children approach resolution, what types of peripheral information are available to them during TOTs, etc.

Another way to examine TOTs as a function of language competence would be with students who are in the process of acquiring a second language. In most academic settings, there exists a good opportunity to examine changes in TOTs related to language evolution within a systematically structured and moderately controlled environment with many possible subjects: students enrolled in foreign language courses (cf., Ecke, 1997).

Tracking these students would provide an excellent way to study the effects of target word strength, operationally defined by tests or exercises using these words. Laboratory manipulations of item strength have been limited by the restriction of a single laboratory session (Ryan et al., 1982; Smith et al. 1994, 1991; Valentine et al., 1996). With students learning a new language, not only could one study TOT rate at a molar level by learning time (semesters/months) and general proficiency (grades), TOTs could also be examined at the micro level with individual words.

# REFERENCES

Abrams, L., & Rodriguez, E. L. (2005). Syntactic class influences phonological priming of tip-of-the-tongue resolution. *Psychonomic Bulletin & Review, 12,* 1018–1023.

Abrams, L., Trunk, D. L., & Margolin, S. J. (2007). Resolving tip-of-the-tongue states in young and older adults: The role of phonology. In L. O. Randal (Ed.), *Aging and the elderly: Psychology, sociology, and health* (pp. 1–41). Hauppauge, NY: Nova Science.

Abrams, L., Trunk, D. L., & Merrill, L. A. (2007). Why a superman cannot help a tsunami: Activation of grammatical class influences resolution of young and older adults' tip-of-the-tongue states. *Psychology and Aging, 22,* 835–845.

Abrams, L., White, K. K., & Eitel, S. L. (2003). Isolating phonological components that increase tip-of-the-tongue resolution. *Memory & Cognition, 31,* 1153–1162.

Alario, F. X., & Ferrand, L. (1999). A set of 400 pictures standardized for French: Norms for name agreement, image agreement, familiarity, visual complexity, image variability, and age of acquisition. *Behavioral Research Methods, Instruments & Computers, 31,* 531–552.

Anderson, J. R. (1974). Retrieval of propositional information from long-term memory. *Cognitive Psychology, 6,* 451–474.

Anderson, M. C., Bjork, R. A., & Bjork, E. L. (1994). Remembering can cause forgetting: Retrieval dynamics in long-term memory. *Journal of Experimental Psychology: Learning, Memory, and Cognition, 20,* 1063–1087.

Anderson, M. C., Bjork, E. L., & Bjork, R. A. (2000). Retrieval-induced forgetting: Evidence for a recall-specific mechanism. *Psychonomic Bulletin & Review, 7,* 522–530.

Angell, J. R. (1908). *Psychology.* New York: Henry Holt.

Askari, N. (1999). Priming effects on tip-of-the-tongue states in Farsi-English bilinguals. *Journal of Psycholinguistic Research, 28,* 197–212.

Astell, A. J., & Harley, T. A. (1996). Tip-of-the-tongue states and lexical access in dementia. *Brain and Language, 54,* 196–215.

Baars, B. J. (1993). Putting the focus on the fringe: Three empirical cases. *Consciousness and Cognition: An International Journal, 2,* 126–136.

Bacon, E., Schwartz, B. L., Paire-Ficout, L., & Izaute, M. (2006). Dissociation between the cognitive process and the phenomenological experience of TOT: Effect of the anxiolytic drug lorazepam on TOT states. *Consciousness and Cognition: An International Journal, 16,* 360–373.

Bahrick, H. P. (2008). Thomas O. Nelson: His life, and comments on implications of his functional view of metacognitive memory monitoring. In J. Dunlosky & R. A. Bjork (Eds.), *Handbook of memory and metamemory: Essays in honor of Thomas O. Nelson.* New York: Erlbaum (pp. 1–10).

Bak, B. (1987). The tip-of-the-tongue phenomenon: A Polish view. *Polish Psychological Bulletin, 18,* 21–27.

Baldwin, J. M. (1889). *Handbook of psychology.* New York: Henry Holt.

Balota, D. A., Dolan, P. O., & Duchek, J. M. (2000). Memory changes in healthy young and older adults. In E. Tulving & F. I. M. Craik (Eds.), *Handbook of memory.* New York: Oxford University Press (pp. 395–410).

Barnhardt, T. M., Glisky, E. L., Polster, M. R., & Elam, L. (1996). Inhibition of associates and activation of synonyms in the rare-word paradigm: Further evidence for a center-surround mechanism. *Memory & Cognition, 24,* 60–69.

Barton, M. I. (1971). Recall of generic properties of words in aphasic patients. *Cortex, 7,* 73–82.

Beattie, G., & Coughlan, J. (1999). An experimental investigation of the role of iconic gestures in lexical access using the tip-of-the tongue phenomenon. *British Journal of Psychology, 90,* 35–56.

Beeson, P. M., Holland, A. L., & Murray, L. L. (1997). Naming famous people: An examination of tip-of-the-tongue phenomena in aphasia and Alzheimer's disease. *Aphasiology, 11,* 323–336.

Bell, B. D., Hermann, B. P., Woodard, A. R., Jones, J. E., Rutecki, P. A., Sheth, R., Dow, C. C., & Seidenberg, M. (2001). Object naming and semantic knowledge in temporal lobe epilepsy. *Neuropsychology, 15,* 434-443.

Biedermann, B., Ruh, N., Nickels, L., & Coltheart, M. (2008). Information retrieval in tip of the tongue states: New data and methodological advances. *Journal of Psycholinguistic Research, 37,* 171–198.

Blumenthal, A. L. (1977). *The process of cognition.* Upper Saddle River, NJ: Prentice Hall.

Bonin, P., Perret, C., Méot, A., Ferrand, L., & Mermillod, M. (2008). Psycholinguistic norms and face naming times for photographs of celebrities in French. *Behavior Research Methods, 40,* 137–46.

Bowles, N. L. (1989). Age and semantic inhibition in word retrieval. *Journal of Gerontology, 44,* 88–90.

Brandreth, G. (1980). *The joy of lex.* New York: William Morrow.

Brédart, S., & Valentine, T. (1998). Descriptiveness and proper name retrieval. *Memory, 6,* 199–206.

Brennen, T., Baguley, T., Bright, J., & Bruce, V. (1990). Resolving semantically induced tip-of-the-tongue states for proper nouns. *Memory and Cognition, 18,* 339–347.

Brennen, T., Vikan, A., & Dybdahl, R. (2007). Are tip-of-the-tongue states universal? Evidence from the speakers of an unwritten language. *Memory, 15,* 167–176.

Browman, C. P. (1978). Tip of the tongue and slip of the ear: Implications for language processing. *UCLA Working Papers in Phonetics and Phonology, #42.*

Brown, A. S. (1979). Priming effects in semantic memory retrieval processes. *Journal of Experimental Psychology: Human Learning and Memory, 5,* 65–77.

Brown, A. S. (1989). *How to increase your memory power.* Glenview, IL: Scott Foresman.

Brown, A. S. (1991). A review of the tip of the tongue phenomenon. *Psychological Bulletin, 109,* 204–223.

Brown, A. S. (1998). Transient global amnesia. *Psychonomic Bulletin & Review, 5,* 401–427.

Brown, A. S. (2003). A review of the déjà vu experience. *Psychological Bulletin, 129,* 394–413.

Brown, A. S. (2004). *The déjà vu experience*. New York: Psychology Press.

Brown, A. S., & Burrows, C. (2009). Structural knowledge about inaccessible target words during TOTs. *Psychonomic Society Annual Convention*, Boston, MA.

Brown, A. S., & Murphy, D. R. (1989). Cryptomnesia: Delineating inadvertent plagiarism. *Journal of Experimental Psychology: Learning, Memory and Cognition, 15*, 432–442.

Brown, A. S., & Nix, L. A (1996). Age-related changes in the tip-of-the-tongue experience. *American Journal of Psychology, 109*, 79–91.

Brown, A. S., & Rahhal, T. A. (1994). Hiding valuables: A questionnaire study of mnemonically risky behavior. *Applied Cognitive Psychology, 8*, 141–154.

Brown, A. S., Zoccoli, S. L., & Leahy, M. M. (2005). Cumulating retrieval inhibition in retrieval from semantic and lexical categories. *Journal of Experimental Psychology: Learning, Memory, and Cognition, 31*, 496–507.

Brown, R. (1970). Psychology and reading: Commentary on chapters 5 to 10. In H. Levin & J. P. Williams (Eds.), *Basic studies on reading*. New York: Basic Books (pp. 164–187).

Brown, R., & McNeill, D. (1966). The "tip of the tongue" phenomenon. *Journal of Verbal Learning and Verbal Behavior, 5*, 325–337.

Brown, S. R. (2000a). Reply to Bruce Mangan's commentary on "What feeling is the 'feeling of knowing?'" *Consciousness and Cognition: An International Journal, 9*, 545–549.

Brown, S. R. (2000b). Tip-of-the-tongue phenomena: An introductory phenomenological analysis. *Consciousness and Cognition: An International Journal, 9*, 516–537.

Bruce, C., & Howard, D. (1988). Why don't Broca's aphasics cue themselves? An investigation of phonemic cueing and tip of the tongue information. *Neuropsychologia, 26*, 253–264.

Buchanan, T. W., Tranel, D., & Adolphs, R. (2006). Impaired memory retrieval correlates with individual differences in cortisol response but not autonomic response. *Learning & Memory, 13*, 382–387.

Buján, A., Lindín, M., & Díaz, F. (2009). Movement related cortical potentials in a face naming task: Influence of the tip-of-the-tongue state. *International Journal of Psychophysiology, 72*, 235–245.

Burke, D. M., & Laver, G. D. (1990). Aging and word retrieval: Selective age deficits in language. In E. A. Lovelace (Ed.), *Aging and cognition: Mental processes, self-awareness, and interventions* (pp. 281–300). Amsterdam, the Netherlands: North-Holland.

Burke, D. M., & Shafto, M. A. (2004). Aging and language production. *Current Directions in Psychological Science, 13*, 21–24.

Burke, D. M., Locantore, J. K., & Austin, A. A. (2004). Cherry pit primes Brad Pitt: Homophone priming effects on young and older adults' production of proper names. *Psychological Science, 15*, 164–170.

Burke, D. M., MacKay, D. G., & James, L. E. (2000). Theoretical approaches to language and aging. In T. J. Perfect & E. A. Maylor (Eds.), *Models of cognitive aging. Debates in psychology*. New York: Oxford University Press (pp. 204–237).

Burke, D. M., MacKay, D. G., Worthley, J. S., & Wade, E. (1991). On the tip of the tongue: What causes word finding failures in young and older adults? *Journal of Memory & Language, 30*, 542–579.

Burke, D. M., Stamatakis, E., Broderick, C., Finan, V., Shafto, M. A., Osborne, G., & Tyler, L. K. (2005). Aging, tip-of-the-tongue experiences, and atrophy of the insula: A voxel-based morphology study. Cognitive Neuroscience Society Annual Meeting, New York City, 2005. *Journal of Cognitive Neuroscience, 17*, Suppl. B195.

Butters, N., & Albert, M. (1982). Remote memory, retrograde amnesia, and the neuropsychology of memory. In L. S. Cermak (Ed.), *Human memory and amnesia.* Hillsdale, NJ: Lawrence Erlbaum (pp. 257–274).

Butterworth, B., & Beattie, G. W. (1978). Gesture and silence as indicators of planning in speech. In R. N. Campbell & P. T. Smith (Eds.), *Recent advances in the psychology of language: Formal and experimental approaches, Vol. 4B.* New York: Kluwer (pp. 347–360).

Caramazza, A., & Miozzo, M. (1997). The relation between syntactic and phonological knowledge in lexical access: Evidence from the "tip-of-the-tongue" phenomenon. *Cognition, 64*, 309–343.

Choi, H., & Smith, S. M. (2005). Incubation and the resolution of tip-of-the-tongue states. *The Journal of General Psychology, 132*, 365–376.

Cleary, A. M. (2006). Relating familiarity-based recognition and the tip-of-the-tongue phenomenon: Detecting a word's recency in the absence of access to the word. *Memory & Cognition, 34*, 804–816.

Cleary, A. M., & Reyes, N. L. (2009). Scene recognition without identification. *Acta Psychologica, 131*, 53–62.

Cleary, A. M., & Speckler, L. E. (2007). Recognition without face identification. *Memory & Cognition, 35*, 1610–1619.

Cleary, A. M., Konkel, K. E., Nomi, J. S., & McCabe, D. P. (2010). Odor recognition without identification. *Memory & Cognition, 38*, 452–460.

Cohen, G., & Faulkner, D. (1984). Memory in old age: 'Good in parts.' *New Scientist, 11*, 49–51.

Cohen, G., & Faulkner, D. (1986). Memory for proper names: Age differences in retrieval. *British Journal of Developmental Psychology, 4*, 187–197.

Connor, L. T., Balota, D. A., & Neely, J. H. (1992). On the relation between feeling of knowing and lexical decision: Persistent subthreshold activation or topic familiarity? *Journal of Experimental Psychology: Learning, Memory, and Cognition, 18*, 544–554.

Cook, G. I., Marsh, R. L., & Hicks, J. L. (2006). Source memory in the absence of successful cued recall. *Journal of Experimental Psychology: Learning, Memory, and Cognition, 32*, 828–835.

Cross, E. S., & Burke, D. M. (2004). Do alternative names block young and older adults' retrieval of proper names? *Brain & Language, 89*, 174–181.

Cycowicz, Y. M., Friedman, D., Rothstein, M., & Snodgrass, J. G. (1997). Picture naming by young children: Norms for name agreement, familiarity, and visual complexity. *Journal of Experimental Child Psychology, 65*, 171–237.

Dagenbach, D., Carr, T. H., & Barnhardt, T. M. (1990). Inhibitory semantic priming of lexical decisions due to failure to retrieve weakly activated codes. *Journal of Experimental Psychology: Learning, Memory, and Cognition, 16*, 328–340.

Dahlgren, D. J. (1998). Impact of knowledge and age on tip-of-the-tongue rates. *Experimental Aging Research, 24*, 139–153.

Dale, H. C. A., & McGlaughlin, A. (1971). Evidence of acoustic coding in long-term memory. *Quarterly Journal of Experimental Psychology, 23*, 1–7.

Delazer, M., Semenza, C., Reiner, M., Hofer, R., & Benke, T. (2003). Anomia for people names in DAT – Evidence for semantic and post-semantic impairments. *Neuropsychologia, 41*, 1593–1598.

Díaz, F., Lindín, M., Galdo-Alvarez, S., Facal, D., & Juncos-Rabadán, O. (2007). An event-related potentials study of face identification and naming: The tip-of-the-tongue state. *Psychophysiology, 44*, 50–68.

Durso, F. T., & Shore, W. J. (1991). Partial knowledge of word meanings. *Journal of Experimental Psychology: General, 120*, 190–202.

Ecke, P. (1997). Tip of the tongue states in first and foreign languages: Similarities and differences of lexical retrieval failures. In *Proceedings of the EUROSLA 7 Conference* (pp. 505–514). Barcelona, Spain.

Ecke, P. (2001). Lexical retrieval in a third language: Evidence from errors and tip-of-the-tongue states. In J. Cenoz, B. Hufeisen, & U. Jessner (Eds.), *Cross-linguistic influences in third language acquisition: Psycholinguistic perspectives* (pp. 90–114). Bristol, UK: Multilingual Matters.

Ecke, P. (2004). Words on the tip of the tongue: A study of lexical retrieval failures in Spanish speakers of the southwestern US and northern Mexico. *Southwest Journal of Psycholinguistics, 23*, 1–31.

Elbers, L. (1985). A tip-of-the-tongue experience at age two? *Journal of Child Language, 12*, 353–365.

Ellis, A. W. (1985). The production of spoken words: A cognitive neuropsychological perspective. In A. W. Ellis (Ed.), *Progress in the psychology of language* (Vol. 2). Hillsdale, NJ: Erlbaum (pp. 107–145).

Erdelyi, M. H., & Kleinbard, J. (1978). Has Ebbinghaus decayed with time?: The growth of recall (hypermnesia) over days. *Journal of Experimental Psychology: Human Learning and Memory, 4*, 275–289.

Evrard, M. (2002). Ageing and lexical access to common and proper names in picture naming. *Brain and Language, 81*, 174–179.

Facal-Mayo, D., Juncos-Rabadán, O., Alvarez, M., Pereiro-Rozas, A. X., & Díaz-Fernández, F. (2006). Efectos del envejecimiento en el acceso al léxico. El fenómeno de la punta de la lengua ante los nombres propios. *Revista De Neurologia, 43*, 719–723.

Faust, M., Dimitrovsky, L., & Davidi, S. (1997). Naming difficulties in language-disabled children: Preliminary findings with the application of the tip-of-the-tongue paradigm. *Journal of Speech, Language, & Hearing Research, 40*, 1026–1036.

Faust, M., Dimitrovsky, L., & Shacht, T. (2003). Naming difficulties in children with dyslexia: Application of the tip-of-the-tongue paradigm. *Journal of Learning Disabilities, 36*, 203–215.

Faust, M., & Sharfstein-Friedman, S. (2003). Naming difficulties in adolescents with dyslexia: Application of the tip-of-the-tongue paradigm. *Brain & Cognition, 53*, 211–217.

Fay, D., & Cutler, A. (1977). Malapropisms and the structure of the mental lexicon. *Linguistic Inquiry, 8*, 505–520.

Ferrand, L. (2001). Grammatical gender is also on the tip of French tongues. *Current Psychology Letters: Behavior, Brain & Cognition, 5*, 7–20.

Finley, G. E., & Sharp, T. (1989). Name retrieval by the elderly in the tip-of-the-tongue paradigm: Demonstrable success in overcoming initial failure. *Educational Gerontology, 15*, 259–265.

Francis, W. N., & Kučera, H. (1982). *Frequency analysis of English usage: Lexicon and grammar*. Boston: Houghton Mifflin.

Freedman, J. L., & Landauer, T. K. (1966). Retrieval of long-term memory: "Tip-of-the-tongue" phenomenon. *Psychonomic Science, 4,* 309–310.

Freud, S. (1960, 1901). *The psychopathology of everyday life*. New York: Penguin.

Frick-Horbury, D., & Guttentag, R. E. (1998). The effects of restricting hand gesture production on lexical retrieval and free recall. *American Journal of Psychology, 111,* 43–62.

Galdo-Alvarez, S., Lindín, M., & Díaz, F. (2009a). Age-related prefrontal over-recruitment in semantic memory retrieval: Evidence from successful face naming and the tip-of-the-tongue state. *Biological Psychology, 82,* 89–96.

Galdo-Alvarez, S., Lindín, M., & Díaz, F. (2009b). The effect of age on event-related potentials(ERP) associated with face naming and with the tip-of-the-tongue (TOT) state. *Biological Psychology, 81,* 14–23.

Gardiner, J. M., Craik, F. I. M., & Bleasdale, F. A. (1973). Retrieval difficulty and subsequent recall. *Memory & Cognition, 1,* 213–216.

Georgieff, N., Dominey, P. F., Michel, F., Marie-Cardine, M., & Dalery, J. (1998) Anomia in major depressive state. *Psychiatry Research, 77,* 197–208.

Geva, A., Moscovitch, M., & Leach, L. (1997). Perceptual priming of proper names in young and older normal adults and a patient with prosopanomia. *Neuropsychology, 11,* 232–242.

Gollan, T. H., & Acenas, L. R. (2004). What is a TOT? Cognate and translation effects on tip- of-the-tongue states in Spanish-English and Tagalog-English bilinguals. *Journal of Experimental Psychology: Learning, Memory, & Cognition, 30,* 246–269.

Gollan, T. H., & Brown, A. S. (2006). From tip-of-the-tongue (TOT) data to theoretical implications in two steps: When more TOTs means better retrieval. *Journal of Experimental Psychology: General, 135, 462–483.*

Gollan, T. H., & Silverberg, N. B. (2001). Tip-of-the-tongue states in Hebrew-English bilinguals. *Bilingualism: Language and Cognition, 4,* 63–83.

Gollan, T. H., Bonanni, M. P., & Montoya, R. I. (2005). Proper names get stuck on bilingual and monolingual speakers' tip of the tongue equally often. *Neuropsychology, 19,* 278–287.

González, J. (1996). The tip of the tongue phenomenon and the lexical retrieval: Study of its properties in Spanish and the effect of the stimulus frequency (Abstract). *Estudint de Psicologia, 56,* 71–96.

Goodglass, H., Kaplan, E., Weintraub, S., & Ackerman, N. (1976). The "tip-of-the-tongue" phenomenon in aphasia. *Cortex, 12,* 145–153.

Goodglass, H., Theurkauf, J. C., & Wingfield, A. (1984). Naming latencies as evidence for two modes of lexical retrieval. *Applied Psycholinguistics, 5,* 135–146.

Gruneberg, M. M., Smith, R. L., & Winfrow, P. (1973). An investigation into response blockaging. *Acta Psychologica, 37,* 187–196.

Hamberger, M. J., & Seidel, W. T. (2003). Auditory and visual naming tests: Normative and patient data for accuracy, response time, and tip-of-the-tongue. *Journal of the International Neuropsychological Society, 9,* 479–489.

Hanley, J. R., & Chapman, E. (2008). Partial knowledge in a tip-of-the-tongue state about two- and three-word proper names. *Psychonomic Bulletin & Review, 15,* 156–160.

Hanly, S., & Vandenberg, B. (2010). Tip-of-the-tongue and word retrieval deficits in dyslexia. *Journal of Learning Disabilities, 43,* 15–23.

Harley, T. A., & Bown, H. E. (1998). What causes a tip-of-the-tongue state? Evidence for lexical neighbourhood effects in speech production. *British Journal of Psychology, 89,* 151–174.

Hart, J. T. (1965). Memory and the feeling-of-knowing experience. *Journal of Educational Psychology, 56,* 208–216.

Hart, J. T. (1966). Methodological note on the feeling-of-knowing experiments. *Journal of Educational Psychology, 57,* 347–349.

Heine, M. K., Ober, B. A., & Shenaut, G. K. (1999). Naturally occurring and experimentally induced tip-of-the-tongue experiences in three adult age groups. *Psychology & Aging, 14,* 445–457.

Hintzman, D. L. (1978). *The psychology of learning and memory.* San Francisco, CA: Freeman.

Hotopf, N. (1980). Slips of the pen. In U. Frith (Ed.), *Cognitive processes in spelling.* San Diego, CA: Academic Press (pp. 287–307).

James, L. (2006). Specific effects of aging on proper name retrieval: Now you see them, now you don't. *Journal of Gerontology: Psychological Sciences, 61B,* 180–183.

James, L., & Burke, D. M. (2000). Phonological priming effects on word retrieval and tip-of-the-tongue experiences in young and older adults. *Journal of Experimental Psychology: Learning, Memory & Cognition, 26,* 1378–1391.

James, W. (1893). *The principles of psychology* (Vol. 1). New York: Holt.

Jones, G. V. (1989). Back to Woodworth: Role of interlopers in the tip-of-the-tongue phenomenon. *Memory & Cognition, 17,* 69–76.

Jones, G. V., & Langford, S. (1987). Phonological blocking in the tip of the tongue state. *Cognition, 26,* 115–122.

Jönsson, F. U., & Olsson, M. J. (2003). Olfactory metacognition. *Chemical Senses, 28,* 651–658.

Jönsson, F. U., Tchekhova, A., Lönner, P. A., & Olsson, M. J. (2005). A metamemory perspective on odor naming and identification. *Chemical Senses, 30,* 353–365.

Juncos-Rabadán, O., Facal, D., Álvarez, M., & Rodríguez, M. S. (2006). El fenómeno de la punta de la lengua en el proceso de envejecimiento. *Psicothema, 18,* 501–506.

Kikyo, H., Ohki, K., & Sekihara, K. (2001). Temporal characteristics of memory retrieval processes: An fMRI study of the "tip of the tongue" phenomenon. *European Journal of Neuroscience, 14,* 887–892.

Kinoshita, S. (2001). The role of involuntary aware memory in the implicit stem and fragment completion tasks: A selective review. *Psychonomic Bulletin & Review, 8,* 58–69.

Kinoshita, S., & Towgood, K. (2001). Effects of dividing attention on the memory-block effect. *Journal of Experimental Psychology: Learning, Memory, and Cognition, 27,* 889–895.

Kohn, S. E., Wingfield, A., Menn, L., Goodglass, H., Berko Gleason, J., & Hyde, M. (1987). Lexical retrieval: The tip-of-the-tongue phenomenon. *Applied Psycholinguistics, 8,* 245–266.

Koriat, A. (1993). How do we know that we know? The accessibility model of the feeling of knowing. *Psychological Review, 100,* 609–639.

Koriat, A. (1994). Memory's knowledge of its own knowledge: The accessibility account of the feeling of knowing. In J. Metcalfe & A. P. Shimamura (Eds.), *Metacognition: Knowing about knowing*. Cambridge, MA: MIT Press (pp. 115–136).

Koriat, A. (2000). The feeling of knowing: Some metatheoretical implications for consciousness and control. *Conscious and Cognition, 9*, 149–171.

Koriat, A., & Levy-Sadot, R. (2001). The combined contributions of the cue-familiarity and accessibility heuristics to feelings of knowing. *Journal of Experimental Psychology: Learning, Memory, and Cognition, 27*, 34–53.

Koriat, A., & Lieblich, I. (1974). What does a person in a "TOT" state know that a person in a "don't know" state doesn't know. *Memory & Cognition, 2*, 647–655.

Koriat, A., & Lieblich, I. (1975). Examination of the letter serial position effect in the "TOT" and the "don't know" states. *Bulletin of the Psychonomic Society, 6*, 539–541.

Koriat, A., & Lieblich, I. (1977). A study of memory pointers. *Acta Psychologica, 41*, 151–164.

Kozlowski, L. T. (1977). Effects of distorted auditory and of rhyming cues on retrieval of tip-of-the-tongue words by poets and nonpoets. *Memory & Cognition, 5*, 477–481.

Kuhlmann, S., Piel, M., & Wolf, O. T. (2005). Impaired memory retrieval after psychosocial stress in healthy young men. *Journal of Neuroscience, 25*, 2977–2982.

la Heij, W., Starreveld, P. A., & Steehouwer, L. C. (1993). Semantic interference and orthographic facilitation in definition naming. *Journal of Experimental Psychology: Learning, Memory, and Cognition, 19*, 352–368.

Langfitt, J. T., & Rausch, R. (1996). Word-finding deficits persist after left anterotemporal lobectomy. *Archives of Neurology, 53*, 72–76.

Lawless, H., & Engen, T. (1977). Associations to odors: Interference, mnemonics, and verbal labeling. *Journal of Experimental Psychology: Human Learning and Memory, 3*, 52–59.

Leeds, M. (1944). One form of paramnesia: The illusion of déjà vu. *Journal of the American Society for Psychical Research, 38*, 24–42.

Lesk, V. E., & Womble, S. P. (2004). Caffeine, priming, and tip of the tongue: Evidence for plasticity in the phonological system. *Behavioral Neuroscience, 118*, 453–461.

Levelt, W. J. M. (1989). *Speaking: From intention to articulation*. Cambridge, MA: MIT Press.

Lindín, M., & Díaz, F. (2010). Event-related potentials in face naming and tip-of-the-tongue state: Further results. *International Journal of Psychophysiology, 77*, 53–58.

Lindín, M., Díaz, F., Capilla, A., Ortiz, T., & Maestú, F. (2010). On the characterization of the spatio-temporal profiles of brain activity associated with face naming and the tip-of-the-tongue state: A magnetoencephalographic (MEG) study. *Neuropsychologia, 48*, 1757–1766.

Linton, M. (1996). The maintenance of a complex knowledge base after seventeen years. In D. L. Medin (Ed.), *Psychology of learning and motivation: Advances in research and theory* (Vol. 35), San Diego, CA: Academic Press (pp. 127–163).

Litman, J. A., Hutchins, T. L., & Russon, R. K. (2005). Epistemic curiosity, feeling-of-knowing, and exploratory behaviour. *Cognition and Emotion, 19,* 559–582.

Logan, J. M., & Balota, D. A. (2003). Conscious and unconscious lexical retrieval blocking in younger and older adults. *Psychology & Aging, 18,* 537–550.

Lovelace, E. (1987). Attributes that come to mind in the TOT state. *Bulletin of the Psychonomic Society, 25,* 370–372.

Lovelace, E. A., & Twohig, P. T. (1990). Healthy older adults' perceptions of their memory functioning and use of mnemonics. *Bulletin of the Psychonomic Society, 28,* 115–118.

Lowenstein, G. (1994). The psychology of curiosity: A review and reinterpretation. *Psychological Bulletin, 116,* 75–98.

MacKay, D. G. (1987). *The organization of perception and action: A theory for language and other cognitive skills.* New York: Springer-Verlag.

MacKay, D. G., & Burke, D. M. (1990). Cognition and aging: A theory of new learning and the use of old connections. In T. M. Hess (Ed.), *Aging and cognition: Knowledge organization and utilization.* Amsterdam, the Netherlands: North-Holland (pp. 213–263).

Mangan, B. (2000). What feeling is the "feeling of knowing"? *Consciousness and Cognition: An International Journal, 9,* 538–544.

Maril, A., Simons, J. S., Mitchell, J. P., Schwartz, B. L., & Schacter, D. L. (2003). Feeling-of-knowing in episodic memory: An event-related fMRI study. *NeuroImage, 18,* 827–836.

Maril, A., Simons, J. S., Weaver, J. J., & Schacter, D. L. (2005). Graded recall success: An event-related fMRI comparison of tip of the tongue and feeling of knowing. *NeuroImage, 24,* 1130–1138.

Maril, A., Wagner, A. D., & Schacter, D. L. (2001). On the tip of the tongue: An event-related fMRI study of semantic retrieval failure and cognitive conflict. *Neuron, 31,* 653–660.

Marshall, J. C. (1979). Disorders of language and memory. In M. M. Gruneberg & P. E. Morris (Eds.), *Applied problems of memory.* New York: Academic Press. (pp. 249–267).

Matison, R., Mayeux, R., Rosen, J., & Fahn, S. (1982). "Tip-of-the-tongue" phenomenon in Parkinson disease. *Neurology, 32,* 567–570.

May, J. E., & Clayton, K. N. (1973). Imaginal processes during the attempt to recall names. *Journal of Verbal Learning and Verbal Behavior, 12,* 683–688.

Maylor, E. A. (1990a). Age, blocking and the tip of the tongue state. *British Journal of Psychology, 81,* 123–134.

Maylor, E. A. (1990b). Recognizing and naming faces: Aging, memory retrieval, and the tip of the tongue state. *Journals of Gerontology: Psychological Sciences, 45,* 215–226.

Maylor, E. A. (1994). Ageing and the retrieval of specialized and general knowledge: Performance of masterminds. *British Journal of Psychology, 85,* 105–114.

Maylor, E. A., & Valentine, T. (1992). Linear and nonlinear effects of aging on categorizing and naming faces. *Psychology and Aging, 7,* 317–323.

Metcalfe, J., Schwartz, B. L., & Joaquim, S. G. (1993). The cue-familiarity heuristic in metacognition. *Journal of Experimental Psychology: Learning, Memory, and Cognition, 19,* 851–864.

Meyer, A. S., & Bock, K. (1992). The tip-of-the-tongue phenomenon: Blocking or partial activation? *Memory and Cognition, 20,* 715–726.

Meyer, G. E., & Hilterbrand, K. (1984). Does it pay to be "Bashful"?: The Seven Dwarfs and long-term memory. *American Journal of Psychology, 97,* 47–55.

Miozzo, M., & Caramazza, A. (1997). Retrieval of lexical-syntactic features in tip-of-the tongue states. *Journal of Experimental Psychology: Learning, Memory, and Cognition, 23,* 1410–1423.

Mitchell, D. B. (1989). How many memory systems? Evidence from aging. *Journal of Experimental Psychology: Learning, Memory, & Cognition, 15,* 31–49.

Morgan, J. J. R., & Gilliland, A. R. (1939). *An introduction to psychology.* New York: Macmillan.

Murakami, Y. (1980). On the memory unit within *kana*-letter and *kanji*-letter words in the tip of the tongue phenomenon. *Japanese Journal of Psychology, 51,* 41–44.

Naito, M., & Komatsu, S. (1989). Effects of conceptually driven processing on perceptual identification. *Japanese Psychological Research, 31,* 45–56.

Nelson, T. O. (2000). Consciousness, self-consciousness, and metacognition. *Consciousness and Cognition, 9,* 220–223.

Norman, D. A. (1969). *Memory and attention.* Toronto: Wiley.

Norman, D. A., & Bobrow, D. G. (1976). On the role of active memory processes in perception and cognition. In C. N. Cofer (Ed.), *The structure of human memory.* San Francisco: W. H. Freeman.

Pease, D. M., & Goodglass, H. (1978). The effects of cueing on picture naming in aphasia. *Cortex, 14,* 178–189.

Perfect, T. J., & Hanley, J. R. (1992). The tip-of-the-tongue phenomenon: Do experimenter-presented interlopers have any effect? *Cognition, 45,* 55–75.

Perlmutter, M. (1978). What is memory aging the aging of? *Developmental Psychology, 14,* 330–345.

Pillsbury, W. B. (1939). *The essentials of psychology.* New York: Macmillan.

Pine, K. J., Bird, H., & Kirk, E. (2007). The effects of prohibiting gestures on children's lexical retrieval ability. *Developmental Science, 10,* 747–754.

Priller, J., & Mittenecker, E. (1988). Experimente zum Unterschied von "Wort auf der Zunge" und "Gefühl des Wissens." *Zeitscrift für Experimentelle und angewandte Psychologie, 35,* 129–146.

Pyers, J. E., Gollan, T. H., & Emmorey, K. (2009). Bimodal bilinguals reveal the source of tip-of the-tongue states. *Cognition, 112,* 323–329.

Ralph, M. A. L., Sage, K., & Roberts, J. (2000). Classical anomia: A neuropsychological perspective on speech production. *Neuropsychologia, 38,* 186–202.

Rastle, K. G., & Burke, D. M. (1996). Priming the tip of the tongue: Effects of prior processing on word retrieval in young and older adults. *Journal of Memory and Language, 35,* 586–605.

Ravizza, S. (2003). Movement and lexical access: Do noniconic gestures aid in retrieval? *Psychonomic Bulletin & Review, 10,* 610–615.

Read, J. D., & Bruce, D. (1982). Longitudinal tracking of difficult memory retrievals. *Cognitive Psychology, 14,* 280–300.

Reason, J. (1984). Lapses of attention in everyday life. In R. Parasuraman & D. R. Davies (Eds.), *Varieties of attention.* Orlando, FL: Academic Press (pp. 515–549).

Reason, J., & Mycielska, K. (1982). *Absent-minded? The psychology of mental lapses and everyday errors.* Englewood Cliffs, NJ: Prentice-Hall.

Reason, J. T, & Lucas, D. (1984). Using cognitive diaries to investigate naturally occurring memory blocks. In J. E. Harris & P. E. Morris (Eds.), *Everyday memory, actions, and absent mindedness*. London: Academic Press (pp. 53–70).

Reder, L. M., & Kusbit, G. W. (1991). Locus of the *Moses Illusion*: Imperfect encoding, retrieval, or match? *Journal of Memory and Language, 30*, 385–406.

Reed, G. (1974). *The psychology of anomolous experience*. Boston: Houghton Mifflin.

Riefer, D. M. (2002). Comparing auditory vs. visual stimuli in the tip-of-the-tongue phenomenon. *Psychological Reports, 90*, 568–576.

Riefer, D. M., Kevari, M. K., & Kramer, D. L. F. (1995). Name that tune: Eliciting the tip-of-the tongue experience using auditory stimuli. *Psychological Reports, 77*, 1379–1390.

Robinson, V. B., Abrams, L., & Bahrick, H. P. (2004, May). *Restoring access to words following retrieval failures*. Poster presented at the 16th annual convention of the American Psychological Society, Chicago, IL.

Roediger, H. L. (1974). Inhibiting effects of recall. *Memory and Cognition, 2*, 261–269.

Roediger, H. L., & Neely, J. H. (1982). Retrieval blocks in episodic and semantic memory. *Canadian Journal of Psychology, 36*, 213–242.

Roediger, H. L., Neely, J. H., & Blaxton, T. A. (1983). Inhibition from related primes in semantic memory retrieval: A reappraisal of Brown's (1979) paradigm. *Journal of Experimental Psychology: Learning, Memory, and Cognition, 9*, 478–485.

Rubin, D. C. (1975). Within word structure in the tip-of-the-tongue phenomenon. *Journal of Verbal Learning and Verbal Behavior, 14*, 392–397.

Ryan, M. R., Petty, C. R., & Wenzlaff, R. M. (1982). Motivated remembering efforts during tip-of-the-tongue states. *Acta Psychologica, 51*, 137–147.

Salas-Puig, J., Gil-Nagel, A., Serratosa, J. M., Sánchez-Álvarez, J. C., Elices, E., Villanueva, V., Carreño, M., Álvarez-Carriles, J., & Porcel, J. (2009). Self-reported memory problems in everyday activities in patients with epilepsy treated with antiepileptic drugs. *Epilepsy & Behavior, 14*, 622–627.

Schachter, P. (1988). What's in a name? Inferences from tip-of-the-tongue phenomena. In L. M. Hyman & C. N. Li (Eds.), *Language, speech and mind: Studies in honour of Victoria A. Fromkin*. New York: Routledge (pp. 295–321).

Schacter, D. L. (1999). The seven sins of memory: Insights from psychology and cognitive neuroscience. *American Psychologist, 54*, 182–203.

Schacter, D. L. (2001). *The seven sins of memory: How the mind forgets and remembers*. Boston: Houghton Mifflin.

Schriefers, H., & Jescheniak, J. D. (1999). Representation and processing of grammatical gender in language production: A review. *Journal of Psycholinguistic Research, 28*, 575–600.

Schulkind, M. D. (2002). Feature modulation search: A novel memory search model that extends the perceptual interference effect to musical stimuli. *Journal of Experimental Psychology: Learning, Memory, and Cognition, 28*, 346–352.

Schvaneveldt, R. W., Durso, F. T., & Mukherji, B. R. (1982). Semantic distance effects in categorization tasks. *Journal of Experimental Psychology: Learning, Memory, and Cognition, 8*, 1–14.

Schwartz, B. L. (1994). Sources of information in metamemory: Judgments of learning and feelings of knowing. *Psychonomic Bulletin & Review, 1*, 357–375.

Schwartz, B. L. (1998). Illusory tip-of-the-tongue states. *Memory, 6*, 623–642.

Schwartz, B. L. (1999). Sparkling at the end of the tongue: The etiology of tip-of-the-tongue phenomenology. *Psychonomic Bulletin & Review, 6*, 379–393.

Schwartz, B. L. (2001a). The phenomenology of naturally-occurring tip-of-the-tongue states: A diary study. In S. P. Shohov (Ed.), *Advances in psychology research* (Vol. 8). Huntington, NY: Nova Science Publishers (pp. 73–84).

Schwartz, B. L. (2001b). The relation of tip-of-the-tongue states and retrieval time. *Memory & Cognition, 29*, 117–126.

Schwartz, B. L. (2002a). The strategic control of retrieval during tip-of-the-tongue states. *The Korean Journal of Thinking & Problem Solving, 12*, 27–37.

Schwartz, B. L. (2002b). *Tip-of-the-tongue states: Phenomenology, mechanism, and lexical retrieval.* Mahwah, NJ: Erlbaum Associates.

Schwartz, B. L. (2006). Tip-of-the-tongue states as metacognition. *Metacognition Learning* (online journal).

Schwartz, B. L. (2008). Working memory load differentially affects tip-of-the-tongue states and feeling-of-knowing judgments. *Memory & Cognition, 36*, 9–19.

Schwartz, B. L. (2010). The effects of emotion on tip-of-the-tongue states. *Psychonomic Bulletin & Review, 17*, 82–87.

Schwartz, B. L., & Frazier, L. D. (2005). Tip-of-the-tongue states and aging: Contrasting psycholinguistic and metacognitive perspectives. *The Journal of General Psychology, 132*, 377–391.

Schwartz, B. L., & Smith, S. M. (1997). The retrieval of related information influences tip-of the-tongue states. *Journal of Memory and Language, 36*, 68–86.

Schwartz, B. L., Benjamin, A. S., & Bjork, R. A. (1997). The inferential and experiential bases of metamemory. *Current Directions in Psychological Science, 6*, 132–137.

Schwartz, B. L., Travis, D. M., Castro, A. M., & Smith, S. M. (2000). The phenomenology of real and illusory tip-of-the-tongue states. *Memory & Cognition, 28*, 18–27.

Seifert, C. M., Meyer, D. E., Davidson, N., Patalano, A. L., & Yaniv, I. (1995). Demystification of cognitive insight: Opportunistic assimilation and the prepared-mind perspective. In R. J. Sternberg & J. E. Davidson (Eds.), *The nature of insight.* Cambridge, MA: MIT Press (pp. 65–124).

Shafto, M. A., Burke, D. M., Stamatakis, E., Tam, P. P., & Tyler, L. K. (2007). On the tip-of the-tongue: Neural correlates of increased word-finding failures in normal aging. *Journal of Cognitive Neuroscience, 19*, 2060–2070.

Shafto, M. A., Stamatakis, E. A., Tam, P. P., & Tyler, L. K. (2010). Word retrieval failures in old age: The relationship between structure and function. *Journal of Cognitive Neuroscience, 22*, 1530–1540.

Shore, W. J., & Durso, F. T. (1990). Partial knowledge in vocabulary acquisitions: General constraints and specific detail. *Journal of Educational Psychology, 82*, 315–318.

Siefert, C. M., Meyer, D. E., Davidson, N., Patalano, A. L., & Yaniv, I. (1995). Demystification of cognitive insight: Opportunistic assimilation and the prepared-mind perspective. In R. J. Sternberg & J. E. Davidson (Eds.), *The nature of insight.* Cambridge, MA: MIT Press (pp. 65–124).

Skinner, B. F., & Vaughan, M. E. (1983). *Enjoy old age.* New York: W. W. Norton.

Smith, S. M. (1994). Frustrated feelings of imminent recall: On the tip of the tongue. In J. Metcalfe & A. P. Shimamura (Eds.), *Metacognition: Knowing about knowing*. Cambridge, MA: MIT Press (pp. 27–45).

Smith, S. M., Balfour, S. P., & Brown, J. M. (1994). Effects of practice on tip-of-the-tongue states. *Memory, 2*, 31–49.

Smith, S. M., Brown, J. M., Balfour, S. P. (1991). TOTimals: A controlled experimental method for studying tip-of-the-tongue states. *Bulletin of the Psychonomic Society, 29*, 445–447.

Snodgrass, J. G., & Vanderwart, M. (1980). A standardized set of 260 pictures: Norms for name agreement, image agreement, familiarity, and visual complexity. *Journal of Experimental Psychology: Human Learning and Memory, 6*, 174–215.

Snow, W. G. (1992). The Toronto Television Test: A pilot study of a new test of remote memory (abstract). *Journal of Clinical and Experimental Neuropsychology, 14*, 46.

Sun, Y., Vinson, D. E., & Vigliocco, G. (1998). Tip-of-the-tongue and tip-of-the-pen in Chinese. *Psychonomic Society Convention. Dallas, TX.*

Sunderland, A., Watts, K., Baddeley, A. D., & Harris, J. E. (1986). Subjective memory assessment and test performance in elderly adults. *Journal of Gerontology, 41*, 376–384.

Taylor, J. K., & MacKay, D. G. (2003). Tip-of-the-tongue phenomena: Gold mine or can of worms? Review of B. L. Schwartz "Tip-of-the-tongue states: Phenomenology, mechanism, and lexical retrieval." *American Journal of Psychology, 116*, 291–297.

Thompson, P. J., & Corcoran, R. (1992). Everyday memory failures in people with epilepsy. *Epilepsia, 33* (Supplement 6): S18–S20.

Thompson, R., Emmorey, K., & Gollan, T. H. (2005). "Tip of the fingers" experiences by deaf signers. *Psychological Science, 16*, 856–860.

Thorndike, E. L., & Lorge, I. (1952). *The teacher's word book of 30,000 words*. New York: Columbia University Press.

Tomlinson, T. D., Huber, D. E., Rieth, C. A., & Davelaar, E. J. (2009). An interference account of cue-independent forgetting in the no-think paradigm. *Proceedings of the National Academy of Sciences of the United States of America,15*, 15588–15593.

Tulving, E., & Arbuckle, T. Y. (1966). Input and output interference in short-term associative memory. *Journal of Experimental Psychology, 72*, 145–150.

Tweney, R. D., Tkacz, S., & Zaruba, S. (1975). Slips of the tongue and lexical storage. *Language and Speech, 18*, 388–396.

Valentine, T., Brennan, T., & Brédart, S. (1996). *The cognitive psychology of proper names*. New York: Routledge.

Vigliocco, G., Antonini, T., & Garrett, M. F. (1997). Grammatical gender is on the tip of Italian tongues. *Psychological Science, 8*, 314–317.

Vigliocco, G., Vinson, D. P., Martin, R. C., & Garrett, M. F. (1999). Is "count" and "mass" information available when the noun is not? An investigation of tip of the tongue states and anomia. *Journal of Memory and Language, 40*, 534–558.

Vihman, M. M. (1980). Phonology and the development of the lexicon: Evidence from children's errors. *Journal of Child Language, 8*, 239–264.

Vitevitch, M. S. (1997). The neighborhood characteristics of malapropisms. *Language and Speech, 40*, 211–228.

Vitevitch, M. S., & Sommers, M. S. (2003). The facilitative influence of phonological similarity and neighborhood frequency in speech production in younger and older adults. *Memory & Cognition, 31*, 491–504.

Warriner, A. B., & Humphreys, K. R. (2008). Learning to fail: Reoccurring tip-of-the-tongue states. *The Quarterly Journal of Experimental Psychology, 61*, 535–542.

Watkins, M. J. (1990). Mediationism and the obfuscation of memory. *American Psychologist, 45*, 328–335.

Wellman, H. M. (1977). Tip of the tongue and feeling of knowing experiences: A developmental study of memory monitoring. *Child Development, 48*, 13–21.

Wenzl, A. (1932). Empirische und theoretische Beiträge zur Erinnerungsarbeit bei erschwerter Wortfindung. *Archiv für die gesamte Psychologie, 85*, 181–218.

White, K. K., & Abrams, L. (2002). Does priming specific syllables during tip-of-the-tongue states facilitate word retrieval in older adults? *Psychology and Aging, 17*, 226–235.

Whitten, W. B., & Leonard, J. M. (1981). Directed search through autobiographical memory. *Memory & Cognition, 9*, 566–579.

Widner, R. L., Otani, H., & Winkelman, S. E. (2005). Tip-of-the-tongue experiences are not merely strong feeling-of-knowing experiences. *The Journal of General Psychology, 132*, 392-407.

Widner, R. L., Smith, S. M., & Graziano, W. G. (1996). The effects of demand characteristics on the reporting of tip-of-the-tongue and feeling-of-knowing states. *American Journal of Psychology, 109*, 525–538.

Wing, A. M., & Baddeley, A. D. (1980). Spelling errors in handwriting: A corpus and a distributional analysis. In U. Frith (Ed.), *Cognitive processes in spelling*. San Diego, CA: Academic Press (pp. 251–285).

Wood, G. (1983). *Cognitive psychology: A skills approach*. Monterey, CA: Brooks/Cole.

Woodworth, R. S. (1929). *Psychology*. Oxford, UK: Holt.

Woodworth, R. S. (1938). *Experimental psychology*. New York: Henry Holt (pp. 37–38).

Woodworth, R. S. (1940). *Psychology*. New York: Holt.

Yaniv, I., & Meyer, D. E. (1987). Activation and metacognition of inaccessible stored information: Potential bases for incubation effects in problem solving. *Journal of Experimental Psychology: Learning, Memory, and Cognition, 13*, 187–205.

Yarmey, A. D. (1973). I recognize your face but I can't remember your name: Further evidence on the tip-of-the-tongue phenomenon. *Memory & Cognition, 1*, 287–290.

Zwicky, A. M. (1982). Classical malapropisms and the creation of a mental lexicon. In L. K. Obler & L. Menn (Eds.), *Exceptional language and linguistics*. New York: Academic Press (pp. 115–132).

# AUTHOR INDEX

# SUBJECT INDEX